Our LORD

Who Becomes the

Righteousness

of God

Our LORD
Who Becomes the
Righteousness
of God
(Ⅱ)

PAUL C. JONG

Hephzibah Publishing House
A Ministry of THE NEW LIFE MISSION
SEOUL, KOREA

Our LORD Who Becomes the Righteousness of God (II)
Copyright © 2002 by Hephzibah Publishing House
Scripture quotations are from *the New King James Version.*

ISBN 89-8314-227-8
Cover Art by Min-soo Kim
Illustration by Young-ae Kim
Printed in Korea

Hephzibah Publishing House
A Ministry of THE NEW LIFE MISSION
48 Bon-dong, Dongjack-gu
Seoul, Korea 156-060

♠ Website: http://www.bjnewlife.org, http://www.baptism-cross.org
♠ E-mail: newlife@bjnewlife.org
♠ Phone: 82(Korea)-16-392-2954
♠ Fax: 82-33-651-2954

Words of Gratitude

Words are inadequate to express my heartfelt gratitude to our Lord Jesus. He always provides me with enough of His words to preach the gospel of the water and the Spirit worldwide, and has encouraged me to write this book according to His will.

I would like to thank all of the individuals involved in this publication. First of all, I owe a debt of gratitude that cannot be repaid to all the members of The New Life Mission. They have been praying for and supporting this task with all their hearts.

I express my special gratitude to my fellow workers Rev. Samuel Kim and Rev. John Shin, who have been in charge of this publication. I cannot thank Sangmin Lee enough for editing, Youngwon Joe for translating, and Suzanne Lee for her faithful proofreading.

I owe all the glory to our Lord God who has made us His children through the riches of His righteousness.

Hallelujah!

PAUL C. JONG

CONTENTS

CHAPTER 9

CHAPTER 10

CHAPTER 11

CHAPTER 12

Preface

If the Doctrine of Justification or the Doctrine of Sanctification that prevails in Christianity nowadays were really true, a lot of people throughout the world would have already been saved from their sins. However, the reality of it is that this is not the case and as a result, no one has been able to obtain deliverance from all his or her sins through the doctrines.

To witness this reality is truly tantalizing. Even though people are able to be saved from all their sins by simply believing in the gospel of the water and the Spirit written in the Bible, they are neither willing to hear nor to believe in this truth, therefore they are on the verge of destruction not knowing God's free gift contained in this truth. It becomes clear that the reason for this phenomenon is due to the preachers, clergymen, and leaders of today's Christianity.

God tells us to get rid of the false prophets. It is deplorable to see that though it is certainly true that there are too many false prophets nowadays, most Christians do not perceive the prophets' false teachings as something false. However, regardless of whom God raises and uses, He raises the servants of the gospel of the water and the Spirit and they shout it out. How many people in this world indeed are willing to listen to those who shout out the gospel of the water and the Holy Spirit, which God acknowledges?

The time has now arrived and God has revealed the truth of the water and the Spirit to the thirsty spirits all over the world through His servants who are bearing witness to it. I hope that you will be able to rebuild your faith, which has been ruined by the false teachers, by believing in the true gospel after rooting out and throwing down the false doctrines in Christianity today. We should be very thankful that there are true servants of God during these last days.

Those who possess the righteousness of God are now shouting out the truth of the water and the Holy Spirit. This truth will be spread to every part of this world, where it has not reached until now. *"For there is nothing hidden which will not be revealed, nor has anything been kept secret but that it should come to light" (Mark 4:22).* The gospel of the water and the Spirit, together with God's righteousness, will bear witness to the only truth that allows all the people in this world to receive the remission of sin.

Therefore, even though every believer in God's righteousness receive salvation from the judgment and punishment of sin, those who don't believe in it will receive the fatal condemnation of eternal death, which God sends down to sinners.

The time has arrived for you to decide whether you will believe in the false doctrines on justification or sanctification instead of believing in God's righteousness, which lies inside the gospel of the water and the Spirit. It is totally up to you whether you believe in this truth or not.

However, it is you who will be bound to the results of the decision. You should not forget that God gave you His righteousness as a gift together with the gospel of the water and the Spirit. It is not too late for you to believe in the true righteousness of God. Only then will you be able to obtain the eternal righteousness inside God and live happily for an eternity.

In Romans, God's righteousness is thought of as most

important and is preciously born witness to. Therefore, we should learn about God's righteousness through Romans since the gospel containing God's righteousness brings this righteousness to us.

Now is the time for Christianity to discard the false gospel, which does not contain God's righteousness, and return to His righteousness. In order to do so, we need to learn what God's righteousness really is and recover the true faith. The time has arrived for us to know about God's righteousness through Romans.

Luther, one of the greatest religious reformers, was in need of God's righteousness. He realized that one could not wash away one's sins through virtuous deeds regardless of whether one believed in God's righteousness or not. God's righteousness, which is talked about in the Bible, is not so called 'the righteousness acquired by faith' that can be obtained by a doctrinal and incomplete faith and most Christians are supporting.

People are trying to build up the moral righteousness of human deeds in a state in which they have not truly realized what God's righteousness really is. Therefore, innumerable Christians have fallen into an ethical faith of Christianity. In fact, we can nowadays often witness that Christians compete with one another while trying to show off their own virtuous deeds.

Though there are many who say that they have obtained the remission of their sins by believing in Jesus, there are rarely those who truly know the righteousness of God and believe in it. Many people believe in the Doctrine of Justification or the Doctrine of Sanctification, which are the pivotal doctrines in today's Christianity, and have fallen into 'self-conceit' of their faith while not knowing God's righteousness. They brag about themselves with their absurd and false faiths saying, "I will go to Heaven even though I have sin, because I believe in Jesus!" Can one truly go to Heaven when he/she possesses sin just because he/she believes in Jesus somehow?

Reconsider this question with your conscience. It is arrogant for one to believe that one can go to Heaven even though one has sin by believing in Jesus somehow. This is a self-justified faith that has sprung out from religion. We should discard the false faith that says that one can go to Heaven even when there is sin by only believing in Jesus. Isn't God holy? Does God acknowledge one just because he/she believes in the Doctrine of Justification that says that he/she has received salvation from his/her own sins even though he/she has sin in his/her heart? Can one obtain the righteousness of the true God by believing in forged doctrines on justification or sanctification? Certainly not.

How could a person say that he/she is sinless though there is evidently sin inside his/her heart? Without knowing and believing in the righteousness of God written in His words, one cannot say that he/she is actually sinless in his/her conscience. The reason some people can say recklessly that they are able to go to Heaven is because they believe in the forged doctrines on justification or sanctification that prevail in today's Christianity. Did your sins really disappear when you relied on these kinds of doctrines? Is it possible? Only one who discovers and believes in God's righteousness by believing in the words of the gospel of the water and the Spirit can say that he/she surely is sinless.

However, one who has faith in the Doctrine of Justification, which is one of the principal Christian doctrines, believes that he/she is sinless only due to the reason that he/she believes in Jesus somehow, though in truth he/she has sin. You should know that the faiths of these kinds of people are faiths that are just like the tower of Babel, built by a human plot against God's word. It is not hard to realize that it is impossible for one to escape from all sins by doctrinal faith. The Lord Jesus revealed God's righteousness through the baptism He received from John, His blood on the Cross, and His resurrection. He gave it to all those who believe in Him. Therefore, Paul said clearly that in the gospel God's righteousness is revealed from faith to faith (Romans 1:17).

There are many Christian leaders who are outstanding in their ethical and moral standards. However, they teach their followers to pursue the human righteousness inside Christianity stirring up the human ethics and morals of Christians. They don't even have the slightest idea about the gospel of the water and the Spirit containing God's righteousness.

Therefore, they can't teach their followers about the righteousness of God. This is the reason why the true gospel in which God's righteousness is revealed cannot be found inside the doctrines and teachings of Christianity nowadays. Christianity has not spread God's righteousness, which is revealed inside the gospel of the water and the Spirit and is considered the most important by God, until now. Therefore, no one is able to soundly encounter God's righteousness with Christian doctrines.

Then where can God's righteousness be found? It is revealed where one can obtain salvation from all sin by discovering and believing in God's righteousness inside the baptism Jesus received and His blood on the Cross. The Bible explains God's righteousness through the gospel of the water and the Spirit. The faith believing in the baptism Jesus Christ received from John the Baptist, His bloodshed on the Cross, and the resurrection leads us to know about God's righteousness.

If we wish to own the righteousness of God, we should believe in the words of the gospel of the water and the Spirit. God's righteousness is abundantly revealed inside the gospel of the water and the Spirit God has given. Therefore, anyone who makes up his/her mind to believe in God's righteousness can find and believe in it right now.

What I want to tell you brethren is that one cannot know about God's righteousness by a doctrinal faith that still prevails inside Christianity. I tell you that this is only possible by believing in the words of the water and the Holy Spirit, which contains God's righteousness. However, most believers and theologians of today's Christianity do not even wish to know about God's righteousness. Rather, they are not able to know it. The reality is that they fear that the doctrinal faiths they had until now would be deteriorated.

However, God's righteousness only can actually bring the remission of sin to all sinners. The reason these people are not able to accept the words containing God's righteousness is that they have been fed with ethical and moral teachings until now. Satan has turned the attention of people elsewhere so that they would not know about the righteousness God has given to them.

What Christian believers need at this time is not the ethical righteousness of religion, but to have faith in God's righteousness. Presently, most people who say that they believe in Jesus as their Savior have not been able to equip themselves with the faith in God's righteousness and are therefore on the verge of spiritual death. Therefore, today's Christian believers should be clothed with God's righteousness in their hearts.

This righteousness of God can only be obtained when our souls believe in the gospel of the water and the Spirit. In order to do that, we need to first discard the doctrinal faiths based on human logic and the false teachings on salvation. Moreover, we should be most concerned with the salvation of our own souls. One can get clothed with God's righteousness only after one's soul has obtained eternal redemption from all the sins of his/her whole life.

Right now, Christianity has departed itself from God and is running on a carriage of theoretical doctrines toward complete darkness. The doctrinal faiths that theologians have forged gave birth to human-centered religious faiths. Now, Christianity might at this moment seem to have obtained great success based on worldly standards, but we see that there isn't the slightest bit of God's righteousness inside it. Rather we can find only human righteousness inside Christianity, and it is human righteousness that blocks God's blessings.

Most Christian souls are about to go to hell after death due to their spiritual starvation and sins. They should realize and believe that only the abundance of God's righteousness can save them from hell. Therefore, we should deliver the abundant truth of God's righteousness to all the sinners who still do not know about it.

Now we will learn and come to know what God's righteousness is. If we don't believe in His righteousness, even though we know about it, we will receive eternal destruction, but we will surely enjoy the spiritual blessings of Heaven if we do believe in it.

Christianity today has degraded itself into a worldly religion due to the Doctrine of Justification and the Doctrine of

Sanctification. This religion is like 'the great harlot' in the Bible. The Doctrine of Justification and the Doctrine of Sanctification that theologians have invented inside Christianity are causing a favorable reaction among people, though they are nothing more than the religious doctrines that have been concocted by human thought. There is not a single person whose sins were perfectly eliminated by believing in these doctrines!

The Doctrine of Sanctification is the same as the doctrine that worldly religions teach on virtuous deeds. It is impossible to obtain the righteousness of God, which is talked about in the Bible, with these kinds of doctrinal faiths. Most Christians regard the doctrinal righteousness in the same light with God's righteousness, and that is a false teaching from Satan. One who blocks people from believing in God's righteousness will remain as a great enemy to God. Therefore, God can't allow people to obtain His righteousness inside worldly religions because it has only been allowed by the gospel of the water and the Spirit.

All of those who eagerly long for God's righteousness! I hope you will obtain the remission of sin and eternal life by believing that Jesus Christ came to this world, took over your sins by the baptism He received from John, died on the Cross, and resurrected on the third day. God's righteousness will bring eternal life and the blessing of becoming God's children to all those who believe in His righteousness. God's righteousness is different from the human righteousness that can be obtained by keeping the law. God's righteousness allows the eternal remission of sin to all sinners at once.

Nothing in heaven or on earth can separate those who possess the faith in God's righteousness from God's love that is revealed inside Jesus Christ. The faith in God's righteousness is true and should be appreciated inside Christianity. God's righteousness can be obtained only by believing in the gospel of the water and the Spirit.

Paul asserted that even the Israelites would receive salvation from sin in the last days by believing in God's righteousness. He believed that since God did not break the promise that He would save the Israelites from sin, God would work in the last days and save them from sin. God always works consistently according to His will. He wants to save all humankind. There is no one from any historical time period who has been left out from the blessing that can be obtained by believing in God's righteousness, just because he/she was not a Jew.

It is really unfortunate that there are people who reject the gospel of the water and the Spirit without knowing that God's love and His righteousness are hidden inside it. We should remember and keep in our hearts the fact that there is only human righteousness remaining for those who say that they believe in Jesus without knowing the abundance of God's righteousness. The salvation from sin God has given to mankind can only be acquired by believing in the righteousness of God.

In conclusion, a person gets saved from sin not by his/her own efforts, but by believing in the abundance of God's righteousness that is revealed inside the gospel of the water and the Spirit. God did not abandon the Jews or leave out the Gentiles from the blessing of being clothed with His righteousness. God allowed His righteousness, which can be obtained by the faith in Jesus' baptism and His blood of the Cross, to be given to both the Israelites and the Gentiles.

Iniquities are prevailing in the present generation we live in. Therefore, we can only receive the remission of sin by believing in God's righteousness right now. Paul the Apostle said, *"In it (the gospel of Christ) the righteousness of God is revealed from faith to faith" (Romans 1:17).* Now is the time we all should believe in the abundance of God's righteousness. We should all obtain the abundance of His righteousness that He has given to all humanity by believing in the words of the gospel of the water and the Spirit. God blessed us so that we could praise Him for eternity by believing in His righteousness, which never changes.

I am sure that this book will be "the bunker-buster" to Christianity's false teachers and their followers in today's world. They are the perpetrators of Satan who have made deep caves of Christian doctrines and dwelt in them. They are so well adapted to the dark caves of Satan that they are unable to see God's life-giving light, unless the bunkers were to be blown out. When these sinners lose their old habitats through this "bunker-buster," they will be blessed abundantly with the righteousness of God.

Let us give thanks and praise to the Holy Triune God— God the Father, Jesus Christ the Son, and the Holy Spirit who has saved us from all the sins in this world through His righteousness. ⊠

CHAPTER

7

Introduction to Chapter 7

Reflecting on the fact that before his redemption his flesh was condemned to death by the Law of God, the Apostle Paul made the confession of faith that he was, by believing in Jesus Christ, dead to sin. Before we met the righteousness of God— that is, before we were born again—those of us who believe in Christ used to live under the dominion and curse of the Law. Thus, the Law would have had dominion over us had we not been redeemed of our sins by encountering Jesus Christ, who brought us the righteousness of God.

Paul spoke of spiritual matters that cannot easily be understood in flesh—that is, those who are dead to sin are no longer under the dominion of sin, just as a woman whose husband has died is completely freed from her obligation to her husband. This passage may sound simple, but it is a spiritually crucial passage. It means that, whether they like it or not, those who have not met the righteousness of God are, as a matter of fact, fated to live under the curse of the Law. This is because they have not yet resolved the problem of their sins.

Romans 6:23 tells us that *"the wages of sin is death,"* meaning that sin will disappear only when its wages have been paid. If one believes in Jesus, yet does not know the righteousness of God given by Jesus, then he is still living in sin and must pay the wages of sin. This is why we have to meet God's righteousness through Jesus Christ. Only by encountering the righteousness of God can we be dead to our sins, freed from the Law, and be married to our new groom Christ Jesus.

We can find God's righteousness through Jesus Christ, but without believing in this righteousness of God, no one can be freed from the Law. The only way to break away from the curse of the Law is to know and believe in God's righteousness. Have you found this righteousness of God through Jesus? If not, now is the time for you to abandon your own righteousness and humbly return to God's Word.

Toward Christ after being dead to sin

Paul told his brethren in Rome, *"You also have become dead to the law through the body of Christ."* You have to have a precise understanding of what it is *'to have become dead to the law through the body of Christ.'* No one can go to Christ without becoming dead to sin through the body of Christ. Our sins, in other words, must die with the body of Jesus Christ. This is possible only when one believes in the baptism of Jesus by John and His death on the Cross.

We can die with Christ to sin by believing in Jesus' baptism by John. Because Jesus died with all the sins of the mankind passed onto His body with His baptism by John, our sins, too, have died with Him when we believed in this. That all the sins of the world were passed onto Jesus through His baptism by John is the truth. This truth should not just be known, but kept in our hearts in faith. We must keep this faith until we enter the Kingdom of God. This is why Paul said that we became dead to the Law through the body of Christ. As such, those who believe in this truth can go to Jesus Christ, live with Him, and bear the righteous fruits for God.

We should not believe in the oldness of the letter, but in the new truth of the Spirit. Sinners actually commit more sins because of the Law. This is because the Law reveals more sins that are hidden inside of them, thereby making them more knowledgeable of their sins and allowing them to sin even more. One of the functions of the Law is to make us recognize our sins, but it also functions to reveal more of the nature of sin and to make us commit more sins. Were it not for the Law that God gave us, we would not know that there was so much sin hiding inside of us. But God gave us His Law, and this Law not only makes sin even more sinful, but it also makes us commit more and more sins.

Therefore, Paul says that since we have become dead to sin through Christ's body, we now have to serve the Lord with the faith of believing in God's righteousness. He is telling us to serve the Lord with the help of the Spirit and the gift of redemption given to us for our faith held deep in our hearts, instead of serving Him with faith in the literal letter of the Word. As the Bible tells us that *"for the letter kills, but the Spirit gives life,"* we must follow the Lord by realizing the true meaning of the gospel of the water and the Spirit, which is God's righteousness. When we believe in the Word of God, in other words, we have to know and believe in the true meaning hidden in the written Word.

Then is the Law sin? Certainly not!

Paul explained the Law of God by emphasizing its functions. This shows how important it is to believe with a proper understanding of the function of the Law. Paul looked at his sins in his own way before, and because of this he did not know his own sins, but through the Law of God he was able to realize that he had a covetous heart in him.

I hope that the believers in Jesus today are also able to reach the same understanding about the Law as the one reached by Paul. There are so many people who, not having realized the truth of the Law, try ever harder to live their lives by the Law. They go to church thinking that if they try a little harder, they will be able to keep all of the Law. But in reality, these people will actually not be able to find God's righteousness at all.

They have not realized the profound meaning of the Law given by God, and have thus become legalists. They are hypocritical blinds unable to see even their own hearts, and they don't know they are standing against the righteousness of God in the Christian community. There are many such people in today's Christianity. Those who do not truly know God's righteousness and have accepted Jesus as their nominal Savior in legalistic faith will not be exempt from the punishment of eternal death.

Paul stated that through God's commandments, he came to realize the covetousness inside his heart. When he realized his sins through the commandments, Paul was still a legalist who thought that he had to keep God's Law. God's commandments revealed the covetousness in Paul's heart and made Paul's sins even more sinful. This is how Paul came to realize that he was nothing but a grave sinner.

There are twelve natures of sin in human mind. When Paul did not know about the actual functions of the Law, he thought of himself as a fine person, not realizing just how sinful he really was. But the result of his effort to live by God's commandments showed to him that he was far from being able to keep the commandments, and that these commandments actually revealed his sins even more.

How are people when they believe in Jesus? When you

first started to believe in Jesus, you might have been all fired up with your faith, but as the time passes, you would have found the many sins that are fundamentally in you. Through what did you find these sins? It is through the written Law and commandments that we have found out just how full our hearts with the twelve kinds of sins. And we shrink from seeing our sinful selves before the Law. This is because we find, through the Law, that we are truly grave sinners.

That is why some people created the Doctrine of Justification to comfort themselves. This doctrine claims that even though we have sin in our hearts, just because we believe in Jesus, God would regard us as righteous. This is only a man-made doctrine. People have made and believed in such a doctrine to hide their sins, trying to live in the complacency of this doctrine. But because they are still revealed as sinners before the Law, their sins come to weigh down heavier and heavier on their minds. To be freed from all our sins, we have no other choice but to believe in the gospel that contains God's righteousness. This is the only way to be delivered from all our sins.

As Paul in his past had thought that God gave the commandments to be followed, he considered it only natural that he would try and do his best to keep them. Yet contrary to this, he found out that these commandments actually put his soul to death because of sin. Paul ultimately realized that he had been misunderstanding and mistakenly believing in God's commandments.

Everyone has in his heart the twelve kinds of sins mentioned in Mark 7:21-23. *"For from within, out of the heart of men, proceed evil thoughts, adulteries, fornications, murders, Thefts, covetousness, wickedness, deceit, lewdness, an evil eye, blasphemy, pride, foolishness. All these evil things come from within and defile a man."*

Paul and all other people ultimately came to recognize their sins through God's commandments. By the Law they realized their sins and were put to death, and then they discovered the righteousness of God through Jesus Christ and believed in it. What is your understanding of the righteousness of God? Are you still trying to observe the commandments while thinking that you can keep them all? God gave us His Law so that we would recognize our sins and return to Him— to be delivered from sin, in other words, by believing in the righteousness of God. We must have a proper understanding as to why God gave us His commandments and believe in them correctly. Once you realize this truth, you will know just how precious the gospel of water and the Holy Spirit is.

Those who believe in God's commandments can realize how great of a sinner they are in the sight of God. People who do not know the role of the commandments and do not believe in God's righteousness will come across great difficulties in their religious lives and ultimately be led to their own destruction. This is because it is simply impossible to stay away from sin while living in a world that is full of sins. This is why some people even seclude themselves in the remote mountains and try to live ascetic lives. They think that by living in deep mountains and retreating away from the sins of the world, they can avoid committing sins, but this is not the case.

We must realize that, though it is true that everyone in this world commits sin and thus has sin in his heart, the redemption from all such sin can be found in knowing and believing in God's righteousness. Even if we were to avoid the world in order to escape from its sins, we would still be unable to escape from the sins of their hearts. This is because our sins are found in our hearts. To truly rid ourselves of sin, we must believe in the gospel of the water and the Spirit. The Law of God and His commandments make our sins even more sinful. Those who know the severity of their sins must know and believe in the righteousness of God, revealed to us through the gospel of the water and the Spirit.

"And the commandment, which was to bring life, I found to bring death. For sin, taking occasion by the commandment, deceived me, and by it killed me" (Romans 7:10-11). We must have a proper understanding of the Law. Those who have not properly understood the Law will spend their whole lifetime drowned in legalism, trying to escape from the Law until their very last day. Only those who know the true role of the Law will love and believe in the righteousness of God fulfilled by Jesus. Do you, then, know this righteousness of God?

Paul the Apostle said that because he was not born again in the past, he had then belonged to his flesh and been sold under sin. He also confessed that although he wished to live by God's Law, he ended up doing that which he did not wish to do—to commit sin, that is. This was because he did not have the Holy Spirit in him, as he did not have the righteousness of God. Paul then admitted that the reason as to why he committed sin against his desire was because of the sins found in his heart, for He was yet to find the righteousness of God at the time.

Nevertheless, Paul realized one law, and that law was the law of sin—his most fundamental realization of the fact that man, who has sin in his heart, cannot avoid sinning. He also realized that the inner person still desired to always live according to the Law of God. But Paul confessed that, just as a tree of sin bears the fruits of sin, he was a sinner who could only continue to live in sin, because he, not having met Jesus Christ yet, had not received the redemption of his sins. It was proper, in other words, for him to be put to death because of his sins.

This is why he confessed that he was a wretched man, lamenting, *"Who will deliver me from this body of death?" (Romans 7:24)* This was Paul's recollection of himself when he had been a sinner. You should consider applying this confession of Paul to yourself. Are you not still imprisoned in this body of death that cannot keep the Law? We must believe in the righteousness of God. In the gospel of the water and the Spirit is this righteousness of God hidden, and we can attain His righteousness by believing in this gospel.

Paul could be freed from all his wretchedness by believing in the baptism of Jesus Christ and His death on the Cross. ⊠

The Gist of Paul's Faith: Unite with Christ after Being Dead to Sin

< Romans 7:1-4 >

"Or do you not know, brethren (for I speak to those who know the law), that the law has dominion over a man as long as he lives? For the woman who has a husband is bound by the law to her husband as long as he lives. But if the husband dies, she is released from the law of her husband. So then if, while her husband lives, she marries another man, she will be called an adulteress; but if her husband dies, she is free from that law, so that she is no adulteress, though she has married another man. Therefore, my brethren, you also have become dead to the law through the body of Christ, that you may be married to another--to Him who was raised from the dead, that we should bear fruit to God."

Have you ever seen an entangled bundle of yarn? If you attempt to understand this chapter without knowing the truth of Jesus' baptism in which Paul the Apostle believed, your faith would only be in a greater state of confusion than before.

Paul says in this chapter that because everyone is utterly sinful before the Law of God, one can go to Jesus Christ and be born again only after dying a spiritual death.

The truth that Paul came to realize

Romans 7:7 states, *"What shall we say then? Is the law sin? Certainly not! On the contrary, I would not have known sin except through the law."* Paul continues, *"For I would not have known covetousness unless the law had said, 'You shall not covet.'"* Moreover, he adds, *"But sin, taking opportunity by the commandment, produced in me all manner of evil desire."* Paul realized that he had been violating all of the 613 commandments of God. In other words, he was no more than a mass of sin who could not do anything but commit sins, because he was a descendant of the first man Adam, was brought forth in iniquity, and was conceived in sin by his mother.

Everyone who is born into this world sins, starting from his very birth to his death. They are thus incapable of keeping God's commandments. How could these masses of sin keep all the 613 commandments and the Law of God? Only when we recognize that we are sinners before the Law of God can we go to Jesus Christ, the righteousness of God, and come to the realization that we can finally be delivered from sin through Christ Jesus. Jesus Christ became the righteousness of God. He brought us this righteousness of God through His baptism by John and His blood on the Cross. We must therefore all know and believe in God's righteousness. The reason as to why we must believe in Jesus is because this righteousness of God is found in Him.

Do you know and believe in God's righteousness? God's righteousness is the secret that is hidden in the gospel of water and the Spirit. This secret is all contained in the baptism that Jesus received from John at the Jordan River. Do you want to know this secret? If you want to believe in this truth, you will get the righteousness of God through your faith.

Before we came to know about God's Law and commandments, it seemed as if we were not sinners, even though we had committed sin on a daily basis. But after we started attending church, we came to realize that we were indeed very sinful, and that we would reach spiritual death because of the sins revealed in us. Thus, in order to lead souls to Jesus Christ, Paul the Apostle recollected his past days when he falsely believed by having misunderstood God's Law and commandments.

Here is an example that will help you understand the role of the Law of God. I am holding the Bible right now. If I hide something of great importance between the leaves of this Bible saying, "Don't ever try to look inside this book to find out what's hidden in it," and then leave it here on the table with you for a while, how will you react? The moment you hear my words, you'll feel a desire to find out what's hidden in that Bible, and as a result of this curiosity, you would violate my instruction. The very moment you wonder to yourself about what might be in hidden in that Bible, you will have no other choice but to find out. But had I not ordered you to never look into the Bible, you would have never felt the temptation. Likewise, when God commands us, the sins that had been latent in us will manifest themselves according to the circumstances.

The Law that God has given to the mankind has the role of revealing sin in people's hearts. He did not give it to us so that we could keep and follow it; rather, the Law was given to us in order to reveal our sins and thus make us sinners. We will all perish if we do not go to Jesus Christ and believe in God's righteousness that is found in the baptism that Jesus received from John and the blood that He shed on the Cross. We should bear in mind that the role of the Law is to bring us to Christ and to help us believe in God's righteousness through Him.

This is why Paul the Apostle testified, *"But sin, taking opportunity by the commandment, produced in me all manner of evil desire" (Romans 7:8).* Through the Law of God, Paul the Apostle showed us what the basic fundamentals of sin are. He confessed that in his fundamentals he had been a sinner, but that he came to have eternal life by believing in the righteousness of God given by Jesus Christ.

Paul's lamentation and faith

Paul thus said, *"O wretched man that I am! Who will deliver me from this body of death? I thank God-through Jesus Christ our Lord!" (Romans 7:24)*

Paul acknowledged the fact that even he, who possessed God's righteousness, still sinned, and that as such, God's righteousness was even more urgently needed not only for him but also for the rest of the mankind.

We should obtain the righteousness of God by correctly knowing the secrets hidden in the baptism that Jesus received and believing in it. You and I should know and believe in God's righteousness found in Christ's baptism and His blood on the Cross. Only then can our souls and flesh, which have no other choice but to sin, be delivered from our sins. We must not forget the fact that Christ's baptism and His blood on the Cross fulfilled God's righteousness.

Those who do not know the righteousness of God can only remain as sinners in the end, however hard they may try to keep His Law. We must realize that God's Law was not given for us to keep them. But legalists do not realize that the secret of redemption lies in the "baptism" that Jesus had received along with His blood on the Cross. As a result of this, they misunderstand God's Law by thinking that it was given to them to obey, and they keep on living in confusion. But we must recognize our sins through the Law and live by our faith in God's righteousness. We must not turn against this righteousness of God to pursue our own righteousness. Rather, we must believe in the righteousness of God fulfilled by the baptism of Christ and His blood on the Cross. We need to, in other words, learn to give thanks to our Lord, who has fulfilled God's righteousness.

This is why Paul, looking at his own flesh, initially cried out, *"O wretched man that I am!,"* but still gave thanks to God through Jesus Christ. The reason Paul made this confession was because the more he had sinned, the more wholly did Jesus' baptism and His blood on the Cross fulfill the righteousness of God. We, too, are able to shout in joy and victory, because we have been saved by our faith in Jesus Christ, even as we also live difficult lives between the law of the flesh and that of God's righteousness. The faith Paul had was one that believed in the baptism of Jesus Christ and in His blood on the Cross. This is how Paul came to dwell in his faith in the righteousness of God, and by believing in this righteousness of God, he could become the one who offered praises to Him.

In Romans chapter 7, Paul talks about his wretched state in the old times, in contrast to his later victorious faith in God's righteousness. Paul's victory of faith was because of his faith in this righteousness of God.

"Or do you not know, brethren (for I speak to those who

know the law), that the law has dominion over a man as long as he lives?" (Romans 7:1).

Reflecting on the fact that before his redemption his flesh was condemned to death by the Law of God, Paul made the confession of faith that he was, by believing in Jesus Christ, dead to sin. Before we met the righteousness of God—that is, before we were born again—those of us who believe in Christ used to live under the dominion and curse of the Law. Thus, the Law would have had dominion over us had we not been redeemed of our sins by encountering Jesus Christ, who brought us the righteousness of God.

Paul spoke of spiritual matters that cannot easily be understood in flesh—that is, those who are dead to sin are no longer under the dominion of sin, just as a woman whose husband has died is completely freed from her obligation to her husband. This passage may sound simple, but it is a spiritually crucial passage. It means that, whether they like it or not, those who have not met the righteousness of God are, as a matter of fact, fated to live under the curse of the Law. This is because they have not yet resolved the problem of their sins.

Romans 6:23 tells us that *"the wages of sin is death,"* meaning that sin will disappear only when its wages have been paid. If one believes in Jesus, yet does not know the righteousness of God given by Jesus, then he is still living in sin and must pay the wages of sin. This is why we have to meet God's righteousness through Jesus Christ. Only by encountering the righteousness of God can we be dead to our sins, freed from the Law, and be married to our new groom Christ Jesus.

We can find God's righteousness through Jesus Christ, but without believing in this righteousness of God, no one can be freed from the Law. The only way to break away from the curse of the Law is to know and believe in God's righteousness. Have you found this righteousness of God through Jesus? If not, now is the time for you to lay aside your own righteousness and humbly return to God's Word.

Toward Christ after being dead to sin

Paul told his brethren in Rome, *"You also have become dead to the law through the body of Christ."* You have to have a precise understanding of what it is *'to have become dead to the law through the body of Christ.'* No one can go to Christ without becoming dead to sin through the body of Christ. Our sins, in other words, must die with the body of Jesus Christ. This is possible only when one believes in the baptism of Jesus by John and His death on the Cross.

We can die with Christ to sin by believing in Jesus' baptism by John. Because Jesus died with all the sins of the mankind passed onto his body with His baptism by John, our sins, too, have died with Him when we believed in this. That all the sins of the world were passed onto Jesus through His baptism by John is the truth. This truth should not just be known, but kept in our hearts in faith. We must keep this faith until we enter the Kingdom of God. This is why Paul said that we became dead to the Law through the body of Christ. As such, those who believe in this truth can go to Jesus Christ, live with Him, and bear the righteous fruits for God.

So, the Scripture tells us that we should serve God in the newness of the Spirit and not in the oldness of the letter (Romans 7:6). Sinners actually commit more sins because of the Law. This is because the Law reveals more sins that are hidden inside of them, thereby making them more knowledgeable of their sins and allowing them to sin even more. The prime function of the Law is to make us recognize our sins, but it also functions to reveal more of the nature of sin and to make us commit more sins. Were it not for the Law that God gave us, we would not know that there was so much sin hiding inside of us. But God gave us His Law, and this Law not only makes sin even more sinful, but it also makes us commit more and more sins.

Therefore, Paul says that since we have become dead to sin through Christ's body, we now have to serve the Lord with the faith of believing in God's righteousness. He is telling us to serve the Lord with the help of the Spirit and the gift of redemption given to us for our faith held deep in our hearts, instead of serving Him with faith in the literal letter of the Word. As the Bible tells us that *"for the letter kills, but the Spirit gives life,"* we must follow the Lord by realizing the true meaning of the gospel of the water and the Spirit, which is God's righteousness. When we believe in the Word of God, in other words, we have to know and believe in the true meaning hidden in the written Word.

Then is the Law sin? Certainly not!

Paul explained the Law of God by emphasizing its functions. This shows how important it is to believe with a proper understanding of the function of the Law. Paul looked at his sins in his own way before, and because of this he did not know his own sins, but through the Law of God he was able to realize that he had a covetous heart in him.

I hope that the believers in Jesus today are also able to

reach the same understanding about the Law as the one reached by Paul. There are some people who, not having realized the truth of the Law, try ever harder to live their lives by the Law. And there are many who go to church thinking that if they try a little harder, they will be able to keep the all the Law. But in reality, these people will actually not be able to find God's righteousness at all.

These people have not realized the profound meaning of the Law given by God, and have thus become legalists. They are hypocritical blinds unable to see even their own hearts, who stand against the righteousness of God in the Christian community. There are many such people in today's Christianity. Those who do not truly know God's righteousness and have accepted Jesus as their nominal Savior in legalistic faith will not be exempt from the punishment of eternal death.

Paul stated that through God's commandments, he came to realize the covetousness inside his heart. When he realized his sins through the commandments, Paul was still a legalist who thought that he had to keep God's Law. However, God's commandments came to reveal the covetousness in Paul's heart and made Paul's sins even more sinful. This is how Paul came to realize that he was nothing but a grave sinner.

There are twelve natures of sin in human mind. When Paul did not know about the actual functions of the Law, he thought of himself as a fine person, not realizing just how sinful he really was. But the result of his effort to live by God's commandments showed to him that he was far from being able to keep the commandments, and that these commandments actually revealed his sins even more.

How are people when they believe in Jesus? When you first started to believe in Jesus, you might have been all fired up with your faith, but as the time passes, you would have found the many sins that are fundamentally in you. Through what did you find these sins? It is through the written Law and commandments that we have found out just how full our hearts with the twelve kinds of sins. And we shrink from seeing our sinful selves before the Law. This is because we find, through the Law, that we are truly grave sinners.

That is why some people created the Doctrine of Justification to comfort themselves. This doctrine claims that even though we have sin in our hearts, just because we believe in Jesus, God would regard us as righteous. This is only a man-made doctrine. People have made and believed in such a doctrine to hide their sins, trying to live in the complacency of this doctrine. But because they are still revealed as sinners before the Law, their sins come to weigh down heavier and heavier on their minds. To be freed from all our sins, we have to believe in the gospel that contains God's righteousness. This is the only way to be delivered from all our sins.

As Paul in his past had thought that God gave the commandments to be followed, he considered it only natural that he would try and do his best to keep them. Yet contrary to this, he found out that these commandments actually put his soul to death because of sin. Paul ultimately realized that he had been misunderstanding and mistakenly believing in God's commandments.

Everyone has in his heart the twelve kinds of sins mentioned in Mark 7:21-23. *"For from within, out of the heart of men, proceed evil thoughts, adulteries, fornications, murders, Thefts, covetousness, wickedness, deceit, lewdness, an evil eye, blasphemy, pride, foolishness. All these evil things come from within and defile a man."*

Like Paul, all people can recognize their sins through God's commandments. By the Law they can realize their sins and are put to death, and then they come to discover the righteousness of God through Jesus Christ and believe in it. What is your understanding of the righteousness of God? Are you still trying to observe the commandments while thinking that you can keep them all? God gave us His Law so that we would recognize our sins and return to Him—to be delivered from sin, in other words, by believing in the righteousness of God. We must have a proper understanding as to why God gave us His commandments and believe in them correctly. Once you realize this truth, you will know just how precious the gospel of water and the Holy Spirit is.

Those who believe in God's commandments can realize how great of a sinner they are before God. People who do not know the role of the commandments and do not believe in God's righteousness will come across great difficulties in their religious lives and ultimately be led to their own destruction. This is because it is simply impossible to stay away from sin while living in a world that is full of sins. This is why some people even seclude themselves in the remote mountains and try to live ascetic lives. They think that by living in deep mountains and retreating away from the sins of the world, they can avoid committing sins, but this is not the case.

We must realize that, though it is true that everyone in this world commits sin and thus has sin in his heart, the redemption from all such sin can be found in knowing and believing in God's righteousness. Even if we were to avoid the world in order to escape from its sins, we would still be unable to escape from the sins of their hearts. This is because our sins are found in our hearts. To truly rid ourselves of sin, we must believe in the gospel of the water and the Spirit. The Law of God and His commandments make our sins even more sinful. Those who know the severity of their sins must know and believe in the righteousness of God, revealed to us through the gospel of the water and the Spirit.

"And the commandment, which was to bring life, I found to bring death. For sin, taking occasion by the commandment, deceived me, and by it killed me" (Romans 7:10-11). We must have a proper understanding of the Law. Those who have not properly understood the Law will spend their whole lifetime drowned in legalism, trying to escape from the Law until their very last day. Only those who know the true role of the Law will love and believe in the righteousness of God fulfilled by Jesus. Do you, then, know this righteousness of God?

Paul the Apostle said that because he was not born again in the past, he had then belonged to his flesh and been sold under sin. He also confessed that although he wished to live by God's Law, he ended up doing that which he did not wish to do—to commit sin, that is. This was because he did not have the Holy Spirit in him, as he did not have the righteousness of God. Paul then admitted that the reason as to why he committed sin against his desire was because of the sins found in his heart, for He was yet to find the righteousness of God at that time.

Nevertheless, Paul realized one law, and that law was the law of sin—his most fundamental realization of the fact that man, who has sin in his heart, cannot avoid sinning. He also realized that the inner person still desired to always live according to the Law of God. But Paul confessed that, just as a bad tree bears bad fruits, he was a sinner who could only continue to live in sin bearing the fruits of sin, because he, not having met Jesus Christ yet, had not received the redemption of his sins. It was proper, in other words, for him to be put to death because of his sins.

This is why he confessed that he was a wretched man, lamenting, *"Who will deliver me from this body of death?"* *(Romans 7:24)* This was Paul's recollection of himself when he had been a sinner. You should consider applying this confession of Paul to yourself. Are you not still imprisoned in this body of death that cannot keep the Law? We must believe in the righteousness of God. In the gospel of the water and the Spirit is this righteousness of God hidden, and we can attain His righteousness by believing in this gospel.

Paul was able to be freed from all his wretchedness by believing in the baptism of Jesus Christ and His death on the Cross.

The climax of chapter 7 is found in verses 24 and 25. Paul wrote, *"O wretched man that I am! Who will deliver me from this body of death? I thank God—through Jesus Christ our Lord! So then, with the mind I myself serve the law of God, but with the flesh the law of sin."*

In Romans chapter 6, Paul talked about the faith that leads us to be buried and resurrected in union with Christ. By uniting ourselves with His baptism and His death on the Cross, we can attain this faith.

Paul realized that he was a wretched man, whose flesh was so insufficient that he broke the Law of God not only before he met Jesus but also kept breaking it even after his encounter with Jesus. He thus lamented, *"Who will deliver me from this body of death?"* He then concluded that he could be delivered from the body of death by believing in the righteousness of God, saying, *"I thank God—through Jesus*

Christ our Lord!" Paul was set free from the sins of the flesh and mind by believing in God's righteousness through Christ and being united with Him.

Paul's final confession was, *"So then, with the mind I myself serve the law of God, but with the flesh the law of sin"* *(Romans 7:25).* And at the beginning of chapter 8, he confessed, *"There is therefore now no condemnation to those who are in Christ Jesus, who do not walk according to the flesh, but according to the Spirit. For the law of the Spirit of life in Christ Jesus has made me free from the law of sin and death"* *(Romans 8:1-2).*

There were originally two laws given by God: the law of sin and death and that of the Spirit of life. The law of the Spirit of life saved Paul from the law of sin and death. It meant that by believing in the baptism of Jesus and His death on the Cross, which took away all his sins, he united himself with Jesus and was saved from all his sins. We must all have the faith that unites us with the Lord's baptism and His death on the Cross.

Paul confessed in Romans chapter 7 that he was previously set to be condemned under the Law, but through Jesus Christ, he came to be delivered from this condemnation. As such, he could serve God through the Holy Spirit, who dwelled in him.

The truth Paul realized

Paul confessed, *"Is the law sin? Certainly not! Indeed I would not have known what sin was except through the law"* *(Romans 7:7).* He could not have known covetousness unless the Law said, "You shall not covet." Paul explained the relationship between the Law and sin, saying, *"But sin, taking opportunity by the commandment, produced in me all manner of evil desire."* This means that human hearts are fundamentally full of sin. From the moment people are conceived in their mother's wombs, they are conceived in sin, and will be born with the twelve kinds of sins.

These twelve kinds of sins are adultery, fornication, murder, theft, covetousness, wickedness, deceit, lewdness, an evil eye, blasphemy, pride, and foolishness. Everyone commits these sins until they die. How can anyone in the world obey the Law and commandments of God when he/she is born into this world with these twelve sins? The very moment when we hear the words of the Law and the commandments that tell us what we "should" or "should not do," sin starts to act in us.

When we did not know the Law and the commandments of God, the sins within us were quietly asleep. But after hearing the commandments, which told us what to do and what not to do, these sins came out and made us sin even more.

Whoever is not born again or does not believe in and understand the truth of the water and the Spirit has sin in him. This sin, having become active by the words of the commandments, then produces even more sins. The Law, which tells people what to do or what not to do, is like a trainer that tries to tame sin. However, sin goes against God's commands and disobeys them. When a sinner hears the commandments, the sins within his/her heart are activated, leading him/her to commit even more sins.

We can realize through the Ten Commandments that we have sin inside us. The role of the Law is thus to reveal the sins inside our hearts, make us realize that God's commandments are holy, and to awaken us to our sinfulness. At our fundamentals, we were born with the covetousness to have greed over everything that God has created, including properties or partners that are not ours. So, the commandment that states, "Do not covet," tells us that we were born sinners and were destined to go to hell from the day of our births. It also shows us the imperative for the Savior, who fulfilled the righteousness of God.

That is why Paul confessed that sin took the opportunity by the commandment to produce in him all manners of evil desire. Paul realized that he had been a great sinner who broke the good commandments of God, for he was originally born sinful and was with sin before believing in God's righteousness.

When we look into chapter 7, we find out that Paul the Apostle was very spiritual, had an extensive knowledge of the Bible, and had great spiritual understanding and experiences. He clearly knew through the Law that there was sin within him, which with the commandments produced all manners of evil desire. He came to know that the Law of God had the role of revealing sins within him. As these sins revived, he also confessed that the commandment, which was to bring life, brought him death.

How is your faith? Is it like Paul's? Isn't there sin in your heart whether you believe in Jesus or not? If so, that means you still do not know God's righteousness, have not received the Holy Spirit, and are a sinner who is destined to go to hell to be judged for your own sins. Do you admit these facts? If you do, then believe in the gospel of the water and the Spirit, in which the righteousness of God is revealed. You will be saved from all your sins, gain the righteousness of God, and have the Holy Spirit come upon you. We must believe in the gospel of the water and the Spirit.

Sin, taking occasion by the commandment, deceived Paul

Paul the Apostle said, *"The commandment, which was to bring life, I found to bring death. For sin, taking occasion by the commandment, deceived me, and by it killed me" (Romans 7:10-11).* Sin, in other words, deceived Paul by taking advantage of the commandment. Paul believed in the commandment that was truly good and just, and yet the twelve kinds of sin were alive and festering in his heart. This meant that he had been deceived by sin because he could not understand the purpose of God's commandments.

At first, Paul thought that God gave the Law for him to obey it. But later, he realized that the Law was not given to be obeyed, but to reveal the sins within people's hearts, along with the holiness of God, and to make unbelievers be judged by God. That is how Paul thought he was deceived by sin, since he did not understand God's commandments and Law correctly. Most people today are also deceived in the same way.

We must realize that the reason God gave us the commandments and the Law was not for us to obey them, but for us to realize our own sins and reach God's righteousness by believing in the gospel of the water and the Spirit. But since we try to live according to the Law with our sins, we end up revealing our sinful nature.

So, a sinner realizes through the Law that even though the Law is holy, he/she does not have any power or the capacity to live a holy life. In that moment, he/she becomes a sinner who has no choice but to be sent to hell by the Law. But sinners who do not believe in the gospel of the water and the Spirit keep on thinking that God gave them the Law for them to obey. They keep on trying to obey the Law, but they will deceive themselves and fall into destruction in the end.

Those who are not born again by remaining ignorant of the righteousness of God commit sin and then try to be forgiven by offering prayers of repentance. In the end, however, they come to realize that they misunderstood the purpose of God's Law and have deceived themselves. Sin, taking occasion by the commandment, has deceived them. The Law of God is holy, but the sins within them instead lead them to death.

Paul said, *"Therefore the law is holy, and the commandment holy and just and good. Has then what is good become death to me? Certainly not! But sin, that it might appear sin, was producing death in me through what is good, so that sin through the commandment might become exceedingly sinful" (Romans 7:12-13).* Those who understand this truth realize their need for God's righteousness, and hence, believe that the gospel of the water and the Spirit is the real truth. A person who believes in the gospel of the water and the Spirit also believes in the righteousness of God. Let us be delivered from all our sins and reach the holiness of God by believing in His righteousness. I wish for all of you to be blessed by this gospel.

How were the flesh and mind of Paul?

Paul was full of the Spirit and had a deep understanding of the Word of God. However, he spoke of his flesh in the following words: *"For we know that the law is spiritual, but I am carnal, sold under sin. For what I am doing, I do not understand. For what I will to do, that I do not practice; but what I hate, that I do. If, then, I do what I will not to do, I agree with the law that it is good. But now, it is no longer I who do it, but sin that dwells in me" (Romans 7:14-17).* He said that he committed sin because he was carnal by nature. Since he was carnal, he saw himself seeking after the desires of the flesh, even though he wanted to do good.

Paul thus realized, *"I delight in the law of God according to the inward man. But I see another law in my members, warring against the law of my mind, and bringing me into capacity to the law of sin which is in my members" (Romans 7:22-23).* This is why he lamented over his flesh, crying out, *"O wretched man that I am!"(Romans 7:24)* Even after Paul was born again, he was still distressed because evil was present within him, though he wanted to do good. When Paul said that evil was present within him, he was referring to his own flesh. He saw another law in his members, warring against the law of the Spirit, making him lose to the flesh, and leading him to commit sins. He could only admit that he had no choice but to be subjected to judgment as he saw his flesh taking control over him to sin. Because Paul, too, had flesh, he lamented over the sins that arose from his flesh.

That is why Paul declared, *"O wretched man that I am!"* But he also thanked Jesus Christ for fulfilling the righteousness of God. This was because he believed that Jesus came to earth, was baptized, and was crucified to give the forgiveness of sins to all of mankind. He could heartily thank God, for he had the faith that united him with the baptism and blood of Jesus Christ.

Paul knew that when John baptized Jesus, all his sins, as well as the sins of the world, were passed onto Jesus once and for all. He also knew that when Jesus died on the Cross, we all died to sin as well. We must therefore have a united faith together with the truth of the water and the Spirit. Is your heart united with the baptism and blood of Jesus Christ? Have you, in other words, united your heart with the gospel of the water and the Spirit, which fulfilled the righteousness of God? We must have our faith united in the baptism that our Lord received from John and the blood that He shed on the Cross. It is very important for us to have united faiths because uniting with the gospel of the water and the Spirit is to unite with the righteousness of the Lord.

Romans 6:3 states, *"As many of us as were baptized into Christ Jesus were baptized into His death."* This means that by believing in Jesus' baptism, we have also been baptized with Him, meaning that we have become united into the death of our Lord. That is, by being baptized in unity through faith, we were spiritually baptized into His death. To be united with the Lord is to be united with His baptism and to die in union with His death.

We must therefore believe in and unite with the baptism of Jesus and His death on the Cross that have fulfilled the righteousness of God. If you do not yet believe in the gospel of the water and the Spirit, which holds the righteousness of God, you are not united with the baptism of Jesus and His death. And it is in this gospel that the righteousness of God has been revealed.

If our hearts do not unite with the baptism of Jesus and His death on the Cross, our faith is merely theoretical and useless. Unite yourself with the baptism of Jesus and His blood on the Cross and believe in them. That is how we should believe. A theoretical faith is useless. What good is a nice house, for example, if it is not yours? To make the righteousness of God ours, we must know that the purpose for Jesus' baptism was to wash away our sins, and that His death on the Cross was for the death of our flesh. Through our faith in the righteousness of God fulfilled by our Lord, we must be redeemed once and for all and walk in the newness of life.

Through your faith thus united with the baptism of Jesus and His blood on the Cross, the righteousness of God will actually become your own. We must unite with the baptism and death of Jesus, for if we do not, our faith would mean nothing.

"O wretched man that I am! Who will deliver me from this body of death?" (Romans 7:24) This is not just Paul's lamentation, but also that of you and I, as well as all those who are still separated from Christ. He who will deliver us from this distress is Jesus, and it can be resolved only by believing in the Lord, who was baptized, crucified, and resurrected for us.

Paul said, *"I thank God—through Jesus Christ our Lord!"* This shows that Paul united himself with the Lord. We must believe that if we unite and have faith that the Lord saved us from our sins through His baptism and blood, we will be forgiven and receive eternal life. All your sins will be passed onto Jesus Christ when you believe in the baptism of Jesus with a united heart. You will have died and be resurrected with Him after acquiring a faith in union with His death on the Cross.

Jesus started His ministry on earth at the age of thirty. The very first thing He did on His mission was to wash away our sins by being baptized by John the Baptist. Why was He baptized? It was for Him to bear all the sins of mankind. Therefore, when we united our hearts with the righteousness of God, carried out by Jesus, all our sins were actually passed onto Jesus through His baptism. All our sins were transferred to Jesus and washed away once and for all.

Our Lord actually came to the world and was baptized to bear all our sins and died to pay their wages. Jesus said to John just before He was baptized, *"It is fitting for us to fulfill all righteousness" (Matthew 3:15)*. *"All righteousness"* refers to Jesus' receiving of the baptism, which washed away all the sins of mankind, who were destined for hell, and also to His death and resurrection. What is the righteousness of God? According to God's promises in the Old Testament, Jesus' baptism and death on the Cross, which saved all sinners, is His righteousness. The reason Jesus came to earth in the appearance of a man and received baptism was to take all the sins of mankind onto Him and wash them away.

Why did John baptize Jesus? It was to fulfill the righteousness of God by taking all the sins of mankind. We, who were baptized into Christ Jesus, were also baptized into His death and now walk in the newness of life, for He was raised from the dead. To have faith in the righteousness of God is to believe and unite our hearts with the baptism of Jesus, His death on the Cross, and His resurrection. It is very important for us to believe that Jesus took all our sins onto Himself when He was baptized. We were buried with Him when He died on the Cross because we were united with Him through His baptism. It is crucial for us to unite our hearts with the Lord by believing in the righteousness of God, even after being delivered from all our sins. We can give thanks to God because we have all died with Christ when He died on the Cross, for He had already taken all our sins through His baptism.

Uniting with Jesus by faith is necessary even after obtaining God's righteousness through our redemption. After receiving the gift of redemption, our faith can deteriorate into a mere convention. But, if we unite our hearts with the righteousness of the Lord, our hearts will live with God. If we unite with the righteousness of God, we will live with Him, but if we do not, then we cannot help but become irrelevant to Him. If we do not unite with the Lord God and just remain spectators to Him, as if we were admiring our neighbor's garden, we would become irrelevant to God by being separated from Him. Therefore, we must unite with the Word of the Lord and the righteousness of God in faith.

If we have the faith in uniting with the baptism of Jesus and His death on the Cross, we are the Christians who are united with the Lord

To believe in the righteousness of God is to unite with the Lord and have the faith to acknowledge His righteousness. Every aspect of our lives should be united with the righteousness of God. That is how we should live. If we do not unite with His righteousness, we will become slaves to our flesh and die, but the very moment that we unite ourselves with the righteousness of God, all our sins will be forgiven. Only when we unite our hearts with the righteousness of the Lord do we become God's servants. All of God's works will then become pertinent to us, and, as such, all His works and power will become ours. However, if we do not unite with Him, we will remain irrelevant to His righteousness.

We are infirm and weak in the flesh, just as Paul was, so we must unite our hearts with the righteousness of God. We must unite and believe that Jesus was baptized by John and crucified to save us from all our sins. This is the kind of faith that pleases God and brings blessings to our bodies and souls. If we believe in the Lord's endeavors with our hearts united in faith, all the promised blessings of Heaven will also be ours. That is why we must be united with Him.

On the other hand, if we do not unite our hearts with the righteousness of God, we won't be serving Him. Those Christians who do not unite their hearts with God's righteousness love worldly values more than anything else. They are no different from the unbelievers in the world. They come to realize the value of God's righteousness only when their possessions, which they love as much as their own lives, are taken away from them. Materials do not have the worth or power to take control over people's lives. Only the righteousness of the Lord can give us the forgiveness of sins, eternal life and blessings. Materials are not worth our lives. We must realize that if we unite with the righteousness of the Lord, we, as well as our neighbors, will live.

Our hearts must be united in the righteousness of the Lord. We must live by faith and unite our hearts with Christ. Faith that is united with the righteousness of Christ is beautiful. What Paul finally says in chapter 7 is that we should live spiritual lives in union with the Lord.

Have you ever seen anyone who has become a servant of God without his heart being united with His righteousness? There is none! Have you seen anyone who acknowledges the gospel of the water and the Spirit as the necessary condition for the forgiveness of sins without being joined to the righteousness of God? There is no one. No matter how much we know about the Bible, our faith will be useless unless we are joined to the righteousness of God and believe that by believing in the baptism of Jesus and His blood on the Cross, we can be delivered from all our sins.

Even if we have once received the forgiveness of sins and attended church, if we are not united with His righteousness, we are sinners who have no part in the Lord's plan.   Though we say that we believe in God, we would be separated from the Lord if we were not joined to His righteousness. We must be united with the righteousness of God if we are to be consoled, helped, and led by Christ.

Have you received God's righteousness and the forgiveness of all your sins by believing in the gospel of the water and the Spirit? Do you serve, just as Paul did, the law of God with your mind while your flesh serves the law of sin everyday? We must be joined to the righteousness of God at all times. What will happen if we do not unite ourselves with the righteousness of God? We will be destroyed. But those who are united with God's righteousness will lead lives that are united with the church of God.

Believing in the righteousness of God means to be joined to the church and servants of God. We can continue to live by faith only when we are united with God's righteousness everyday. Those who are forgiven for their sins by believing in His righteousness must be united with God's church everyday. Since the flesh always wants to serve the law of sin, we must always meditate on God's law and live by faith. We can be united with the Lord if we keep meditating and focusing on the righteousness of God.

We, who believe in the righteousness of God, should unite with the church and servants of God on a daily basis. To do so, we have to always remember the righteousness of God. We have to think about and unite with God's church everyday. We must meditate on the fact that the Lord was baptized to bear all our sins in our stead. When we are joined to this faith and the righteousness of God, we will have peace from God, and you will be renewed, blessed and empowered by Him.

Unite yourself with God's righteousness. You will then

find new strength. Unite with the baptism of Jesus in the righteousness of God now. Your sins will all be taken away. Unite your heart with the death of Christ on the Cross. You, too, will die with Him. Unite with His resurrection. You, too, will live again. In short, when you unite with Christ in your heart, you will die and be resurrected with Christ, and thus become delivered from all your sins.

What happens if we do not unite with Christ? We may be confused and ask, "Why was Jesus baptized? The only difference between the Old Testament and the New Testament is that the former talks about the 'laying on of hands' and the latter talks about baptism. So? What's the big deal?" A knowledge-oriented or theoretical faith is not an actual faith, and it eventually leads believers to wander away from God.

Those who believe in such manner are like a student who accepts only knowledge from his teachers. If the student really respected his teachers, he would also learn from their noble characters, leadership, or great personalities. We should not accept the Word of God as just another piece of knowledge, but should learn of God's personality, love, mercy, and justice with our hearts. We should get rid of the idea of trying to learn His Word only as knowledge, but unite with His righteousness. To be joined to the righteousness of God leads believers to gain true life. Be united with the Lord! A united faith is the true faith. A theoretical and knowledge-oriented faith is not a united faith, but a shallow one.

"The mercy of God," as it is sung in a hymn, "is an ocean divine, a boundless and fathomless flood." When our hearts are united with the righteousness of God, there will be a peace as boundless and fathomless as the mercy of God that has given us His righteousness. But a theoretical and knowledge-oriented faith that is not joined to God is like shallow water. If the sea is shallow, it foams easily, but the magnificent flow of the blue waves, where the ocean water is very deep, is indescribable. But in shallow water, when waves hit the shore, they clot, break, foam, and get jumbled up into a mess. The faiths of those who are not united with God's righteousness are like these waves in shallow water.

The hearts of those who are united with the Word of God are deep, centered around the Lord, steadfast and unshakable in all circumstances. Their hearts move toward the will of the Most High. But those whose hearts are not joined to His righteousness are shaken easily, at the slightest trouble.

We must have faith that is united with the Lord. We must be joined to the Word of God. We must not be shaken at trivial matters. Those who are united with the Lord have been baptized with Christ, died with Christ, and arose again with Christ from death. Since we no longer belong to the world, we must unite with God's righteousness to please Him, who has accepted us as the servants of righteousness.

If we unite with the righteousness of God, we will always be at peace, happy, and full of strength because the Lord's strength will become ours. With His power and blessings made ours, we will live with great blessings. If we are joined to the baptism of Jesus and His death on the Cross by faith, all His power will become our own.

Unite your heart with the Lord. If you unite with the Lord, you will also be united with the church of God. And those who are united with God will unite with each other, doing, in their fellowship, His works and together growing in their faith in His Word.

If we do not unite our hearts with Christ, however, we will

lose everything. Even if our faith is as small as mustard seeds, the Lord has already forgiven our sins once and for all. We should be joined to this truth everyday, despite our weaknesses. Only a united faith will let you live and give thanks to God through Jesus Christ.

When we unite with the righteousness of the Lord, we find new strength and our hearts become steadfast. Our hearts become justified when we unite with God's Word. It is impossible to obtain the determination to serve the Lord by following our own minds. When we unite with the baptism of Jesus, His Cross and resurrection, our faith will grow and stand firmly on the Scripture.

We must unite our hearts with the Lord. Only the faith that is united with Him is the true faith; that which is not united with Him is a false faith.

We give thanks to God for allowing us to unite our faith with the Lord by giving us the baptism of Jesus and His blood on the Cross. We must unite our hearts with Him from this day on, to the last day, when we will meet the Lord again. Let us unite with Him.

We need to unite our hearts with God because we are weak before Him. Paul was also united with God and was delivered from his sins. He became God's precious servant, who preached the gospel all over the world, by knowing and believing in the gospel of the water and the Spirit given by Jesus Christ, the righteousness of God. Because we are weak, serving the law of God with our minds but the law of sin with our flesh, we can live only by uniting with the Lord.

Have you now learned about the faith that unites with the righteousness of Jesus? Is your faith united with the baptism of Jesus? Now is the time for you to have a united faith that believes in the baptism and the blood of Jesus. Those of you whose faith is not united with God's righteousness have failed in their faith, in their salvation, and I their lives.

Therefore, the righteousness of the Lord is the indispensable requirement for your deliverance. Being united with the Lord is the blessing that leads all of us to receive the forgiveness of sins and to become God's children. Receive the righteousness of God by uniting yourself to and believing in His righteousness. The righteousness of God will then become yours, and God's blessing will always be with you.

Thank God for Jesus Christ!

Paul the Apostle said that he thanked God through Jesus Christ our Lord. He thanked for the righteousness of God received by faith through Jesus Christ. Even after Paul believed in God's righteousness, he could not but serve God's law with his mind and the law of sin with his flesh. But since he believed in God's righteousness with all his heart, his heart had no sin.

Paul confessed that he was already condemned by the Law in Jesus Christ, and saved from sin through faith because of God's righteousness. He also said that those who were facing the wrath of God and the punishment of His Law would still be able to bear the fruit of salvation by believing in God's righteousness in their hearts. In the hearts of the born-again, there are wishes of the Holy Spirit as well as the wishes of the flesh. But a person who is not born again only has the lusts of the flesh. Therefore, sinners desire only to sin, and what is more, through their natural instincts, they try to beautify their sins before the others' eyes.

The deacons and the elders who are not born again usually say, "I want to live virtuously, but I don't know why it's so difficult." We must consider why they cannot help but live this way. This is because they are sinners who have not received salvation by believing in God's righteousness. In their hearts is sin because the righteousness of God is not found in them. But in the hearts of the born-again are both the righteousness of God and the Holy Spirit, but no sin.

When Paul had sin in his heart, he lamented, *"For the good that I will to do, I do not do; but the evil I will not to do, that I practice. O wretched man that I am! Who will deliver me from this body of death?"* However, Paul added immediately, *"I thank God—through Jesus Christ our Lord!" (Romans 7:25)* This means that he received salvation from all his sins by believing in Jesus Christ, who has fulfilled God's righteousness.

What Paul was trying to say in chapter 7 is that before, when he was religious without being born again, he had not known what the role of the Law was. But he said that the One who delivered him from that wretched state, caused by sin, was Jesus Christ, who had accomplished God's righteousness. Whoever believes that Jesus Christ fulfilled God's righteousness to deliver us from sin will be saved.

Those who believe in God's righteousness serve the law of God with the mind but serve the law of sin with the flesh. Their flesh still leans toward sin because it has not yet been changed, although they have been born again. The flesh desires sin, but the mind, which believes in God's righteousness, wills to follow God's righteousness. On the other hand, those who have not received the forgiveness of sins will be led by both their mind and flesh to only commit sin, because in the fundamentals of their hearts are found sin. But those who know and believe in the righteousness of God abide by His righteousness.

We thank God through Jesus Christ, for Christ has fulfilled all of God's righteousness. Thanks be to the Lord for giving us His righteousness and leading us to believe in it. ⊠

The Reason Why We Can Praise the Lord

< Roman 7:5-13 >
"For when we were in the flesh, the sinful passions which were aroused by the law were at work in our members to bear fruit to death. But now we have been delivered from the law, having died to what we were held by, so that we should serve in the newness of the Spirit and not in the oldness of the letter. What shall we say then? Is the law sin? Certainly not! On the contrary, I would not have known sin except through the law. For I would not have known covetousness unless the law had said, 'You shall not covet.' But sin, taking opportunity by the commandment, produced in me all manner of evil desire. For apart from the law sin was dead. I was alive once without the law, but when the commandment came, sin revived and I died. And the commandment, which was to bring life, I found to bring death. For sin, taking occasion by the commandment, deceived me, and by it killed me. Therefore the law is holy, and the commandment holy and just and good. Has then what is good become death to me? Certainly not! But sin, that it might appear sin, was producing death in me through what is good, so that sin through the commandment might become exceedingly sinful."

I praise the Lord who has led me until now

I praise the Lord who has led me to meet you, the precious people of God again. I sincerely thank Him for having blessed me to live a happy life to this day. God has been always with me and had mercy on me, even though there have been times when I felt discouraged, experienced hardships, agony and weaknesses within myself on many different occasions. He has been alive and by my side throughout my life, in both my troubles and joys. There never was an instance when He left me alone, not even for a second.

How much God has blessed us! Were God like us, He would perhaps have had mercy on us for two or three times, but would eventually have run out of patience. But God is not man, and His patience has no limit. He continues to bestow His ceaseless mercy on us, regardless of whether we do good deeds or not, whether we obey His Word or not. With such loving God, we cannot help but praise, worship and serve Him. King David praised the Lord throughout his entire life, thanking Him for taking care of him every time he was in trouble through the hardships in his life. He confessed, *"For by You I can run against a troop, by my God I can leap over a wall" (Psalm 18:29).*

How much God has blessed us! We cannot praise Him enough. Would we be satisfied if we built a church as large as the whole world? Would we be satisfied if we built a church that reached the sky? Of course not! We can build the biggest and the most beautiful church that we can ever imagine, but it is not the size or the beauty of the church that matters, but the fact that God works preciously at calling souls, making them hear His Word and allowing them to be born again by believing in His Word. And there is nothing we can do but only praise our Lord for all these blessings. We give thanks to God for allowing us to serve Him, bearing the fruits of His works from what, surely, would have been only wasted lives otherwise.

Aren't you thankful that God lets you sit in this new retreat center? Our God has blessed us with His boundless grace and has kept us as the apple of His eye. Who are we and what have we done to deserve all His love? We are no one, and we have done nothing. And yet God has made us precious before Him, not because we have anything to show for, but because we have been born again. We were anything but precious before we met Jesus Christ. God made us, who were foaming in our madness and wandering in the desert, destined to die and vanish away into dust and ashes, His children.

How beautiful and great is the love that God has given us! Praise the Lord! Of the many souls in this world, God has saved us with His unconditional love in His righteousness. There is more to salvation than just deliverance. It means that our souls are now in communion with God. It means that His love is now ours. It means that His blessings, too, are ours to claim.

It is by the amazing guidance and encouragement of God that we still find ourselves in His church. Had God not kept us here, how could we be here? Had He not loved us and blessed us, how would we have been able to preach the gospel and serve Him? We can serve God because He is alive, is with us, and has blessed us.

If the Lord had neither kept nor blessed us, we couldn't have praised Him before, or even now. God has loved, blessed, encouraged and covered us with His merciful hands so that we might serve, follow, praise and worship Him. Is this not true? We praise the Lord with all our hearts for His amazing work and His endless love for us.

God has done so much for those whom He has saved. That He has delivered us, and that He continues to strengthen the faith of the born-again saints, are the proof that God is holding us, and that He is protecting us. God works and fulfills His will through us.

I believe that God has blessed all His churches, the congregations of the born-again, around the world and will bless them forever. We have experienced much hardships, yet God has always been with us, made us endure and continue doing His works, strengthened our spirits and prepared our hearts to have the faith needed to receive more blessings. How great His grace is! I give thanks to the Lord once again.

We can praise the Lord with our whole hearts

"For when we were in the flesh, the sinful passions which were aroused by the law were at work in our members to bear fruit to death. But now we have been delivered from the law, having died to what we were held by, so that we should serve in newness of the Spirit and not in the oldness of the letter" *(Romans 7:5-6)*. The Bible says that when we were in the flesh, the sinful passions that were aroused by the law were at work in our members to bear fruit to death. However, the Bible also says, *"Now we have been delivered from the law, having died to what were held by, so that we should serve in newness of the Spirit and not in the oldness of the letter."*

Can the flesh be delivered from sinful passions? A human being has two facets of existence. One is the flesh and the other is the heart. The flesh cannot reach the righteousness of God however hard it may try. Nor can it keep the Law of God. Our flesh can never keep the Law of God even after we are born again, no matter how hard we try. So the Apostle Paul says, *"For when we were in the flesh, the sinful passions which were aroused by the law were at work in our members to bear fruit to death. But now we have been delivered from the law, having died to what were held by."*

Romans 4:15 states, *"Because the law brings about wrath; for where there is no law there is no transgression."* We must praise our God with our hearts. God made us praise Him in the newness of the Spirit, not in the oldness of the letter, because we who were held by the Law were already cursed by the wrath of the Law.

The flesh is different from the heart. The flesh is limited but the heart can receive God's Word and praise Him by faith. The heart can also be delivered from sin.

We have died to the Law. I am dead because I have died to what I was held by. Our flesh is already dead to God. With the flesh, we can neither reach His righteousness nor become justified before the Law of God. The flesh cannot avoid being judged. Yet God the Father sent us His only begotten Son, Jesus Christ, and passed the whole wrath of the Law onto Him, who was then crucified in our place. God thus has enabled us to serve the Lord by faith in the newness of the Spirit, not in the oldness of the letter, which had held us by the Law, under its wrath.

We can now praise the Lord by faith. The heart can praise the Lord, though we still have the flesh. Our hearts can believe that the Lord loves us. We can praise our Lord because we believe that we have died in Christ. God has saved us from the wrath of the Law. God the Father sent His only begotten Son for us, who were held by the curse of the Law and the judgment of God, and when the fullness of the time came, He passed all our sins and the wrath of the Law onto His Son. God has thus saved those who accept His love and believe in Him from their sins, His judgment, and the wrath of the Law. We praise the Lord for wholly saving us from all our sins.

We believe wholeheartedly that God has saved us to His righteousness. We give thanks, praise and glory to God with all our hearts for His love. But can we do these things with the flesh? No. When we were in the flesh, the sinful passions, which were by the Law, worked in our members to bear fruit to death. The flesh dwells only under the wrath of God.

We are now delivered from this wrath of the Law by faith. God made us serve Him by our faith in His love and salvation, not by the oldness of the letter and not by the Law of God's wrath, even though we are to be judged by the Law.

None of us can serve the Lord with our deeds. Though we have been born again, we cannot serve Him with our flesh. Is there anyone among us who has been disappointed while trying to serve the Lord with the flesh? We can never serve the Lord with the flesh. The sinful passions always reign the flesh. We cannot serve the Lord with our flesh even after we are born again. We can praise God and serve Him only with our hearts by faith. Therefore, when you praise God, believe with your heart and give thanks for His love. Then, the flesh can become an instrument that follows faith.

I praise the Lord who has saved us from all the wrath of the Law, for I believe in Him with my heart. I give thanks to the Lord. He has wholly saved me. He has delivered me from my daily sins and from the curse of the Law. Let there be no doubt: our Lord has saved us. Despite all our weaknesses and shortcomings, God has saved us because He loves us. How marvelous is it that God would make us righteous, even though we are full of shortcomings? How wondrous is it that God would make us His servants?

We can praise God because He has saved us from the wrath of the Law. We can serve the Lord with the Spirit and with our hearts. We can follow the Lord. We give thanks to the Lord, who has delivered us from our sins and His wrath. Do you give thanks to Him? Did our salvation not reveal just how weak we are? How many times have we failed to live by His will, even though we have tried our best to do so? How many times have we been boastful? How many weaknesses do we have? We can never praise the Lord with our flesh and deeds, not now, nor in the future. We praise God for what He has done with our hearts. Only with our hearts and by our faith can we praise the Lord.

We can't praise the Lord with the flesh

Our own righteousness comes to be broken into pieces while we follow the Lord. The world of the mind and the world of the flesh must be separated. This is the separation of the spirit from the flesh.

Do you believe this? It is useless for us to try with the flesh. When we sing, rejoice, praise, believe, follow and give thanks with our hearts, our flesh can serve the Lord, yielding to our hearts. We praise the Lord and give thanks to Him for our salvation, singing, *"♫All my sins are gone, because of Calvary; Life is filled with song, all because of Calvary; Christ my Savior lives to set me free from sin; Someday, He's coming O wondrous blessed day! All, yes, all because of Calvary. ♫"* But we stumble sometimes because of the flesh. We think to ourselves, "Why am I so weak, though I have no sin?" Then we wonder to ourselves, "♪ *All my sins are gone* ♪ '—that's right—'♪ *Life is filled with song* ♪ '—that's right too— '♪ *All because of Calvary* ♪ '—that's all right, but why am I so weak? I should give thanks and follow the Lord more joyfully with time, but why am I so full of shortcomings? Ah, my pitiful flesh!"

When we feel sad, God says to us, "Why are you cast down, O my soul? Don't you know that I am your Savior? I made you righteous." We can neither serve nor follow God with the flesh. We can serve God by believing in what He did to save us, by loving Him, giving thanks and glorifying Him with our hearts.

I want you to praise God with your heart. I also want you to believe and give thanks to Him with your heart. These things are possible only through our hearts. They are impossible with the flesh. The flesh always remains unchanged even after we are saved. What the Apostle Paul says in the above passage applies to both before and after being saved. God's Word is the same to those who are saved and to those who are not saved.

Have you continued pleasing God with the flesh after you were saved?

Have you continued pleasing God with the flesh after you were saved? Do you think that you can please God because you are different from the others and that you serve God more than they do? Those who are filled with their own righteousness will someday fall into a ditch. There are some people who have already experienced falling into a ditch and a tub of manure.

There is a sister who fell into a tub of manure in this

Summer Bible Meeting. I mean it was a real outhouse, but fortunately it had not been used yet. If somebody had used it before, she would have been mired in real trouble. We dug some deep holes and made some outhouses on that green hill when we prepared this Bible Meeting. Then, we put a footrest on each toilet, but we hadn't fixed the footrests to each outhouse yet. So, this sister slipped and fell into the hole. God has dug such a hole for those who are filled with their own righteousness. God wants us to glorify only Him.

My soul feels uncomfortable and unsatisfied when I veer from the right path after being saved. When I ponder on why I feel this way, I realize that my clothes are stained with filthiness. I come to know that I am not supposed to go that way, but I soon forget. As soon as I realize this I repent, saying, "I should not do this. What was I thinking? Oh, Lord. I praise You for washing away all my sins." But I come to sin again in no time. Sometime I dwell in God's grace and suddenly fall into sin. Then, I find myself escaping from sin to the grace of God. Back and forth I waver. So I sigh in grief and despair at my existence.

I came to know just how dirty I was after all my sins were forgiven. I came to deeply understand and thought, "It's terrible. Why am I so infirm and weak, though I believe in You, God?" The sinful passions, which are aroused by the Law, work in our members. I realized that the more I tried to live according to the Law, the more my flesh fell into the sinful passions. I came to know that the flesh could never follow God. I came to serve the Lord by presenting my flesh as an instrument of the righteousness to God and praised what God blessed after believing in Him with my heart.

The flesh is but a mass of sinful passions

Those who do not know that they are masses of sinful passions are surprised at how quickly they slip into sin when they quit serving the Lord for a while. We must believe in the Lord, praise Him, glorify Him and follow Him with our hearts. To follow Him with the heart is the blessing of the grace of the Lord. Only when we believe in Him with our hearts can we follow Him. When we are in the flesh, the sinful passions, which were aroused by the Law, work in our members to bear fruit to death. When we do not praise or follow the Lord with our hearts, our flesh quickly falls into the sinful passions. All of us have this tendency; so did the Apostle Paul.

Paul remained single all his life, preaching the gospel. But he came to know that sin was revived through the sinful passions of the flesh. He might have thought, "I am afraid. I was filled with joy some time ago, but why am I so gloomy now? What's wrong with me? I was so spiritual a little while ago but I feel like trash now." After thinking it over, he came to understand that he could not serve the Lord without separating the flesh from the heart. "O wretched man that I am! I can't do good with the flesh."

The flesh yields to the heart when we praise and follow God with our hearts. Paul realized this truth. We cannot help but sin. Do you understand this? When those who are sinless praise, believe and follow the Lord with their hearts, the flesh follows the heart. A person may think at first, "I have been saved from all my sins. Hallelujah. I am so happy." But more and more sinful passions are revealed from the person with time. Those who are filled with their own righteousness are more easily disappointed at their own self as the sinful passions come out of them little by little. Though they may not think so, they are actually worse than what they think of themselves.

We must know that our flesh is a mass of sinful passions. We have no confidence in the flesh; you must not depend on it. Instead, believe in God's grace, glorify the Lord, and follow Him with all your heart. These are possible only through the heart. Praise the Lord, for it is the grace of God that allows me, who was horrible at speaking and was full of my own righteousness, to preach the gospel! How can I do so without the grace of the Lord? I can only praise my Lord.

I give thanks to the Lord who enabled me to praise Him

I give thanks to the Lord who washed away all our sins and gave us the Holy Spirit to make us praise Him with our hearts, not with our flesh. We can praise and glorify Him because we believe in Him with our hearts.

"So we are always confident, knowing that while we are at home in the body we are absent from the Lord" (2 Corinthians 5:6). I praise the Lord who saved us from all our sins. I praise and thank the Lord. I glorify and believe in Him. The Lord saved us from all our sins, even as we were destined to die after living for sinful passions. He allowed us be saved by believing in God with our hearts. He made us praise Him and gave us joy.

Do not try to serve God with the flesh—it is impossible. Do not try to have godliness with the flesh—it cannot be attained. Give up all such efforts of the flesh. How, then, can we follow God? The answer is with our hearts. We can serve Him with the heart, in the newness of the Spirit. Our God has saved us, so follow Him with your heart, which enabled you to receive salvation.

I praise God. How many people lament over themselves? They sigh with grief and torment themselves, saying, "Why do I behave like this?" Do not be like them. It is impossible for you not to commit sin with your flesh. Don't try to make what is impossible possible. I want you to believe in God and praise Him with your heart. The flesh will then follow the heart. Have you tried to follow the Lord with your flesh for a long time after you were saved? Do you have a problem doing what you are supposed to be doing? If so, the problem is that you have been trying to serve the Lord with the flesh, not with the heart. Do you know what those who disrespect and slander me say? They laugh at me, scorning at me. But I just smile at them, because I know that they don't know what's going on in me.

I can preach the gospel because the Lord already washed away all my sins. If the Lord had not washed away all my sins, I would have already been judged and dead to God. God made us perfect by making us one with the Spirit. He made us the ones who praise Him. He made us live with thankful minds. He made us rejoice in His blessings. Praise God! Praise the Lord who made us His children! May all the glory be His and only His!

It is never too late. Put no confidence in your flesh. Sinful passions come out of us at the first and the slightest chance. The flesh always wants to make itself a priority before the will of God. This is why following God's will is possible only by faith. It is not possible with the flesh. Do not deceive yourself even after being saved. It is still possible for us to fall, despite our salvation, under the dominion of the flesh, because we know well that the flesh is always imperfect and weak.

We are the people of the Spirit, the people of faith. Put no confidence in your flesh. Repeat after me: "My flesh is like a garbage can." I want you to remember this. Do not trust yourself. We must believe in and follow God with our hearts. I give thanks to the Lord and praise Him for saving us from all the wrath of God's law. Hallelujah! ⊠

Our Flesh That Serves Only the Flesh

< Romans 7:14-25 >

"For we know that the law is spiritual, but I am carnal, sold under sin. For what I am doing, I do not understand. For what I will to do, that I do not practice; but what I hate, that I do. If, then, I do what I will not to do, I agree with the law that it is good. But now, it is no longer I who do it, but sin that dwells in me. For I know that in me (that is, in my flesh) nothing good dwells; for to will is present with me, but how to perform what is good I do not find. For the good that I will to do, I do not do; but the evil I will not to do, that I practice. Now if I do what I will not to do, it is no longer I who do it, but sin that dwells in me. I find then a law, that evil is present with me, the one who wills to do good. For I delight in the law of God according to the inward man. But I see another law in my members, warring against the law of my mind, and bringing me into captivity to the law of sin which is in my members. O wretched man that I am! Who will deliver me from this body of death? I thank God—through Jesus Christ our Lord! So then, with the mind I myself serve the law of God, but with the flesh the law of sin."

How amazing His grace is!

We give thanks to our God who has permitted us this

Summer Bible Meeting and reigned over the weather, preventing typhoons to give us these beautiful days. He has sent souls and gathered His people together to give us His Word and to let us rejoice in fellowship with each other and the Holy Spirit.

God is alive! How amazing His grace is! People now think that typhoon "Doug" will surely come to our country, so officials patrol to withdraw all the campers in the In-Jae valley area. I went to downtown In-Jae this afternoon. I heard people talking to each other, worrying over the typhoon, speculating on how powerful and destructive this typhoon was going to be.

But will everything happen in the way they expect, even as we, the children of God, have gathered here for the summer retreat? If we pray, it will not rain by the mercy of God. Will God blow away His people? God reigns the weather, but He does so on account of our faith. He works wisely, and this means that He will not test those of us whose faith has just begun by making them wonder, "Why does God give us a typhoon when we have this summer retreat?"

I had no power to prevent typhoon "Doug" when I heard about it in the news. All that I could do was pray. This Summer Bible Meeting had already been scheduled, we had already gathered, and there was nothing I could do about it. And I was worried that this chapel might not be strong enough to withstand the typhoon, given the fact that it was built with prefabricated materials. So I couldn't help but rely on God. I prayed, "Help us God. Protect us. In Jesus' name I ask, Amen." And sure enough, God prevented typhoon Doug! I believe God knows everything. He leads us to safety because He understands our situations better than we do.

The weather shows us so minutely that God is alive. I

heard a peal of thunder like a boom of guns in my tent. So, I came out of my tent and looked at the sky. The sky was dark and thick clouds were coming over the valley. So I asked, "Lord, are clouds coming?" My faith began to weaken, "Lord, what's going on? Has the typhoon reached here? Is it really here?" But I had prayed and believed in God, and held on to this faith, saying to God, "I believe You will take care of us, Lord. I believe in You. I already believed that You would work for us." God really blessed us, as we believed. We thank Him with our hearts.

The flesh is selfish and evil

We cannot do anything if God does not work for us. Our God keeps and helps us. Let's take a look at God's Word. Romans 7:14-25 tells us that the Apostle Paul saw himself as staying in the flesh and having been sold under sin. He also discovered that it was a law that the flesh could not help but sin while he was alive.

We who are born again also do evil, though we want to do good with the flesh. Romans 7:19 states, *"For the good that I will to do, I do not do; but the evil I will not to do, that I practice."* We come to see that no good dwells in us. Because of that, we sigh in grief, thinking, "Will I be able to keep my faith?" We are greatly grieved because of our hopeless and evil flesh. Do you know how selfish the flesh is? Romans 7:18 states, *"For I know that in me (that is, in my flesh) nothing good dwells; for to will is present with me, but how to perform what is good I do not find."*

We are always taking our own side, even as we are the seeds of evildoers. Do you know how selfish we, all human beings, are? We certainly know we are evil, but we do not side with the Lord; we take our own side. The Lord is certainly good and His will is also good. We know that we are evil, yet we love ourselves too much. God commanded us not to have other gods before Him. God told us this to give us the knowledge of sin.

We love ourselves and do everything for ourselves, though we know how selfish and self-righteous we are. We fret when there is something beneficial to us, but how stingy and miserly we are to the Lord! It's because we have no sense. Children never let go of their cookies. They seize what is in their hands until it breaks, and they never share it because they are young and have no sense. They don't know that there are more precious things in the world than cookies. Children are like that; we are like that.

Our sins were washed away, but we are still selfish. We give thanks to the Lord for making us sinless and giving us the Holy Spirit by His power. But a war begins within ourselves after receiving the remission of sins and being born again. This war is between the flesh and the Spirit. We are happy after we are born again, but we are soon tormented by this war. But the Lord now wants us to work for the Kingdom of God.

Our Lord abandoned His glory for us. He was sent in the likeness of the flesh. He was not sent to the world as a handsome man. He came to the world as a humble man, maybe as a short-legged and ugly man. In fact, it is said that Jesus was not at all handsome. Isaiah said, *"For He shall grow up before Him as a tender plant, and as a root out of dry ground. He has no form or comeliness; and when we see Him, there is no beauty that we should desire Him"* (Isaiah 53:2). Still, the Lord has taken away all our sins.

Our flesh serves only sin. Paul knew that his flesh was a mass of sin, so he said, *"For what I will to do, that I do not practice; but what I hate, that I do,"* and yet he did not elaborate in detail because he was ashamed of his sins.

We are like garbage cans. We are masses of sin. How deplored would we be to see ourselves leaving a trail of trash behind us. Yet stung by our conscience, we say to God, "Lord, I should not do this, and I want to live according to Your will, but I did it again. How can I stop this, Lord?"

We can thank God when we know our evilness

We must think about the grace that Jesus Christ, our God, gave us. We must think about what God did with our hearts. Only then can we come to know what is right, and only then can we begin to serve the Lord. It is by the grace of God and our faith in Him that we seek God, offer ourselves to Him, and overcome any challenge that may await us as we follow God with our hearts and walk with Him.

We begin to deny ourselves when we come to know that we are evil and useless before God. We realize that avoiding sin is impossible without serving the Lord because of our flesh, and that we cannot do anything, though we are blessed greatly, because of our weaknesses. I give thanks to God who blessed me to serve Him. If God had not put me into the ministry to serve the gospel, I would have remained merely a mass of sin that was still in the flesh and would never do anything righteous before Him.

I give thanks to God for enabling me to serve Him. That's why I offer a prayer like this. "Thank you, Lord. Lord, I need money, but I have nothing. I want to do all these things for You, though I have nothing. Please help me. I will not spend the money for me, but for the Lord. If I spend money on myself, the flesh will be comfortable. But I want to spend it for the Lord and for the righteous work. This money is precious for me, because I worked very hard for it. And because it is precious to me, I offer it to You. Please spend it for your righteous works."

Those who know their evilness know that no good thing dwells in them. What do I mean by the words, 'No good thing dwells in them'? It means that they have only evil things in their flesh. It is evil to live only for oneself.

We thank God through Jesus Christ our Lord

Paul confessed, *"O wretched man that I am! Who will deliver me from this body of death? I thank God—through Jesus Christ our Lord! So then, with the mind I myself serve the law of God, but with the flesh the law of sin" (Romans 7:24-25)*. What does the flesh serve? The flesh always serves sin. However, we serve God with our hearts. Through whom do we thank God? We thank God through Jesus Christ, our Lord.

Paul said, *"I thank God—through Jesus Christ our Lord!"* So do I. If the Lord had not taken out all my sins, I couldn't have been saved because the flesh still serves sin now.

"I thank God—through Jesus Christ our Lord!" We give thanks to the Lord because He took away all the sins of all the flesh. Our flesh serves only sin, even after we receive the forgiveness of our sins. But the heart wants to serve God. The reason why we thank God and why the heart is made righteous is through Jesus Christ. Do you believe this? We thank God and serve Him because He took away our sins. If the Lord had not taken away and saved us from the sins of the flesh, we

would have eternally perished. Do you believe this?

Had the Lord not taken away all our sins, how could we have peace, how could we give thanks to the Lord, and could we serve the Him? How can a person who is under sin help other people? How can a person in jail rescue other people in jail? *"I thank God—through Jesus Christ our Savior."* The Lord cleansed away all our sins for us to serve Him, and He has given us peace in our hearts.

We are already dead in the world

How can we preach the gospel, serve God, work for Him, and contribute to His ministry, without our Lord? We do all these things through our Lord. We continue to follow the Lord today, tomorrow, and the day after tomorrow—never changing. This is the right faith. Those who serve the Lord are like a virtuous and wise woman who keeps her house well. Do not lead a fickle religious life like a frying pan that cools down as easily as it heats up in no time. You should follow the Lord all the time, until He comes again. Consider yourself as cut and perished from the world after you are born again. I want you to remember that you are not a person of the world anymore. We have already become dead to the world.

Our names are eliminated from the family tree of the world. Do you understand? Our names are not in there.

The world may say to you, "Long time no see. What's up? I heard you attend church. I also heard that all your sins are forgiven. So, you have no sin, huh?"

"No, I have no sin."

"That's strange. I think you might have fallen into a wrong church."

"No, don't look at it like that. Come to my church. You'll
see how nice it is."

"I still think you are weird."

Then we think, "Why don't they understand me? I wish
they would understand me." But can those who are yet to be
born again understand us? How can those who do not know
that people can become sinless understand us? How can they
understand that Jesus took away all the sins of the world? They
can't. So don't expect them to understand you. The Lord said
good-bye to the world for us. He waved a yellow handkerchief
on the Cross. He said, *"It is finished" (John 19:30)*, for the fear
that we wouldn't be able to say good-bye to the world because
we are easily moved by pity. He also said, "I eliminated your
names from the family tree of the world."

The Lord enabled us, who could never serve Him, to serve Him by taking away all our sins

We, who could never serve the Lord, were made to be
those who could serve Him through Jesus Christ. By nature, we
were the ones who could never serve the Lord. We must praise
the Lord for bringing us into His church and qualifying us to
serve Him. The Lord uses us. It's not true that we do His works.
Do you understand? The righteous Lord, in other words, uses
us in His righteous works.

Evangelist Lee once referred to the manure-series in his
sermon and said that he was as filthy and disgusting as a heap
of smelly manure. But even that is a gentle expression.
Anything else that you can ever imagine, we are still filthier.
Jeremiah 17:9 states, *"The heart is deceitful above all things."*
God enabled those whose hearts are deceitful above all things

to live for the glory of God, the Lord and the Highest of all. He called us to do His righteous work.

We can follow the Lord and live in His grace because the Lord washed away all our sins. We can suffer with Him and be glorified together with Him. We had already died but for the Lord. If the Lord had not taken away all our sins, we would have been left out of salvation. We would have still remained worldly people if we had lived according to the flesh.

The Lord eternally saved us once and for all. He saved us and made us the instruments of His eternal ministry. How evil and dirty we are! After meeting the Lord, we come to find out more and more just how evil and dirty we are with time. This is why we rejoice when we see the light. But when we look at ourselves, we sigh in grief, just as Paul confessed, *"O wretched man that I am! Who will deliver me from this body of death?" (Romans 7:24)*

But Paul immediately praised the Lord, *"I thank God— through Jesus Christ our Lord!"* The Lord washed away all our sins. He blotted out all the sins of the flesh. How many sins do our flesh commit everyday? Don't pretend as if your flesh does not sin.

Do you thank the Lord?

The Lord blotted out all the sins that we commit with the flesh. Do you believe? That the Lord took away the sins of the world may not seem like much to you, but when you realize that He took away all the sins that are committed by your own flesh, you will shout out, "I thank God—through Jesus Christ our Lord! Thank you, Lord! I praise You!"

Sin has its own weight. The Lord has taken away all the

sins that we commit in our entire lifetime, until our last day. How thankful we are! Had we sinned just a little, we may ask the Lord for His forgiveness with our prayers of repentance. But our sins are countless and ceaseless to the end of our lifetime. When we realize this, we can do nothing but to praise God, "Thank you, Lord. You've blotted out all my sins! I praise You!" We thank God, in other words, *through Jesus Christ our Lord!"* Do you thank God and confess like this? "Thank you, Lord. I give thanks to You for calling and saving me to serve Your righteousness. I give thanks to the Lord who saved me from all the sins of the flesh." Do you thank the Lord? The true redemption of sins looks this simple, but at the same time it is not something to be taken lightly. It is very profound, great, wide, precious and eternal.

We must follow the Lord because there is nothing beneficial in us

We are a mass of sin. We must know that we ourselves are darkness itself. "I am darkness, but You are the light. You are the true light, while I am complete darkness. You are the sun. I am the moon." The moon can lighten the earth only by receiving the light from the sun.

The moon itself cannot lighten. It lightens by reflecting the light that it receives from the sun. Everything is darkness. Are you light or darkness? We are in darkness without the Lord. We can thank, serve, and follow God because of Jesus Christ, and because in Him there is no condemnation. To serve only our flesh, on the other hand, is to serve only darkness. Give it up as early as you can. Our flesh does not change however hard we may try. There is nothing special in us. Our flesh is not everlasting, and so we must live for eternal things. One who lives for eternal things is a wise person. We must know ourselves early and give ourselves up early. We must know that there is nothing to expect from ourselves, and that there is nothing good in us. We are a mass of sin that always and only serves our flesh. The flesh says, "Give me anything I want," and acts like a leech that sucks blood, attaching itself to the body (Proverbs 30:15).

We feel hungry as soon as we go to the toilet after eating something. We are not satisfied with the flesh however hard we may try to serve it. We feel hungry in a matter of hours, regardless of how much and how delicious food we just had. But if we thank the Lord and follow Him, our joy becomes only bigger.

We don't feel empty when we follow our Lord. Do you want to have everlasting joy after your redemption? Then follow the Lord. Do you want to lead a life of light? Follow the Lord. Do you want to live a life of grace? Follow the Lord. Do you want to lead a fruitful life? Know that you are in darkness and just follow the light.

We follow the Lord wherever He goes and we stop wherever He stops. We do what the Lord wants us to do, and not do what the Lord does not want us to do. We must walk with Him and follow Him. Do you have anything to expect from yourself? Of course not! We must follow Him because there is nothing to be expected from ourselves. Is your flesh eternal? Of course not! Then why are you following something that can neither offer anything nor is everlasting?

A long time ago, I used to sing a song that goes like this. "♪ Give me back my youth♪ " But now, I'm okay even if God does not give me back my youth. On a second thought, I realized that I wouldn't be that happy if I returned to my youth. If we follow the Lord, who is the light of our lives, the crown of glory is laid up for us. You don't need to return to your childhood again. Instead we sing, "♪ I will not deny the Lord and I will follow Him everyday for the rest of my days♪ " This shows the true faith with which we do not deny the Lord in our lives and with which we always thank God. Let's sing this gospel song!

"♪ I love God the Lord who formed man from the dust of the ground; Who breathed into his nostrils the breath of life; ♫And who sent His Son for us. I am formed after His likeness, so I will dedicate my body to the Lord. ♫I will not deny the Lord and I will follow Him everyday for the rest of my days.♪ "

I give real thanks to the Lord

I give real thanks to the Lord. The Lord took away our sins and enabled us to serve Him, follow Him, and do His righteous work. If the Lord had not blotted out all the sins that we commit with our flesh and taken them all away, how could we do His righteous work? Not even 0.1%! A sinner is still evil no matter how good-natured he/she may seem. How wonderful is it that the Lord would wash away our sins and enable us to serve Him? How marvelous is it that the Lord would eliminate all our sins and bless us, who had been immersed in filthiness all our lives, lived like a miser, been bound to hell, and lived a vain life without the Lord?

That the Lord has chosen us to serve Him by taking away all our sins and blessing us with our redemption by faith shows just how great God's grace is. How can we be righteous with sin in our hearts? The fact that we have no sin is surely an extraordinary grace. Praise God! The flesh will certainly commit sin again. Even though we hear God's Word now, we will sin again, perhaps as soon as we step out of this chapel. Because of that, I praise the Lord for washing away all our sins. Have no doubt—our Lord Jesus Christ took away all our sins by His baptism in the Jordan River and ended the judgment for sin on the Cross! I believe and praise God! How, then, can we praise God? We can praise God through Jesus Christ!

Beloved saints! We cannot recompense for God's grace however hard we may try for the rest of our lives. It is not enough even if we eternally give thanks to the Lord, who enabled us to do His righteous and fruitful work by taking away all our sins, however weak we may be. We cannot praise Him enough even if we praise Him for the rest of our lives.

We deeply know in our minds that nothing good dwells within us. Think it over. Will you sin as long as you live? You surely will sin, but the Lord has taken away your sins already. The Lord blessed us to do the work of God. The Lord enabled us to serve Him. We cannot help but give thanks to our Lord. I want you to praise the Lord and live a life of thankfulness to Him through Jesus Christ for all your life. Our God enabled us to live a thankful life to God. God saved us from all the sins that we commit with the flesh. He saved us from all our sins in order to for us to serve Him with our hearts. Because the grace of our Lord is so great, we want to follow and serve Him. Let us thank Him with all our hearts.

How amazing the grace of God given to us through Jesus Christ is! I really want you to know just how wicked and weak your flesh is, to look into what you are doing, to think about whether the Lord really took away your sins or not, to give thanks to the Lord, and to live by faith. I give thanks to the Lord who enabled us to live precious lives. *"I thank God— through Jesus Christ our Lord. So then, with the mind I myself serve the law of God, but with the flesh the law of sin"* *(Romans 7:25).* We love God with our hearts, but with our flesh we love sin. But our Lord is lovelier. It would not be a sin until we commit a lawless deed with our flesh, but the Lord has already blotted out even the sins that we would commit in future. This is why our Lord is lovelier, and why He is to be thanked.

Thank You, Lord. I praise You for giving us the hearts to serve You, and for saving us wholly from all the sins of our flesh, committed throughout our lives. ⊠

The Flesh Serves
The Law of Sin

< Romans 7:24-25 >
"O wretched man that I am! Who will deliver me from this body of death? I thank God—through Jesus Christ our Lord! So then, with the mind I myself serve the law of God, but with the flesh the law of sin."

It is the law that the flesh serves sin

How is your life of faith? *"The spirit indeed is willing, but the flesh is weak" (Matthew 26:41).* Are you not like this?

The Bible also tells us, *"So then, with the mind I myself serve the law of God; but with the flesh the law of sin."* And those are the laws that dominate us. Our hearts are made to love God and to love the truth, but it is only natural for the flesh to serve the law of sin. The Word of God tells us that the heart serves the gospel and His righteousness, while the flesh serves only sin.

Do you know what the law of sin is? We want to lead faithful lives, so we, the saints and the servants of God, feel as bold as lions when our flesh actually does not serve sin. But we have no power when our flesh serves and is indulged in sin. We may think that we will be happy and full of courage by not sinning anymore, but in reality, we do not really have the confidence not to sin any longer. The hearts of saints and the hearts of the servants of God are shrunken because of this.

"♬All my sins are gone! ♪ Through the grace of Calvary!♬" Though we have redemption and praise God like this, we have no self-confidence to live when we think of our future lives of faith. We think about the weaknesses of the flesh and come to this conclusion: "I shouldn't live this way in the future; I shouldn't sin anymore." But when we depend on the Lord once again and stand firm on the righteousness of God again, we make promises to God, saying, "Lord, thank You. Hallelujah. I will follow You until my dying day." We then powerfully serve the Lord in a blaze, but that does not last long because we soon become disappointed again with ourselves when we sin again. In fact, all the saints and the servants of God who have been saved are like this. We thus come to be repressed by the fact that the flesh serves only sin.

I know the Lord does not want us to be bound by the weakness of the flesh. This is also the reason why Paul separated the spirit from the flesh. *"So then, with the mind I myself serve the law of God; but with the flesh the law of sin."* Our flesh cannot be improved. The flesh serves only the law of sin. Paul says that this is the law. The flesh is made to follow and serve only sin. Do you understand this? It's the law. Who can change the law? Neither you nor I can. Whom should we serve with our hearts then? We should serve God. We should love God, the truth, the souls and His righteousness with all our hearts.

Do not expect much from the flesh

The flesh wants to amplify carnal pleasure, comfort, peace, joy and its pride, not the righteousness of God. The flesh wants everything to be done as it pleases.

Do not expect much from the flesh, saying, "Listen flesh, I want you to do a good job." Give up your expectations that the flesh will get better. Don't assume that our flesh loves God and His righteousness, or that it wants to serve God's righteousness and suffer for Him.

Those who expect something good from the flesh are foolish. What, then, should we do? Everything is done according to the law of the Lord. Can we change God's law, even if we know it? Of course we cannot change it, for it is the law of the Lord.

It is God's law that makes the flesh serve sin. If we feel depressed and our face is dark, this is because we are serving the flesh. Our flesh wants to live well, so the flesh always justifies itself. Let us not justify ourselves; rather, let us leave the flesh as it is. I want you to live by the faith in the Lord with your heart. The flesh cannot escape from sinning until it dies, because the flesh serves only sin. We cannot escape from sinning by ourselves. You may think, "The flesh may become better." But this is never the case. Or when you unconsciously commit sins, you may think, "It's due to the bad environment." No! It's not due to the circumstances at all—the flesh was meant to serve sin form the very beginning!

The flesh never does anything good. The flesh sins until it dies. "Will the flesh get better?" Do not expect such a thing, for you will be thoroughly disappointed. No matter how frequently you make up your mind and tell yourself, "I will not act as such," the flesh cannot help but to do evil things, even against your wishes. Who among us have not resolved in our minds not to sin? Everyone has! But it is the law of God for the flesh to serve only sin.

Catholic priests and nuns as well as the monks and

hermits of every religion try to live holy lives with their flesh. But it is impossible for the flesh to live a life without blemishes. They live their lives as hypocrites. It is impossible for us to do good with our flesh. The flesh serves the law of sin. This is the law that God has established. Just as a maggot cannot fly while a cicada enjoys flying in the sky, this is the law. Just as a maggot likes to eat dirty mud, human flesh likes to commit sins. Can you honestly say that there is something that you can expect from your flesh? Of course not. This is why the Apostle Paul said, *"So then, with the mind I myself serve the law of God; but with the flesh the law of sin" (Romans 7:25).*

Our flesh sins until we die. It cannot help but sin. Would the flesh not sin anymore after a long period of training? No! The flesh cannot be improved. Is it then okay for the flesh to sin as much as it wants? No! That is not what I am saying here. I just mean that the flesh cannot help but sin. Our sins do not depend on our wills or abilities. We cannot help but sin, even if we do not want to sin, and we sin even more if we try harder not to sin.

"But I see another law in my members, warring against the law of my mind, and bringing me into captivity to the law of sin which is in my members. O wretched man that I am! Who will deliver me from this body of death?" (Romans 7:23-24) It is impossible for the flesh to do good because the flesh brings us into captivity to the law of sin.

People hate to say this truth and they are ashamed of this. They say, "How can you openly say this?" But was it not Paul himself who said this so blatantly? The flesh serves the law of sin. We serve sin, regardless of our will, until we die. We are not born just to sin. Still, it is undeniable that the flesh is an instrument of sin.

The Lord enabled us to serve Him sufficiently

Beloved saints, what do you think? Do you think that you can serve the Lord with your flesh if you keep on trying? Is it possible? No!

Who saved us from all our sins? Jesus did. Did Jesus Christ, then, deliver us from all the sins of the flesh that serves the law of sin? Did Jesus Christ really save us, who serve the law of sin and commit sins all our lives, from all the sins of the flesh? Did the Lord really save us from all our sins? The answer is an emphatic yes! Of course He did! It is impossible for the flesh not to sin, and it is impossible for you to be forgiven of your sins and be delivered from the condemnation of God through your flesh. But the Lord made it possible. The Lord made us righteous and He saved us from all our sins, even if we constantly sin.

Jesus Christ our Lord has saved us. Who is the Lord that has saved us? It is Jesus Christ. Who is Jesus then? He is the Son of God and the Lord of all believers. He is the Lord who has saved us. Jesus Christ our Lord made us perfect from all sins. Jesus Christ enabled us to serve Him.

The Lord enabled us to live without sin. The omnipotent Lord who created us saved us from all our sins. Our Lord wholly saved us and made us righteous, even though the flesh serves the law of sin until it dies. This is why Paul the Apostle thanked God through Jesus Christ the Lord. We also cannot thank God enough for sending Jesus Christ, our Lord.

We must know how amazing the salvation of the Lord is, just how great and gracious it is. We cannot but give thanks to the Lord for His almighty power that has saved our corrupt flesh that does nothing but sin until it dies. The Lord saved us with His power and made our members His instruments to serve Him by faith. The Lord perfectly saved us so that we would no longer be servants of sin anymore.

Has not our Lord perfectly saved us? Of course He did! He has wholly and perfectly saved us. He enabled us to serve Him sufficiently. Who did this great thing? Our Lord did! Who turned those who cannot help but commit sin with their flesh to become righteous and to serve God? Our Lord did! The Lord saved us, who sin throughout our lives, from all our sins. He also changed us so that we could serve His righteousness.

The Lord has saved us from all our sins

We must think this over because we are human beings. I think of how amazing the salvation of the Lord is because I am a human being. Had I not known that the flesh serves only sin, I would always have been disappointed with it. I would probably have given up the life of faith because of my sins, even though I had already received the forgiveness of my sins.

"Before I was saved, I could stand, even if I sinned. But if I still sin now, it makes no difference whether I was saved or not. What's the use of being born again?" You may think that you should become better than before. You might feel that your flesh would be, now that you have been saved, better than when you were not. Those who have not been born again yet cannot understand what I am saying.

We can thank Jesus only when we know and believe that all the sins of the flesh have been forgiven. I give thanks to the Lord, who took away all the sins that I commit until I die.

In the previous edition of the Korean hymnbook, there was a hymn that went: "♪ Hallelujah! Praise Him! ♫All my past sins have been forgiven! And I walk with the Lord Jesus, then everywhere I go is the Kingdom of Heaven♪ " What does this mean? If the Lord took away only our past sins, what are we to do next? We should not sin with the flesh anymore; we should thoroughly pray for forgiveness whenever we commit sins, and we should live well anyway. But this is only Satan's awful trick.

Nothing is sweeter than this trick. Satan beguiles us, saying, "All your past sins have been forgiven. So if you walk with Jesus, and if you don't sin anymore, you can enter the Kingdom of Heaven. But whenever you sin in the future, you must offer prayers of repentance to be forgiven, so that you can enter the Kingdom of Heaven. Do you understand?" Most people then believe this when they read the Bible. They sing hymns, weeping, "♪ Hallelujah! Praise Him! ♫All my past sins have been forgiven! And I walk with the Lord Jesus, then everywhere I go is the Kingdom of Heaven ♪ "

But they cannot stop sinning. It is God's law on flesh. The flesh cannot help but sin again and again. So they think they have to pray for forgiveness. They diligently say prayers of repentance to receive the forgiveness for their daily sins. They sing hymns after the prayers, "♪ Hallelujah! Praise Him! ♫All my past sins have been forgiven! And I walk with the Lord Jesus, then everywhere I go is the Kingdom of Heaven ♪ " But does it last even for two or three days? They sin again in a manner of hours, not even days. They may pray and fast for forgiveness, but they cannot escape from this unchangeable law of God while living in their flesh.

Are the words of the hymn true? Are only your past sins forgiven? Our Lord has taken away all our sins, not only our past sins. We can praise Him now, "♪ Hallelujah! Praise Him! ♫ALL of my sins have been forgiven! And I walk with the

Lord Jesus, then everywhere I go is the Kingdom of Heaven♪ ”

Those who have been saved may be confused after sinning again, when they do not know that it is God's law for their flesh to sin until they die. They easily lose the peace of their mind whenever they find the evilness of their flesh just like those who are not born again. They are peaceful only when they do not sin. This is the phenomenon that can be found in every Christian's life who has not received the forgiveness of their sins yet. They may just sing with their lips, “♫All my sins are gone.♪ All your sins are also gone. All our sins are gone!♫” But if they sin again, they think that they have to ask for forgiveness once again. The more frequently they sin, the softer they sing, “♫My sins are gone, ♫your sins are gone...,” and they come to be disappointed with themselves as time goes by.

Our Lord has perfectly saved us from all our sins. Our Lord has saved us from all the sins so that we could praise and thank Him anytime and in any situation. We can enjoy peace with Him and pray to God for help at all times through Jesus Christ.

If we know that the flesh only serves the law of sin, we can escape from sin by faith

Why is your life of faith so hard? You are beset by the hard life of faith because you do not know the truth, that the flesh serves only the law of sin? We must lead spiritual lives by knowing this truth.

We come to know God's truth and change when we diligently listen to His Word and have fellowship with each other. *"If you abide in My word, you are My disciples indeed. And you shall know the truth, and the truth shall make you free" (John 8:31-32). "I thank God—through Jesus Christ our Lord!"* The Lord has perfectly saved us from all our sins so that we can thank God all the time. Do you believe this? The Lord has saved us from all our sins.

Never be overwhelmed and closed down by your own thoughts—they will lead you to nowhere. We can follow the Lord, thank Him, and live a life of faith only when we are not under the yoke of sin. If our faith is correlated with our deeds, and if we know we will sin again, we cannot always rejoice and follow the Lord. If the Lord's salvation were even a little imperfect, we would not be able to follow the Lord with much assurance.

We thank the Lord because He took away all our sins. We praise and follow Him with power. If I cannot solve the problem of my own sins, how can I save others from their sins? How can I preach the gospel to others? How can a drowning man save other drowning men? If we admit that our flesh cannot help but sin, we can escape from sin. But if we do not admit this truth, then we would be influenced by the false doctrines of a religion called "Christianity."

There is a funny story, and you may know it. Once upon a time, a young Catholic priest got on a carriage with two nuns from his church to visit a dying believer in a remote village. He came to sit between the two to drive the horses. The pretty young nun was sitting on the right side of him and the ugly old nun was sitting on the left side of him. There was no problem when the carriage was on the smooth and wide road of the town, but as soon as they were on the narrow and rough road in the mountains, the carriage began to sway terribly. Guess what the Catholic priest was thinking in his mind. When the carriage inclined to the right side, he prayed "Oh, God. Please, do as you please!" But when it inclined to the opposite side, he cried out in his heart desperately, "Oh, Lord. Don't lead me into temptation!" He prayed two things: "Oh, Lord. Do as you please" and "Oh, Lord. Don't lead me into temptation."

We are all the same as him. Our flesh only serves the law of sin, but we must know the Lord's will and follow Him with faith according to His will, because we have nothing to expect from ourselves. We are dead and there is no possibility for our flesh to be improved.

We follow the Lord because He has perfectly saved us

How heavy would we feel if we entered the Kingdom of Heaven by doing good deeds, or if our salvation depended on how much we did good deeds or committed sins? The Lord says to us, "You are committing sins all your life. But I had taken away all the sins that are to be committed until you die. I made you righteous. I made you a righteous person who has no sin. I have perfectly saved you. Do you thank me?" What is our answer? "Yes, we thank You, my Lord!" He asks again, "Will you follow me?" How do we answer? "Yes, we will."

Do you want to follow God? Of course we want to follow the Lord, because He has took away all our sins. Had the Lord taken away only 90% of your sins, you wouldn't be able to follow Him. You may complain to God saying, "You should also have taken away the remaining 10% of my sins! How can I solve the problem of these sins by myself? How can I follow You while I have to wash away my filthiness?" Then, because of these sins, we come to quit following God.

However, now we want to follow the Lord voluntarily because He has perfectly saved us from all our sins. "Yes, You've saved me perfectly. I can follow You from now on! Thank You, Lord! I praise You. I glorify You. I love You!" We come to dedicate ourselves to serving the Lord because we love Him and we want to follow Him. We want to follow the Lord from the bottom of our hearts because He has saved us from all our sins, and because we have been touched by His love.

The same goes for attending church. Attending Sunday services is infinitely easier if we have the desire to attend; if we do not feel like attending for some reason, then even going to church once a week becomes a chore for us. If you have to listen to the same tragic words during every worship service— "Ladies and gentlemen, repent all the sins you committed during the last week,"—you would quit going to church after a couple of years. Those who have a strong will might last longer, perhaps a decade or even two, but they, too, will eventually quit. Many false prophets force people who suffer from their sins to repent. This is why many people quit going to church, as they think it is too arduous and difficult to believe in Jesus.

We follow the Lord, being impressed with His love. We cannot help but praise the Lord, singing, "♪ I love Jesus! I can't change Jesus with anything else in the world♪ " We follow Jesus because we really love Him.

How amazing His salvation is. The Lord enabled us to serve Him without the slightest bit of sin. *"There is therefore now no condemnation to those who are in Christ Jesus, who do not walk according to the flesh, but according to the Spirit. For the law of the Spirit of life in Christ Jesus has made me free from the law of sin and death" (Romans 8:1-2).* The Lord blesses us to always thank and praise Him. He wants us to rejoice and follow Him all the time. He saved us. Do you believe this?

Do not be beset by your own weaknesses. The Lord took away all the sins of those whose tempers are uncontrollable. He also took away all the sins of the lewd and ill-natured people. Now, doesn't this just make you want to follow the Lord? This is why we love our Lord. Our Lord does not force us to follow Him or coerce us to worship Him either. God has blessed us. He became our Father and we became His children, and God tells us to follow Him. He tells His servants to serve Him.

All those who have been saved by God are His servants. God blesses all His workers and tells them to follow Him. The Lord does not call us for our deeds. The Lord tells us, "I perfectly saved you from all sins. Your temper is intolerable. You have lewdness within you. You are beyond description. You are foolish. You should be cursed because of the sins of your forefathers. But I saved you and I don't care about the other things. You can't help but sin all your life, yet I took away all your sins. I had suffered for you and rose again from the dead to blot out all your sins. I did these things because I love you. I love you. Do you love me?" What is our answer? "Yes, I love You, my Lord. You know that I also love You. Thank You, Lord!"

"Follow Me, and I will make you fishers of men." "Most assuredly, I say to you, he who believes in Me, the works that I do he will do also; and greater works than these he will do, because I go to My Father," said the Lord. Do you believe this? How ill natured we are! How many sins have we committed before God? Don't pretend not to sin.

We sin countless times throughout our lives. But the Lord

has eternally taken away our all our sins, even when our sins are as many as the stars in the sky. The Lord Jesus completely and sufficiently taken away all our sins.

God made us His workers by clothing us in His righteousness

At times we may think that we cannot follow God anymore when we observe ourselves. Our hearts sometimes seem as bright as sunny days, but quite gloomy other times. And from time to time, we find ourselves in darkness while following the Lord after being born again. We change as if we were going through the four seasons. God gave Noah eight kinds of seasons when Noah went out of the ark. God said, *"While the earth remains, Seedtime and harvest, Cold and heat, Winter and summer, And day and night Shall not cease"* *(Genesis 8:22).*

The ups and downs of our faith do not cease, either. We praise Jesus joyously on some days, but turn angry in no time when we face difficulties.

"Then He adds, 'Their sins and their lawless deeds I will remember no more.' Now where there is remission of these, there is no longer an offering for sin." This is what the Lord said (Hebrews 10:17-18).

The flesh cannot help but sin until it dies. It is the law of the flesh. The flesh serves the law of sin. This means that the flesh can only sin. But God made those who can only sin His own servants. How does God make us His servants? Surely He cannot make those who have sin His servants.

God made you His servants by taking away all the sins that your flesh commits to your very last day and paid off all the wages of your sins to make you perfect. He sanctified and called you to become His holy laborers. He made us His servants. Though we are weak, we now have the power. "What power," you may ask. We have the power of His righteousness. We have the perfect power by putting on the righteousness of the Lord. We have been made perfect, in other words. Though we are weak in the flesh, we are strong in the Spirit.

Who can serve the Lord?

"As sorrowful, yet always rejoicing; as poor, yet making many rich; as having nothing, and yet possessing all things" (2 *Corinthians 6:10)*. We have no sin, even though we look sinful. We have no sin, though we sin. We can therefore help many people to be saved with the gospel of the water and the Spirit. This is the mystery of Christ and the secret of the Kingdom of Heaven.

I praise the Lord who has wholly saved us. Who can serve the Lord? Those who want to serve the Lord by trying not to sin, or those who believe that the Lord took away all their sins that are committed in their lifetime? Only the latter can serve the Lord and pleases Him. Only those who believe that the Lord perfectly washed away all their sins can serve Him. They willingly devote themselves to the Lord and invest all their belongings in His works. They are proud of being His workers, for being able to do something, however small, for the Lord.

Some people are afraid of their own righteousness being broken, so they never get angry, even when they are in a situation where they should be angry. Their self-righteousness should be broken. We should throw away our righteousness in trashcans as we throw our wastes away. Our righteousness must be broken. We must stamp and cut it out and throw it away in a trashcan. We can give thanks to the Lord and exalt His righteousness only when we discard our own righteousness.

Such people can praise and thank the Lord singing, *"Enter into His gates with thanksgiving, And into His courts with praise. Be thankful to Him, and bless His name" (Psalms 100:4)*. Those who have their own righteousness, though they may be saved, cannot serve or love the Lord to the end. Those who know that the flesh serves only sin throughout their lives and believe that the Lord took away all their sins, including those to come, want to love and serve the Lord patiently. In their hearts is found an urge to love the Lord.

Do you have the heart that loves and wants to serve the Lord? Do you have the heart that thanks Him?

The Lord enabled us to live happy lives without sin

We, the servants of God, live in affluence and are happier than those who make a million dollars a year. We eat watermelons in the summer and eat peaches and grapes when they are in season. We can eat anything we want. We are not poor. Have you ever lived poorly after being redeemed? We have lived in affluence.

We can live in abundance if we walk with the Lord. One who walks with the Lord shall not want. Do you believe this? We live without shortage, even though we are not rich by the worldly standard. Do you believe this? Do you have unmet needs and desire after things even after you met the Lord? We lack nothing. We live more richly now than we ever did in the past. I, for one, have lived and slept better now than I ever did.

Our Lord has perfectly saved us. Words cannot express this

blessing. Our Lord has wholly saved us, and has enabled you and me to thank God through Him. How great His grace is!

"O wretched man that I am!" Paul said, seeing his flesh. *"Who will deliver me from this body of this death?"* We sin throughout our lives. Who saved us from all the sins that we commit with the flesh? The Lord Jesus Christ has saved us. As Paul did, I, too, thank God through Jesus Christ our Lord. Thank You, my Lord. Thank You for taking away all our sins.

The Apostle Paul did not live with his own righteousness after he obtained God's righteousness. He confessed many times that his flesh was sold under sin. Some people claim that Paul wrote chapter 7 before he was saved and chapter 8 after he was saved. That's just not right.

The Word of God is applicable to both those who are saved and those who are not saved. It is applicable to everyone. Most theologians, not knowing the Word of God, are apt to separate chapter 7 from chapter 8, and apply the former chapter to those who are not saved and the latter chapter to those who are saved. They arbitrarily separate the Word of God into paragraphs, even though they do not know how to separate the paragraphs. There are many smart and yet deceitful men in this field.

The Lord has absolutely and completely taken away all our sins. I want you to live by faith, by thanking God. I want you to iron out the wrinkles on your face. The Lord has taken away all the dark sins from your heart. I give thanks to the Lord who has saved us from all the sins of the flesh. ✉

Praise the Lord, The Savior of Sinners

< Romans 7:14-8:2 >

"For we know that the law is spiritual, but I am carnal, sold under sin. For what I am doing, I do not understand. For what I will to do, that I do not practice; but what I hate, that I do. If, then, I do what I will not to do, I agree with the law that it is good. But now, it is no longer I who do it, but sin that dwells in me. For I know that in me (that is, in my flesh) nothing good dwells; for to will is present with me, but how to perform what is good I do not find. For the good that I will to do, I do not do; but the evil I will not to do, that I practice. Now if I do what I will not to do, it is no longer I who do it, but sin that dwells in me. I find then a law, that evil is present with me, the one who wills to do good. For I delight in the law of God according to the inward man. But I see another law in my members, warring against the law of my mind, and bringing me into captivity to the law of sin which is in my members. O wretched man that I am! Who will deliver me from this body of death? I thank God—through Jesus Christ our Lord! So then, with the mind I myself serve the law of God, but with the flesh the law of sin. There is therefore now no condemnation to those who are in Christ Jesus, who do not walk according to the flesh, but according to the Spirit. For the law of the Spirit of life in Christ Jesus has made me free from the law of sin and death."

Man is a sinner who inherited sin

All human beings inherited sin from Adam and Eve and became the seeds of sin. We are thus originally born as the offspring of sin and inevitably become sinful beings. All the people in the world cannot help but become sinners due to one ancestor, Adam, though none of them wants to be a sinner.

What is the origin of sin? It is inherited from our parents. We are born with sin in our hearts. This is the inherited nature of sinners. We have 12 kinds of sins that are inherited from Adam and Eve. These sins—adulteries, fornications, murders, thefts, covetousness, wickedness, deceit, lewdness, an evil eye, blasphemy, pride and foolishness—are intrinsic in our hearts from the very time when we are born. The basic nature of man is sin.

We are thus born with twelve kinds of sins. We cannot but confess that we are sinners because we are born with sin in our hearts. A human being is born a sinner and is inevitably a sinner because he/she originally has sin within himself/herself, even if he/she does not sin all his/her life. One becomes a sinner because one is born with sin in one's heart. Even if we do not sin with our flesh, we cannot avoid becoming sinners because God looks on the heart. So all human beings are sinners before God.

Man commits the sin of transgression

A human being also commits the sin of transgressions. He/she commits sins with the flesh, sprouting original sin from within. We call these sins "iniquities" or "transgressions." They are the offenses of our outward behaviors that originate from the twelve kinds of sins in our hearts. The evil sin from within makes a human being commit lawless deeds and thereby makes all human beings sinners without exception. A human being does not seem to be a sinner when he/she is very young. Sin does not remarkably come out of an infant when he/she is very young, just as a young persimmon tree does not bring forth persimmons. But sin begins to come out more and more from within as we get older, and we come to know that we are sinners. We call these sins iniquities or transgressions, and they are the sins that are committed through behavior.

God says that both these are sins. The sin in the heart and the lawless deeds of our flesh are both sins. God calls a human being a sinner. All sins are included in the sins of the heart and in the sins of behavior. So, all people are born sinners in the sight of God, whether they sin through their behavior or not.

Unbelievers insist that man is born good originally, and that nobody is born evil. But David confessed to God, *"Against You, You only, have I sinned, And done this evil in Your sight— That You may be found just when You speak, And blameless when You judge. Behold, I was brought forth in iniquity, And in sin my mother conceived me" (Psalms 51:4-5).* This passage means, "I cannot but commit sin like this, because I am originally a seed of sin. I am a grave sinner. So, if You take away my sins, I can be redeemed from all my sins and become righteous. But if You do not take them away, I have to go to hell. I have sin, if You say I have sin. But I have no sin, if You say I have no sin. Everything depends on You, God, and Your judgment."

Strictly speaking, in the sight of God, all human beings cannot help but be sinners because they inherited sin from their parents. They are born sinners regardless of their behavior. The only way to escape from sin is to believe in the salvation of Jesus. Public education teaches our children the false claim, whose key message can be summed up in the following manner: "All people are born good natured. So live virtuously according to the good nature of human beings. You can do good if you just try." They say only positive things. Humans live under the teachings of moral principles. But why do they commit sin in their hearts or with their flesh in their society or at their home? They do so because they are originally born with sin. Humans are born as the seeds of sin. A human being cannot help but commit sins, though he/she wants to do good. This proves that we are born with sin.

You must know yourself

People cannot help but commit sin with the flesh throughout their lives because they are born with sin. This is the original state of mankind—we must know ourselves first. Socrates said, "Know yourself!" And Jesus said, "You are a sinner because you were conceived in sin and brought forth in iniquity. So you must receive the forgiveness of your sins." Know yourself. Most people misunderstand themselves. Almost all people live and die without knowing themselves. Only wise people know themselves. Those who perceive and believe in the truth of Jesus after knowing that they are the seeds of evildoers are the wise ones. They have the right to enter the Kingdom of Heaven.

Those who do not know themselves teach people to play the hypocrite and not to sin anymore. They teach people not to express the sins that are within. Religious educators train them not to sin and to suppress their sins whenever they try to wiggle out of them. They are all on their way to hell. Who are they? They are the servants of Satan, the false shepherds. What they teach is not what our Lord taught us. Of course, our Lord did not tell us to commit sin. But He does tell us, "You have sin, you are a sinner, and the wages of sin is death. You are on your way to destruction because of your sins. So, you must be redeemed of sins. Receive the gift of salvation that saves you from all your sins. Then, all your sins will be forgiven and you will receive eternal life. You will become a righteous, a precious saint and God's child."

Why did God give human beings the Law?

Paul said, *"Moreover the law entered that the offense might abound. But where sin abounded, grace abounded much more" (Romans 5:20).* God gave us the Law so that through it our sins would be revealed even more sinfully (Romans 7:13). He gave the sinners His Law so that they would recognize their sins seriously.

God gave the Law to the Israelites when the descendants of Jacob lived in the wilderness after the Exodus. He gave 613 kinds of commandments. Why did God give human beings the Law? God gave them the Law, first, because He wanted to let them recognize their sins, as they did not know about their sins, and secondly, because they are born with sin.

The ten commandments of the Law show what grave sinners human beings are. *"You shall have no other gods before Me. You shall not make for yourself a carved image... You shall not take the name of the Lord your God in vain, for the Lord will not hold him guiltless who takes His name in vain. Remember the Sabbath day, to keep it holy... Honor your father and your mother, that your days may be long upon the land which the Lord your God is giving you. You shall not murder. You shall not commit adultery. You shall not steal. You shall not bear false witness against your neighbor. You shall not covet your neighbor's house…, nor anything that is your neighbor's" (Exodus 20:3-17).*

God gave all of us the Law, and through it He taught us exactly what kind of sin we have in our hearts. God taught us that we are total sinners before God, and He enlightened us of the truth that we are sinners because we cannot keep the Law.

Can a human being possibly keep the Law of God? When God told the Israelites and the Gentiles to have no other gods before Him, He wanted to enlighten them that they were sinners who, from the very beginning, could not keep even the first commandment. Through the commandments, they came to know that they loved other creatures more than the Creator. They realized that they took the name of God in vain, that they made and served idols that God hated, and that they did not even rest when God gave them rest for their own sake. They also found out that they did not honor their parents, they murdered, they committed adultery, and they did all the lawless deeds that God told them not to do. They could not, in short, keep the Law of God.

The Law has dominion over those whose sins are not forgiven yet

Do you now understand why God gave us the Law? God gave the Law first to those who are not born again. *"Or do you not know, brethren (for I speak to those who know the law), that the law has dominion over a man as long as he lives?"*

(Romans 7:1) God gave the Law to those who inherited sin from their ancestors and have not been born again yet to make them mourn under sin. The Law has dominion over a person as long as he/she lives. Every descendant of Adam has the twelve kinds of sin in his/her heart. God gave the Law to those who have sin in their hearts and He told them that they had fatal sins. Thus, whenever the sins of murder or adultery come out of us and make us sin, the Law tells us, "God told you not to commit adultery. But you committed adultery again. So you are a sinner. God told you not to murder, but you have murdered with your hatred. You are a sinner who murders and commits adultery. God told you not to steal, but you stole again. So you are a thief." Like this, sin comes into existence where the Law exists.

This is why Paul said, *"Or do you not know, brethren (for I speak to those who know the law), that the law has dominion over a man as long as he lives?"* The law has dominion over those whose sins are not forgiven yet. To the Gentiles, who do not know God's Law, their conscience becomes the Law to them. When they do evil, their conscience tells them that they had sinned. Likewise, the unbelievers' conscience functions as the Law to them, and they recognize sins through their conscience (Romans 2:15).

Why do you not serve the Creator, when even your conscience tells you that there is the Creator? Why do you not seek God? Why do you deceive your heart? You should be ashamed of your sins and afraid that other people will find out about your sins. But sinners who do not admit God and who deceive their hearts have no shame.

We are ashamed of ourselves when we look at the sky, the earth, other people, or any other creature, if we have sin. God gave human beings conscience and the law of conscience points out sin. But most of them live without God, playing the hypocrite in the sight of God and living as they please. They are bound to hell. As Paul reminds them to pay attention to the Law, *"Or do you not know, brethren (for I speak to those who know the law), that the law has dominion over a man as long as he lives?"* A human being must be born twice—once as a sinner, and then born again by the grace of God's redemption to live as a righteous.

Paul explained how the Lord saved us from the curse of the law of sin in the following manner: *"For the woman who has a husband is bound by the law to her husband as long as he lives. But if the husband dies, she is released from the law of her husband. So then if, while her husband lives, she marries another man, she will be called an adulteress; but if her husband dies, she is free from that law, so that she is no adulteress, though she has married another man" (Romans 7:2-3).*

If a married woman has an affair, she is called an adulteress. But if her husband is dead and she then marries another man, there is nothing wrong with it. The same logic applies to our deliverance from the law of sin. The Law has dominion over all the descendants of Adam whose sins are not forgiven yet. It tells them, "You are sinners." So they come to confess their sinfulness under the Law saying, "I must go to hell. I am a sinner. It's natural for me to go to hell because of the wages of my sins." But if we become dead to the Law through the body of Christ, the Law can no longer have dominion over us, because our old selves were crucified with Christ by being baptized into Him.

Our old selves are dead

Our Lord took care of our old husbands and He enabled us to be married to Him. *"Therefore, my brethren, you also have become dead to the law through the body of Christ, that you may be married to another—to Him who was raised from the dead, that we should bear fruit to God" (Romans 7:4).* God gave the Law to all human beings, who were born with sin due to their common ancestor, Adam, so that sin through the commandment might be revealed even more. He had made them dwell under the judgment of God, but He saved them through the body of Christ. Jesus Christ died in our place. Is it not right for us to go to hell according to the Law of God? That's right. However, the Lord was sent to the world, took upon all our sins with His baptism in the Jordan River, was crucified, judged and cursed by the wrath of the Law in our stead. Through this and this alone can now be saved and born again by believing it.

Those who are not born again must go to hell. They should believe in Jesus and be saved. We must die once with Jesus Christ. If our old selves do not die once, we cannot become new creatures and enter the Kingdom of Heaven. If our old selves have not been judged according to the Law through our united faith in Jesus, we must be judged and be sent to hell. All those who are not born again should go to hell.

Unbelievers live well, enjoying everything that a good life can provide, but they do not care about their eternal punishments. All human beings should receive the forgiveness of sins by the Lord Jesus while they live on this earth. Every old self has to die once in union with Jesus through faith, because we cannot be born again after our departure from this world. We must be killed once and delivered from our sins through our faith in Jesus Christ. Through whom? Though the body of Jesus Christ. How? By believing that Jesus came to this world and took away all our sins. Are you dead? Is there anyone who is not dead yet? You may wonder, "How can I become dead? How am I alive now, if I was dead?" This is the secret; it is the mystery that no religion can ever solve.

Only the born again can say that their old selves are already dead in union with Jesus. Sinners can be born again and their old selves can be dead only when they listen to God's Word from the born-again. And through this they can become the servants of God. All human beings must listen to the Word of God from the born again saints. You cannot be born again when you ignore their teachings. Even Paul could not be born again without Christ, though he had learned the Word of God from Gamaliel, one of the most prominent teachers of the Law at that time. How thankful we are! We can bring forth the fruits of the righteousness for God by believing in Jesus Christ, who rose again from the dead, when we become dead through the body of Jesus Christ by faith. We can then bring forth the nine kinds of the fruits of the Holy Spirit.

The sinful passions in our members were at work to bear fruit to death

"For when we were in the flesh, the sinful passions which were aroused by the law were at work in our members to bear fruit to death" (Romans 7:5). "When we were in the flesh" means "before we were born again." The sinful passions in our members were at work to bear fruit to death when we did not have faith through the body of Jesus Christ. The sinful passions were constantly at work in our members at that time. There are

twelve kinds of sins in heart. Put differently, this means that there are twelve kinds of outlets of sin in our hearts. Today, for instance, the sin of adultery may come out of its outlet and agitate the heart. Then the heart commands to the head, "Adultery comes out of its hole and it tells me to commit adultery." Then, the head answers, "Okay. I will command the arms and legs to execute it. Listen, arms and legs, do as you want. Hurry up!" The head commands its members to go to the place where the flesh commits adultery. Then, the body goes and does as the head commands. Likewise, when the sin of murder comes out of its hole, it agitates the heart and the heart makes its head get angry with someone. Then, the head commands the body to prepare for it. Sin works in our members like this.

This is the reason why we should receive the forgiveness of our sins. If we do not have the forgiveness of sin, we cannot help but do just as the heart commands, though this is not what we want to do. Everyone should be born again by the true gospel. One can become whole when one is born again, just as a maggot becomes a cicada. Pastors can really serve the Lord only after they are born again. Before being born again, all that they can say is, "Beloved saints, you must do good." This is akin to telling the sick to heal themselves. They urge their congregations to cleanse their hearts for themselves, though they themselves do not know how to cleanse their own sinful hearts.

The sinful passions in our members were at work to bear fruit to death. Does a person commit sin because he/she wants to sin? We commit sin as the servants of sin because we were born with sin, because all our sins have not been blotted out yet, and because we are yet to die through the body of Jesus Christ.

We sin, though we hate to do so. Everyone must therefore receive the forgiveness of sin.

It is better for the pastors whose sins have not been taken away yet to quit serving the Lord. It would be better for them to sell Chinese cabbages. I recommend them to do so. It would be better for them to do so than deceive people by telling lies to make big money and take up offerings for themselves, becoming fat like pigs.

If one has not been saved from all his/her sins, the sin and its passion in his/her members are at work to bear fruit to death. We can serve the Lord under His grace by receiving the Holy Spirit after all our sins are taken away. But we cannot serve the Lord under the Law. Our Lord thus tells us, *"But now we have been delivered from the law, having died to what we were held by, so that we should serve in the newness of the Spirit and not in the oldness of the letter" (Romans 7:6).*

The Law makes our sins become exceedingly sinful

"What shall we say then? Is the law sin? Certainly not! On the contrary, I would not have known sin except through the law. For I would not have known covetousness unless the law had said, 'You shall not covet.' But sin, taking opportunity by the commandment, produced in me all manner of evil desire. For apart from the law sin was dead. I was alive once without the law, but when the commandment came, sin revived and I died. And the commandment, which was to bring life, I found to bring death. For sin, taking occasion by the commandment, deceived me, and by it killed me. Therefore the law is holy, and the commandment holy and just and good. Has then what is good become death to me? Certainly not! But sin, that it might

appear sin, was producing death in me through what is good, so that sin through the commandment might become exceedingly sinful" (Romans 7:7-13).

Paul said that God gave us the Law to make our sins become exceedingly sinful. He also said, *"Therefore by the deeds of the law no flesh will be justified in His sight, for by the law is the knowledge of sin" (Romans 3:20).* However, most Christians are trying to live by the Law while pursuing the righteousness of the Law. So many pastors, who are not born again, are sure that people are taken ill due to their disobedience to the Law, and that they can recover from their illness, if they would only live by the Law.

Can we really conclude that our disobedience of the Law causes all our diseases? Many Christians, ministers as well as their followers, think that things are not going well because they had failed to live according to the Word of God. They think that they are sick because of their sins. So they are afraid of sin. They weep everyday. They might as well add a passage to the Bible that says, "Weep evermore. Weep without ceasing. In every thing weep," even though the Bible tells us to, *"Rejoice always, pray without ceasing, in everything give thanks; for this is the will of God in Christ Jesus for you" (1 Thessalonians 5:16-18).* But false pastors teach people to weep evermore, to weep without ceasing, as if the wrinkles from so much crying are indicators of their faith.

Those with legalistic faith claim that weepers have good faiths. False pastors, who are not born again, appoint a woman who weeps well as a senior deaconess and a tear-prone male Christian as an elder. Do not weep in church; weep at home, if you really have to weep. Why was Jesus crucified? To make us crybabies? Of course not! Jesus took away all our grief, curses, illnesses and pains once and for all, so that His crucifixion would make us not weep anymore and instead live happily. So why do they weep? They must be sent back to their home if they try to weep in the born-again church of God.

What is the difference between the born again and those who are not born again?

The Law is never wrong. The Law is holy. It is truly righteous while we are not righteous at all. We are opposite to the Law because we are born with sin as the descendants of Adam. We do what we should not do, while we cannot do what we should do. So the Law makes us become exceeding sinful.

"For we know that the law is spiritual, but I am carnal, sold under sin. For what I am doing, I do not understand. For what I will to do, that I do not practice; but what I hate, that I do. If, then, I do what I will not to do, I agree with the law that it is good. But now, it is no longer I who do it, but sin that dwells in me. For I know that in me (that is, in my flesh) nothing good dwells; for to will is present with me, but how to perform what is good I do not find. For the good that I will to do, I do not do; but the evil I will not to do, that I practice. Now if I do what I will not to do, it is no longer I who do it, but sin that dwells in me. I find then a law, that evil is present with me, the one who wills to do good. For I delight in the law of God according to the inward man. But I see another law in my members, warring against the law of my mind, and bringing me into captivity to the law of sin which is in my members. O wretched man that I am! Who will deliver me from this body of death?" (Romans 7:14-24)

Prior to this passage, Paul says that all of us, including

himself, should be judged once by the Law. He says that only those who have received all the wrath and the judgments of the Law through the body of Jesus Christ can bear the fruits of righteousness for God. He also says that no good thing dwells in him, and that one who is not born again cannot help but sin. So does one who is born again. But there is an obvious difference between the two. Those who are born again have both the flesh and the Spirit, so there are two kinds of desires in them. But those who are not born again yet have only the lust of the flesh, and they only want to sin. So, all that they are concerned about is how beautifully and constantly they commit sin. This is their goal in life, common to those who are not born again.

Sin makes people commit sin. Romans 7:20 says, *"Now if I do what I will not to do, it is no longer I who do it, but sin that dwells in me."* Is there sin in the heart of the born again? No. Is there sin in the hearts of those who are not born again then? Yes! If you have sin in your heart, sin works in the flesh and it makes you commit even more sins. *"For the good that I will to do, I do not do; but the evil I will not to do, that I practice. Now if I do what I will not to do, it is no longer I who do it, but sin that dwells in me."* Human beings cannot help but to commit sin all their lives, because they are born with sin.

The born again can bear the fruits of the Spirit spontaneously. But those who are not born again cannot bring forth such fruits. They do not have mercy on others. Some of them even kill their own children, if their children disobey them. Cruelties come out of their hearts and kill their children in their hearts when their children disobey them. Though they do not actually kill their children, with their hearts they murder them countless times.

Do you understand what I am trying to say here? But the righteous can do no such thing. They may get into arguments, but they cannot and will not have such cruel hearts, filled with so much bitterness and anger as others have.

Instead, the righteous want to have mercy on the people with their hearts, even those with whom they may be arguing over their different opinions. *"I find then a law, that evil is present with me, the one who wills to do good."* Human beings want to do good because they were created in the image of God. But while their sins still exist in their hearts, only evil things come out of them.

Christians who are not born again talk to each other, lamenting, "I really want to do good, but I can't. I don't know why I can't." They must know that they cannot do so because they are sinners who have not been saved yet. They cannot do good because they have sin in their hearts. The born again have the desires of the Spirit as well as the lusts of the flesh, but those who are not born again yet do not have the Spirit. This is the key difference that distinguishes the born again from those who are not.

Paul talks about the state of his not being born again in chapter 7. Explaining the Law from Romans 7:1 and on, He says that he could not do the good which he wanted to do, but he did the evil which he did not want to do. Paul, in other words, had no desire to sin and only wanted to do good, and yet he could only do exactly what he did not wish to do, while what he really wanted to do in his heart he found it impossible to do. *"O wretched man that I am! Who will deliver me from this body of death?"* He laments this sorry fate of his, but immediately praises the Lord, saying, *"I thank God—through Jesus Christ our Lord!"*

Do you understand what this means? We, the born again, can understand his saying, but those who are not born again can never understand it. A maggot that has never become a cicada can never understand what a cicada says. "Wow! I sing songs for several hours a day on the tree. How cool the wind is!" A maggot might reply from the ground, "Really? What is the wind?" It can never understand what the cicada is saying, but the cicada knows what the wind is.

Because Paul had been born again, he could explain exactly what the difference between those who are born again and those who are not is. He says the Savior who saved him is Jesus Christ. Did Jesus Christ save us? Of course He did! *"So then, with the mind I myself serve the law of God, but with the flesh the law of sin."*

Those whose sins have been taken away serve the law of God with their hearts. What, then, do they serve with the flesh? They serve the law of sin with their flesh. The flesh likes to sin because it has not changed at all. The flesh wants the things of the flesh and the Spirit wants the things of the Spirit. So those whose sins have been taken away can and want to follow the Lord because the Holy Spirit now dwells in them. But those whose sins have not been taken away cannot help but follow sin with both their minds and flesh. The born again, whose sins have now been taken away, can follow God with their minds even as their flesh follows sin.

The law of the Spirit of life in Christ Jesus has made us free from the law of sin and death

Let's skip to Romans 8:1 for now. Those whose sins have been taken away by believing in the salvation of Jesus are no longer judged by the Law of God, though they were born as sinners. *"There is therefore now no condemnation to those who are in Christ Jesus, who do not walk according to the flesh, but according to the Spirit. For the law of the Spirit of life in Christ Jesus has made me free from the law of sin and death"* *(Romans 8:1-2).*

There is therefore now no condemnation to those who are in Christ Jesus. There is no condemnation! Those who are born again have no sin, and there can be no judgment on them. No sin remains in their hearts because the law of the Spirit of life in Christ Jesus has made them free from the law of sin and death. Our Lord is the origin of life. He became the Lamb of God, being conceived by the Holy Spirit, and took upon all the sins of the world on Himself at the Jordan River through His baptism by John. Judged in our place, He was crucified for us. Through this He completely took away all our sins.

Do we, then, have to die again because of our sins? Do we have something to be judged? Do we have sin within us, if all our sins were passed onto Jesus Christ through His baptism? Of course not! We do not have to be judged, for the Lord was baptized in the Jordan River, crucified in our place, and rose again from the dead on the third day to save all sinners.

The salvation of God frees us from His judgment while the Law brings about wrath. *"For the law of the Spirit of life in Christ Jesus has made me free from the law of sin and death."* The wrath of God is revealed to those who have sin. God sends them to hell. But the Lord has freed us from the law of sin and death by taking away all the sins from our hearts. He made believers, who are in Jesus Christ, free from sin. Have your sins been taken away?

"For what the law could not do in that it was weak

through the flesh, God did by sending His own Son in the likeness of sinful flesh, on account of sin: He condemned sin in the flesh, that the righteous requirement of the law might be fulfilled in us who do not walk according to the flesh but according to the Spirit" (Romans 8:3-4).

Our Lord tells us clearly here that the flesh is weak and cannot obey the righteous requirement of the Law. The Law of God is surely good and beautiful, but we cannot live by it because our flesh is too weak. The Law of God requires us to be perfect. It requires us to reach the full obedience of God's Law, but our flesh cannot live by all the requirements of the Law because of its weakness. The Law thus brings its wrath on us. But what is Jesus for, if we are going to be judged after all?

God sent His only Son to save us. God gave us His righteousness by sending His own Son in the likeness of sinful flesh, on account of our sins. Jesus was sent to the world in the likeness of the flesh. *"He condemned sin in the flesh."* God passed all our sins onto Jesus so that the righteous requirement of the Law might be fulfilled in us, who walk not after the flesh, but after the Spirit. Our sins are taken away by our belief in Jesus Christ with our hearts. Our sins are blotted out when we admit what Jesus Christ did for us.

Those who live according to the Spirit and those to the flesh

There are two kinds of Christians: those who follow their own thoughts and those who follow the Word of truth. The latter can be saved and become righteous, while the former will perish.

"For those who live according to the flesh set their minds

on the things of the flesh, but those who live according to the Spirit, the things of the Spirit. For to be carnally minded is death, but to be spiritually minded is life and peace" (Romans 8:5-6). Those who think that believing in God is to live according to the Law can never be perfect. *"For those who live according to the flesh set their minds on the things of the flesh."*

It is the things of the flesh to clean only the outward self. Those who do so dust off the Bible and go to church every Sunday with their holy gaits, though they fight with their wives and are evil at home. They become angels on Sundays.

"Hi, how have you been?"

"Nice to meet you again."

They say "Amen" many times whenever their pastor preaches in a holy voice and a merciful manner. They gently come out of the church after the worship service, but they become different as soon as the church disappears from their sight.

"What did the Word of God say to me? I can't remember; let's just go to drink?"

They are angels in the church but they become carnal beings in no time when they are away from the church.

Sinners, therefore, must pray to God like the following: "God, please save me, a wretched being. I cannot enter the Kingdom of Heaven and will go to hell if You do not save me. But if You wash away all my sins that I commit until I die, I can enter the Kingdom of Heaven by faith." They must fully rely upon God.

Every believer can receive the redemption of their sins and lead a spiritual life when he/she follows the Word of God. *"Those who live according to the Spirit (set their minds on) the things of the Spirit. For to be carnally minded is death, but to be spiritually minded is life and peace."* If we think and believe according to the truth of God, peace will come to us. *"Because the carnal mind is enmity against God; for it is not subject to the law of God, nor indeed can be. So then, those who are in the flesh cannot please God" (Romans 8:7-8).* Those whose sins are not taken away yet and who are still in the flesh can never please God.

"But you are not in the flesh but in the Spirit, if indeed the Spirit of God dwells in you. Now if anyone does not have the Spirit of Christ, he is not His" (Romans 8:9). People are confused with these passages because Paul speaks in profoundly spiritual words. Those who are not born again are confused with Romans chapters 7 and 8. They can never understand this part of the Bible. But we, the born again, are not in the flesh, and do not live only for the flesh.

Read carefully to what Paul says in the above passage. Does the Holy Spirit dwell in you? If anyone does not have the Spirit of Christ, the person is not His. If not His, then it means that this person is of Satan and is a sinner bound for hell.

"And if Christ is in you, the body is dead because of sin, but the Spirit is life because of righteousness. But if the Spirit of Him who raised Jesus from the dead dwells in you, He who raised Christ from the dead will also give life to your mortal bodies through His Spirit who dwells in you" (Romans 8:10-11). Amen.

Our Lord was conceived by the Holy Spirit, was sent to the world in the flesh, and took away all our sins. The Lord has come into the hearts of believers, who believe in the redemption of sins, and is sitting down in every one of their hearts. The Holy Spirit comes into the heart and proves that our Lord Jesus washed away all our sins, as white as snow. God will also give life to our flesh when Jesus comes to the world again. *"He who raised Christ from the dead will also give life to your mortal bodies through His Spirit who dwells in you."*

The Spirit bears witness with our spirits that we are the children of God

We must live by the faith in God and by the Holy Spirit after we are born again. *"Therefore, brethren, we are debtors— not to the flesh, to live according to the flesh. For if you live according to the flesh you will die; but if by the Spirit you put to death the deeds of the body, you will live. For as many as are led by the Spirit of God, these are sons of God. For you did not receive the spirit of bondage again to fear, but you received the Spirit of adoption by whom we cry out, "Abba, Father." The Spirit Himself bears witness with our spirit that we are children of God, and if children, then heirs—heirs of God and joint heirs with Christ, if indeed we suffer with Him, that we may also be glorified together" (Romans 8:12-17).* We cry out, "Abba, Father," because we have received the Spirit of adoption, not the spirit of bondage and fear.

"The Spirit Himself bears witness with our spirit that we are children of God." First of all, the Holy Spirit bears witness that we have received the remission of sins through the concrete Word of God. The second witness is that we have no sin. The Spirit has born witness that we are saved. The Holy Spirit has done so in the hearts of those whose sins have been taken away. *"There is none righteous, no, not one"(Romans 3:10).* True, but this is before God delivered us. Below that passage, it is written that we are justified freely by His grace through the redemption that is in Christ Jesus (Romans 3:24). It

is also written that the Spirit itself bears witness that we are the children of God. The Spirit comes to us when we admit in our hearts what God has done for us, but if we do not believe it, the Spirit is nowhere to be found within us. If we receive what God has done for us into our hearts, the Spirit bears witness, "You are righteous. You are my children. You are just. You are my people." *"Then heirs—heirs of God and joint heirs with Christ, if indeed we suffer with Him, that we may also be glorified together."* It is entirely proper for God's children to suffer with the Lord, as well as to be glorified with Him. Those who have the Holy Spirit, being led by the Spirit, rest their hope on their entrance to the Kingdom of Heaven.

We live in the hope of the Millennial Kingdom and the Kingdom of Heaven in spite of the sufferings of this present time

Let us turn to Romans 8:18-25. *"For I consider that the sufferings of this present time are not worthy to be compared with the glory which shall be revealed in us. For the earnest expectation of the creation eagerly waits for the revealing of the sons of God. For the creation was subjected to futility, not willingly, but because of Him who subjected it in hope; because the creation itself also will be delivered from the bondage of corruption into the glorious liberty of the children of God. For we know that the whole creation groans and labors with birth pangs together until now. Not only that, but we also who have the first fruits of the Spirit, even we ourselves groan within ourselves, eagerly waiting for the adoption, the redemption of our body. For we were saved in this hope, but hope that is seen is not hope; for why does one still hope for what he sees? But if we hope for what we do not see, we eagerly wait for it with perseverance."*

We are the first fruits of the Spirit. We who are born again are the first fruits of resurrection. We will take part in the first resurrection. Jesus Christ is the first fruit of resurrection and we are the ones who stick to Him. Those who are Christ's take part in the first resurrection; then comes the end. The ungodly will take part in the second resurrection to be judged. This is why Paul says, *"For I consider that the sufferings of this present time are not worthy to be compared with the glory which shall be revealed in us."* By the glory here, he is referring to the Millennium and the Kingdom of Heaven. We will all be changed when that blessed time comes. The children of God will wholly rise again from the dead and each of them will receive the eternal life of the Lord. The flesh will actually rise again from the dead (our souls have already risen again from the dead.) God will renew all things and the righteous will live happily as kings for a thousand years.

All the creatures of the universe wait for the manifestation of God's children. The creation will be changed as we will be changed. There will be no such thing as pain, suffering, or death at the time of the Millennium. But we groan now. Why? Because the flesh is still weak. What do our souls groan for? They groan for the redemption of our bodies.

"Even we ourselves groan within ourselves, eagerly waiting for the adoption, the redemption of our body. For we were saved in this hope, but hope that is seen is not hope; for why does one still hope for what he sees? But if we hope for what we do not see, we eagerly wait for it with perseverance" (Romans 8:23-25).

We are eagerly waiting for the adoption, for we are saved

in this hope. We, whose sins have been completely taken away, will enter the Millennium and the Kingdom of Heaven. We will not perish, even if the world suddenly comes to its end. Our Lord will come to this world again at the end of the world. He will make all things new and will raise the renewed flesh of the righteous. He will make them reign for a thousand years.

The end of this world is despair to sinners, but new hope to the righteous. Paul hoped for it. Do you groan, and are you waiting for the redemption of your body? Is the Spirit waiting also? We will be changed to spiritual bodies, like the resurrected body of Jesus Christ, feeling neither pain nor weakness.

The Holy Spirit helps the righteous to have faith

The Holy Spirit helps us to have faith. Do we hope for what we see? No, we hope for what we cannot see yet. *"Likewise the Spirit also helps in our weaknesses. For we do not know what we should pray for as we ought, but the Spirit Himself makes intercession for us with groanings which cannot be uttered. Now He who searches the hearts knows what the mind of the Spirit is, because He makes intercession for the saints according to the will of God" (Romans 8:26-27).*

What does the Spirit really want within us? What does He help us to do? What do you hope for? We hope for new heavens and a new earth (2 Peter 3:13), the Kingdom of Heaven. We do not want to live in this perishing world anymore. We are tired, and thus hope for the Day of our Lord. We want to live eternally with no sin, no illness, no evil spirit; we want to live there happily with joy, peace, love and meekness in full fellowship with the Lord Jesus and with each other.

So, the Spirit groans and makes intercessions for us, waiting for new heavens and a new earth. Frankly speaking, we, the righteous, have no pleasure in this world except for, perhaps, playing soccer once in a while with our fellow servants of God. We live on earth because we are interested in preaching the gospel. But for this Great Commission, the righteous would have no reason for being in this world.

God lets all things work together for good to the born again who love Him

Let us read Roman 8:28-30. *"And we know that all things work together for good to those who love God, to those who are the called according to His purpose. For whom He foreknew, He also predestined to be conformed to the image of His Son, that He might be the firstborn among many brethren. Moreover whom He predestined, these He also called; whom He called, these He also justified; and whom He justified, these He also glorified."*

In Romans 8:28 Paul says, *"And we know that all things work together for good to those who love God, to those who are the called according to His purpose."* This passage is very important. Many people think, "Why was I born? God should have made me in a place where Satan did not exist, and He should have allowed me to live in the Kingdom of Heaven from the beginning. Why did He make me like this?" Some people who were born into bad situations hold a grudge, first against their parents, and then against God. "Why did You make me to be born with such suffering?"

This passage provides us with the right answer to such an

inquiry. We were born as creatures of God. Is this right? We are of His creation. God created us in His image according to the likeness of God, but we are still His creatures. There is a purpose for God to place us in this world. The Scripture says, *"And we know that all things work together for good to those who love God, to those who are the called according to His purpose."* Because of the original sin inherited from Adam and Eve, our ancestors, who were beguiled by the Devil, we were born as sinners and suffered. But God sent Jesus Christ for us in order to make us His children through faith. That is the purpose of His creating us. He is also willing to give us happy and eternal lives of gods, with Jesus Christ and God the Father in the Millennial Kingdom and the Kingdom of Heaven.

"And we know that all things work together for good to those who love God, to those who are the called according to His purpose." God's will for us was all accomplished when our sins were taken away. Is this not right? Should we not be happy that we were born into this world? When we think of the glory we will enjoy in the future, we cannot help but be happy for being born. But most people are not happy, and this is because they reject the love of God.

Do you know why there are sins and diseases, and why everything seems to go just fine for the evil people while those who try to do good seems to only suffer? It is because only when we suffer will we come to seek God, meet Him and become His children by receiving the forgiveness of our sins. God let the evil people still live in the world to make all things work together for the good of those who love Him.

Do not think like this: "I don't know why God made me so. Why did God let me be born into such a poor family and suffer?" God let us be born into this world under the reign of

Satan and the Law to make us His children and to make us live eternally as kings with our Lord in His Kingdom. All things worked together for the better and God made us His children. This is the purpose of God in making us this way. We do not have anything to complain and murmur against God. "Why was I made so? Why am I this way?" The good will of God is accomplished through these hardships.

Do not complain about your sufferings. Do not sing such pessimistic songs about your life anymore. *"And as it is appointed for men to die once, but after this the judgment" (Hebrews 9:27).* There is the grace of God's salvation between one's birth and the judgment. We believe in Jesus Christ, all our sins have been taken away by God's grace, and we will eternally reign in the Millennium and in the Kingdom of Heaven. We are to be called "the lord of all creation." Do you now understand why God made you suffer? He gave us sufferings and hardships to bless us to be His children by making us come back to God.

God predestined us to be conformed to the image of His Son

It takes no time for us to receive the remission of sins, to be saved from the judgment of God and to become righteous. We are made righteous once and for all, and we can instantly become God's children by faith. The salvation of God is not the result of a long-term process of our own sanctification. God saved us once and for all and made us righteous at once.

"For whom He foreknew, He also predestined to be conformed to the image of His Son, that He might be the firstborn among many brethren. Moreover whom He

predestined, these He also called; whom He called, these He also justified; and whom He justified, these He also glorified" *(Romans 8:29-30).*

Many people base "the five doctrines of Calvinism" on these passages. But they are wrong. Here, Paul says, *"For whom He foreknew, He also predestined to be conformed to the image of His Son."* God predestined us to be His children in Jesus. God predestined us to be born into this world under His plan. He made us. To be conformed to whose image? To be conformed to the image of God, the image of His Son.

God allowed us to be born, and set to adopt us as His children through Jesus Christ, according to the good pleasure of His will. He promised to send his Son to make us His children, who are conformed to the image of His Son. God called us through Jesus Christ when we were sinners, as the descendants of Adam. *"Come to Me, all you who labor and are heavy laden, and I will give you rest" (Matthew 11:28).* He called us after taking away all our sins. He called us in order to make us righteous by faith.

God made us righteous and He glorified us

God called sinners and made them righteous once and for all. We are made to be righteous once and for all by believing in Jesus Christ as our Savior, not by being sanctified incrementally, as theologians insist. God calls sinners and make them righteous—this is the reason why He calls sinners.

"Whom he called, these He also justified." Those who are called by God and who believe in what Jesus Christ did become righteous. We surely had sin as the descendants of Adam before, but our sins were all taken away when we

believed in the truth that Jesus has indeed taken them all away. Do you then have sin or not? Of course not! We no longer have any sin left in us. *"Whom he called, these He also justified."*

The righteous are those who became the children of God. It is not true that we become His children in stages, step by step. Instead, we are at once glorified as the children of God by His redemption.

"And whom He justified, these He also glorified." God made us His children. I cannot understand why so many Christians believe in the so-called "five steps to salvation." Salvation and becoming God's children are done once and for all. It takes some time for us to take part in the resurrection of our bodies, for we have to wait for the second coming of our Lord, but the deliverance from sin is attained at once, in the blink of an eye. We can have redemption instantly when we respond to the Word of the remission of our sins that God, our caller, has offered to us, and accept what He has done to save us. "Thank You, Lord. Hallelujah! Amen! I am saved because You saved me. I could not have been redeemed if You had not washed away all my sins. Thank You, my Lord! Hallelujah!" Our sins are blotted out in this way.

Redemption requires neither our deeds nor our time. Our deeds have no role to play, even 0.1%, in our redemption. Calvinists say that one has to be justified step by step to be redeemed and to enter the Kingdom of Heaven. Just as a worm cannot run 100 m in a second no matter how hard it tries, people cannot become righteous by their own effort, regardless of how good they may be, or how hard they may try to keep the Law. A worm is still a worm however hard it may wash itself and put on make-up with expensive cosmetics. Likewise, as long as sinners have sin in their hearts, they are still merely sinners no matter how good they may seem.

How can a sinner be completely righteous by being sanctified step be step? Does the flesh get better as time go by? No, the flesh gets ungodly and more evil as it gets older. But the Bible says, *"Moreover whom He predestined, these He also called; whom He called, these He also justified; and whom He justified, these He also glorified."* This passage arranges in a row what happens at once by the grace of God; it does not say that redemption and justification are accomplished in stages. One can be made righteous once and for all by having faith in the Lord, not incrementally.

Many theologians, not knowing what they are doing, insist on unreasonable theories and send people to hell. God promised us redemption and called us through Jesus Christ, made us righteous, and glorified those who came forth to answer His call. *"But as many as received Him, to them He gave the right to become children of God, to those who believe in His name" (John 1:12).* Did God glorify us? Of course! Could we be glorified by doing good deeds and by trials? Do we have to try harder to become righteous? Of course not! We have already become righteous.

None can separate us from the love of God

Who can be against us, if God is for us? None. *"What then shall we say to these things? If God is for us, who can be against us? He who did not spare His own Son, but delivered Him up for us all, how shall He not with Him also freely give us all things? Who shall bring a charge against God's elect? It is God who justifies. Who is he who condemns? It is Christ who died, and furthermore is also risen, who is even at the right hand of God, who also makes intercession for us. Who shall separate us from the love of Christ? Shall tribulation, or distress, or persecution, or famine, or nakedness, or peril, or sword? As it is written: 'For Your sake we are killed all day long; We are accounted as sheep for the slaughter.' Yet in all these things we are more than conquerors through Him who loved us. For I am persuaded that neither death nor life, nor angels nor principalities nor powers, nor things present nor things to come, nor height nor depth, nor any other created thing, shall be able to separate us from the love of God which is in Christ Jesus our Lord"* (Romans 8:31-39).

None can separate us from the love of God. None can make us, the righteous, sinners again. None can hinder those who have become the children of God and who will live in the Millennium and the Kingdom of Heaven. Can tribulations make us sinners? Can distress make us sinners? Can persecution make us sinners? Can famine, nakedness, peril, or the sword make us sinners again? *"He who did not spare His own Son, but delivered Him up for us all, how shall He not with Him also freely give us all things?"* God gives us the Kingdom of Heaven. He freely gives us all things because He did not spare His only begotten Son to save us. When God was willing to make the greatest sacrifice for us, why, then, would He not make us His children?

The redemption that God bestows on us is…

God says that to be redeemed of our sins, we must first of all admit that Jesus Christ was sent in the flesh according to the will of God the Father. Secondly, we must admit that Jesus took upon all our sins on Himself through His baptism in the

Jordan River. Thirdly, we must confess that Jesus was crucified for us, and, finally, that He was resurrected. We cannot be saved if we do not believe in every single one of the above requirements.

Those who do not believe that Jesus is God's Son, or that He is God and the Creator, are excluded from God's salvation. If a person denies the divinity of Jesus Christ, he/she becomes the child of Satan. Those who deny the fact that Jesus took upon all our sins when He was baptized by John the Baptist cannot be saved, either. Jesus cannot become their Savior. They cannot be saved in their hearts, though they believe in Jesus with their thoughts. They go to hell, though they know Jesus. Jesus Christ died in our place because He took upon all our sins with His baptism. Jesus died because of our sins, not because of His sins. He then rose again from the dead to justify all those who believe and raise them up in resurrection.

We are saved by faith in His baptism

I have so far preached on chapter 7 in connection with chapter 8. Chapter 7 says that one who has sin cannot do good. But chapter 8 says that there is now no condemnation to those who are in Christ Jesus and that our faith in Jesus Christ makes us sinless. We are weak and cannot live according to God's will, so God the Father sent Jesus Christ as our Savior, and He took upon all our sins with His baptism when we were still sinners. We are saved from all our sins and made righteous through Jesus Christ. This is the truth that Paul teaches through chapters 7 and 8.

"There is therefore now no condemnation to those who are in Christ Jesus, who do not walk according to the flesh, but

according to the Spirit. " We now have no sin. Are you in Jesus Christ? Do you admit what Jesus Christ did for you? Just like Paul was redeemed of his sins, all our sins have been also taken away, through our faith in the baptism of Jesus and His blood on the Cross. We have been redeemed by believing in the baptism, the blood and the resurrection of Jesus. If a person arrogantly refuses to believe in the baptism of Jesus Christ, and if the person insists that Jesus was baptized only to show us His modesty, God will send that person to hell. Do not be arrogant before the Word of God. How can pastors and ministers ignore Jesus' baptism when Paul himself talked so much about it? How could they ignore the faith of no other than Paul, one of the greatest fathers of faith? How could they ignore the teachings of the servant of God, whom God Himself made an apostle?

If we want to preach about Jesus Christ, we must preach as it is written in the Bible, and we must believe according to the Bible. The Lord tells us, *"If you abide in My word, you are My disciples indeed. And you shall know the truth, and the truth shall make you free" (John 8:31-31).* You and I came to believe in Jesus' baptism like Paul.

When were your sins passed onto the body of Jesus Christ? All our sins were passed onto Jesus Christ when He was baptized by John the Baptist. Jesus said to John, *"Permit it to be so now, for thus it is fitting for us to fulfill all righteousness. "* Here, "for thus" is *"hutos"* in Greek, which means "in this way," "most fitting," or "there is no other way besides this." This word shows that Jesus irreversibly took upon the sins of the mankind onto Himself through the baptism that He received from John. Baptism means "to be washed." For all the sins in our hearts to be washed away, our sins should be passed onto Jesus Christ.

Jesus Christ took upon our sins, was crucified in our stead, and was buried in union with us. Paul thus declared, *"I have been crucified with Christ" (Galatians 2:20)*. How could we be crucified, when in fact it was Jesus who was put to death on the Cross? We are crucified with Christ because we believe that Jesus took upon all our sins on Himself and was crucified for these sins.

I praise the Lord who has saved me from all my sins. We can boldly preach the gospel because Jesus has made us righteous. I give thanks to our Lord for saving us, whose flesh is so weak and who have come so short of His glory, from all our sins. ✉

CHAPTER

8

Introduction to Chapter 8

Chapter 8 can perhaps be described as the most important chapter of the Book of Romans. Through the several themes that are present in this chapter, Paul reveals to us just how wondrous the work of the righteousness of God is.

The first theme is: *"There is therefore now no condemnation to those who are in Christ Jesus" (Romans 8:1).* This means that regardless of how vulgar and degraded we may be in our flesh, the righteousness of God has freed us from all our sins.

The second theme is: *"For what the law could not do in that it was weak through the flesh, God did" (Romans 8:3).* This means that because people in their flesh could not follow the Law given by God, Jesus Christ, by taking all their sins upon Himself with His baptism and His death on the Cross, saved them from their sins and judgments. It is because Jesus came to this earth and took upon all the sins of the mankind at once with His baptism by John that He could carry all the sins of the world on His Cross, be crucified on it, and arise from death to save all those who believe in this truth. All these works of our Lord were meant to fulfill the righteousness of God to save the sinners from their sins, in obedience to the will of our God the Father.

The third theme is: *"For those who live according to the flesh set their minds on the things of the flesh, but those who live according to the Spirit, the things of the Spirit" (Romans 8:5).* This means that when we decide to believe in God, we should believe in Him not by following our own thoughts, but by following the Word of God.

The fourth theme is: *"But you are not in the flesh but in the Spirit, if indeed the Spirit of God dwells in you" (Romans 8:9).* Those who believe in the righteousness of God have received the Holy Spirit in their heart and become the children of God. This also means that you cannot become God's child just because you attend church diligently.

The fifth theme is: *"Therefore, brethren, we are debtors—not to the flesh, to live according to the flesh" (Romans 8:12).* This theme tells us that those who have been saved from all their sins by believing in the gospel of our Lord that has fulfilled the righteousness of God cannot be debtors to their flesh and slaves to it.

The sixth theme is: *"For you did not receive the spirit of bondage again to fear, but you received the Spirit of adoption by whom we cry out, 'Abba, Father'" (Romans 8:15).* Because those who believe in God have received the Holy Spirit, they now call God the Father, *"Abba, Father."*

The seventh theme is: *"The Spirit Himself bears witness with our spirit that we are children of God, and if children, then heirs—heirs of God and joint heirs with Christ" (Romans 8:16-17).* Those who believe in the righteousness of God are those who have received the Holy Spirit, and those who have received the Holy Spirit are those who will become, together with Christ, heirs to His Kingdom of Heaven.

The eighth theme is: *"For we know that the whole creation groans and labors with birth pangs together until now" (Romans 8:22).* This tells us that even the believers in the righteousness of God face suffering in this earthly world, along with all other creatures, but it also tells us that in their next world there will be neither groans nor pain.

The ninth theme is: *"Moreover whom He predestined, these He also called; whom He called, these He also justified;*

and whom He justified, these He also glorified" (Romans 8:30).
This tells us that God has called the sinners in His Son Jesus
Christ, and that He has made them His children by taking away
all their sins at once with His righteousness.

Finally, the tenth and last theme is: *"Who shall bring a
charge against God's elect? It is God who justifies" (Romans
8:33).* No one can judge God's children who have received the
Holy Spirit as their gifts for their deliverance from sin by
believing in the righteousness of God.

These ten themes are then the basic outlines of Romans
chapter 8. We will now turn to examine them in detail with our
main discussion. ⊠

The Righteousness of God, The Fulfillment of the Righteous Requirement of the Law

< Romans 8:1-4 >

"There is therefore now no condemnation to those who are in Christ Jesus, who do not walk according to the flesh, but according to the Spirit. For the law of the Spirit of life in Christ Jesus has made me free from the law of sin and death. For what the law could not do in that it was weak through the flesh, God did by sending His own Son in the likeness of sinful flesh, on account of sin: He condemned sin in the flesh, that the righteous requirement of the law might be fulfilled in us who do not walk according to the flesh but according to the Spirit."

Romans 8:1-4 tells us what kind of faith those who are in Christ have. The secret of this passage is that we can meet, with our faith in the righteousness of God, all the demands of the Law.

What, then, is the faith that believes in the righteousness of God? This is the faith that has received the remission of sins by believing in the baptism of Jesus and His blood, through which our Lord took away all the sins of the world. We can therefore win over sin by believing in Jesus, who has fulfilled all righteousness by pursuing the righteousness of God, as our Savior. This is the faith that follows God's righteousness and our victory in faith.

First of all, Romans 8:1 tells us, *"There is therefore now no condemnation to those who are in Christ Jesus."* Those who dwell in Jesus Christ by believing in the righteousness of God assuredly have no sin. Such a faith is based on the baptism of Jesus and His blood that have fulfilled all the righteous requirement of the Law. Faith in the righteousness of God is the most pivotal faith to the born again saints. How else can mere mortals become sinless? And yet with their unwavering faith in the righteousness of God through Jesus Christ, their sins have all disappeared. This is because Jesus took upon on His flesh all the sins of the world through His baptism, for the sake of those who believe in the righteousness of God.

Romans 8:3 tells us that God sent *"His own Son in the likeness of sinful flesh, on account of sin,"* and that *"He condemned sin in the flesh."* By condemning sin in Jesus' "flesh," in other words, God the Father passed all the sins of the world onto His only begotten Son. This Word of truth is revealed in Matthew 3:13-17 (a much more detailed discussion on this subject can be found in my book, *"Have You Truly Been Born Again of the Water and the Spirit?"*). Those who believe in this truth have no sin, because God has forgiven all the sins of the world with His righteousness.

"O wretched man that I am!"

The passages from Romans 7:24 to 8:6 contain two very contrasting themes. One of them is a discussion of the problem of sin, in other words, the disobedience to God due to the lusts of his own flesh, and the other is a discussion of the solution to this problem of sin that he found in Jesus Christ.

Romans 7:24-25 says, *"O wretched man that I am! Who will deliver me from this body of death? I thank God—through Jesus Christ our Lord! So then, with the mind I myself serve the law of God, but with the flesh the law of sin."* Paul cried out that he was a wretched man when he looked at his own flesh, but he thanked God because he was delivered from his flesh through Jesus Christ. We can also realize that even Paul served the law of God in his mind, but in his flesh he served the law of sin.

Paul confessed that his flesh was following the law of sin, unpleasing to God, instead of living a life pleasing to Him. And yet he said that in his mind he still followed the law of the Spirit of God. Sandwiched between these two laws, Paul felt wretched and desperate, but he nevertheless declared victory of faith by thanking God for delivering him from his sins through his faith in Jesus Christ, the fulfillment of the righteousness of God.

Paul could give such thanks only because he believed that Jesus Christ has atoned all his sins as well as the sins of all mankind. To take upon these sins of the world, Jesus put into His body all the sins of the mankind by being baptized by John. And by being judged of sin on the Cross, He has saved all those who believe in Him from all the sins of the world. This is why Paul declared in Roman 8:1, *"There is therefore now no condemnation to those who are in Christ Jesus."* That there is no condemnation means that there is absolutely no sin in those who believe in the righteousness of God. Those who are in Christ Jesus by believing in the righteousness of God can never have sin in their hearts. They may be weak in their flesh, but they have no sin whatsoever.

In contrast, condemnation means the existence of sin, that is, the state of being condemned. When someone does something wrong, we usually call it a sin. But it is because he does not believe in the righteousness of God that he is a sinner. Yet above passage tells us that there is no condemnation to those who are in Christ Jesus.

This declaration is not, however, based upon the so-called Doctrine of Justification, which the world's religions claim to stand for. 'The credo of being regarded as righteous by faith' means a hypothetical claims that God considers someone righteous even though he is not actually righteous and has sin in his heart just because of his faith in Jesus. But this is mistaken. How can God lie and call a sinner to be without sin? This He does not do. He would instead call such a sinner by saying, "You are facing your certain death from your sins; believe in My righteousness shown in the gospel of the water and the Spirit!"

Nowadays many people try to rationalize their mistaken faith and earn the righteousness of God by sticking to such doctrines. But this kind of faith is very wrong and dangerous. Were Jesus not the God of truth, He could perhaps call a sinner His follower. But you must realize that Jesus, the Truth, does not call a sinner righteousness and sinless. Calling a sinner righteous and sinless is impossible before the righteousness of God, His justice and holiness.

You must realize that your deliverance from sin comes not just by believing in Jesus, but by believing in the righteousness of God, which then becomes yours. Even if you believe in Jesus, God will not call you righteous if you do not know and thus not believe in the righteousness of God. But today's reality is that such doctrines as the Doctrine of Incremental Sanctification and the Doctrine of Justification are accepted by many as the orthodox Christian doctrines. But few realize that such so-called orthodox doctrines can actually prevent one from knowing or earning the righteousness of God. By believing in these doctrines without realizing that they actually are against the righteousness of God, many people have failed to receive the righteousness of God, as such doctrines have ended up becoming their own stumbling blocks.

If you want to be a true Christian, you must measure yourself with the Word of God to see whether you are truly in Christ or not. And to do so, you must hear, see, and understand the Word of the water and the Spirit. Ask yourself, "Is my faith in Jesus a correct one? When I say that I believe in Jesus, am I not just practicing religion? Am I straddling halfway, neither in nor out of Jesus?" It is now time for you to receive the righteousness of God by believing in it and to dwell in the faith of truth that *"There is therefore now no condemnation to those who are in Christ Jesus."*

In Ephesians we can often encounter the passage, "through the redemption that is in Jesus." This means that God has predestined and selected us in Christ Jesus to save us from all our sins. Those who have been atoned by the righteousness of God in Jesus and have entered into Christ are those whose sins have been completely blotted out. Those who believe in the gospel of the water and the Spirit given by our Lord, therefore, face no condemnation in Jesus Christ. When one believes in the gospel of the water and the Spirit, he becomes the one who has received the righteousness of God in the Lord and who preaches this gospel.

Those who believe in the righteousness of God in Jesus

Christ and who have entered into His open arms have no sin. This is the truth and the correct answer. Because Jesus' baptism and His blood on the Cross have made all the sins disappear for those who are in Christ by believing in the righteousness of God, it is impossible for them to have sin. Those who are in Christ therefore truly have no sin. This truth—that there is no sin for those who are in Christ—is the answer found in the Word of the water and the Spirit, and as such, there is nothing complicated about the problem of sin. When you believe in the righteousness of God revealed through the gospel of the water and the Spirit, you too can become truly righteous. Know and believe in the gospel of the water and the Spirit that has the righteousness of God in it. You will then become a righteous saint who dwells in Christ.

Suppose that we are facing a very difficult problem. If we really want to find a solution to this problem, we must continue to search for the answer regardless of the difficulties and troubles that we might face. Similarly, those who believe in Jesus and yet have not entered into Him must search for the righteousness of God revealed in the gospel of the water and the Spirit.

Some people think of Christianity just one of the many religions of the world, and try to find the solution to their sins by coming up and believing in such doctrines as the Doctrine of Incremental Sanctification. But they will soon realize that neither such doctrines nor their own righteousness can cleanse away their sins. They will instead discover that their problem of sin can easily be resolved by believing in the gospel of the water and the Spirit.

If you want to be a true Christian, you must receive the righteousness of God by believing in the gospel of the water and the Spirit in your heart. But the religious people try to earn the righteousness of God by measuring up to such doctrines as the Doctrine of Incremental Sanctification and the Doctrine of Justification, in their attempt to resolve all their problems of sin with their own works. Such faith comes to rely on the prayers of repentance, which ultimately cannot deliver them from their certain destruction because they become more and more sinful whenever they see their sins while resort to such prayers.

But those who believe in the gospel of the water and the Spirit, though they may be weak in their flesh, have resolved all the problems of sin by believing in the righteousness of God. Those who have received the righteousness of God by believing thus have no sin in their minds, and as such there is no condemnation against them.

Because the righteousness of God is in Jesus

Verse 2 says, *"For the law of the Spirit of life in Christ Jesus has made me free from the law of sin and death."* God has given man two laws, the law of the Spirit of life in Jesus and the law of sin and death. As Paul tells us, the law of the Spirit of life has freed us from the law of sin and death, from all our sins. You must realize and understand this truth spoken by Paul to receive new life. This truth applies equally to everyone in this world.

We, too, have been set free from the law of sin and death by believing in the law of the Spirit of life; otherwise, we would have reached our certain destruction under the law of sin and death. But by believing in our hearts in the righteousness of God in Jesus—that is, the baptism of Jesus and His blood on the Cross—we have received His righteousness, come under

the law of the Spirit of life, and received eternal life prepared
for us. Where can you, then, find the gospel of the water and
the Spirit that can forgive all your sins? This is in the baptism
that Jesus received from John and the Cross on which He shed
His blood. The righteousness of God, in other words, is found
in the gospel of the water and the Spirit.

What, then, is the gospel of the righteousness of God that
sets us free from the law of sin and death? It is the gospel that
our Lord was born onto this earth, was baptized by John at the
age of thirty to take upon all the sins of the world on Himself,
was crucified on the Cross, and arose from death, all to deliver
us from our sins—this is the gospel made of the righteousness
of God.

God, knowing that mankind was bound to commit sin
because of its weakness, has planned to save all the sinners
from their sins by giving them the gospel of salvation that can
set them free from the law of sin and death. This is precisely
the gospel of atonement found in Jesus' baptism by John and
His blood on the Cross. By believing in this gospel, all men can
be freed from the law of death of their sins—this righteousness
of God is the law of life that has delivered the mankind from
all its sins.

God gave to man the Word of the Law and has set that any
failure to live by His Law would be a sin. At the same time,
God has also set a law that can deliver sinners from their sins.
This law of salvation is the truth hidden in the righteousness of
God, the law of grace that gives eternal life to all those who
believe in it. The law of atonement that God has set for the
mankind is the law of faith in the gospel of the water and the
Spirit—that is, Jesus' baptism and His blood on the
Cross—and this faith is the law of life that can clothe them the

righteousness of God.

Who, then, can turn against this law of life? Anyone who believes in the gospel of the water and the Spirit given by God will be delivered from all the sins of the world, and by this faith he/she will receive the righteousness of God.

How has God given you the law of the Spirit of life? By sending His Son Jesus to this earth, born from a virgin, by putting all the sins of the world on Him through His baptism by John, by having Him die on the Cross for the wages of these sins, and by resurrecting Him from death—eliminating, thus, all the sins of world and making Jesus the Savior of the sinners. To all those who believe in this truth God has given forgiveness and new life, and this is the law of the Spirit of life that He has given to us.

What, then, is the law of sin and death? This is the commandments that God has given to the mankind. The Law set by God details His commandments on "do's and don't," and any failure to deviate from these commandments would make it a sin, whose wages of death should be paid by punishment in hell.

Thus everyone was placed under the law of death, but Jesus Christ has delivered us from this law of death with His baptism and bloodshed on the Cross. There is no one but Jesus who can save sinners from their sins, and there is no other way but by the gospel of the water and the Spirit given by Him that can deliver us from all our sins. You must therefore know and believe how Jesus came to this earth to save you, and what the righteousness of God is.

Nowadays, however, there are many who profess faith in Jesus and are in highly detailed knowledge of the Law—that is, the law of sin and death—and yet are completely ignorant of the gospel of the water and the Spirit that has delivered them from all their sins. Many still continue to believe in Jesus with this ignorance. From this we can see just how long the gospel of the water and the Spirit has been hidden. This gospel of the water and the Spirit is different from the gospel that contains faith only in the Cross. Many people place great importance only on Jesus' blood on the Cross, but the Scripture tells us that Jesus bled on the Cross because He took upon all the sins of the world when He was baptized by John, not when He was crucified.

You must realize that this difference in knowledge makes all the difference between going to heaven and hell. It may look like a minor difference, but these two understandings profoundly differ from each other, entailing fundamentally different consequences. This is why when you wish to believe in Jesus as your Savior, you must center your faith around the gospel of the water and the Spirit. Only by doing so can you be delivered from all your sins. And yet all too often many who profess faith in Jesus nowadays continue to remain ignorant of the righteousness of God.

Such people try to stand before God as whole by attempting to commit as few sins as possible and by trying to be sanctified for themselves. But the righteousness of God is not something that can be attained by man's own thoughts, efforts, or works. Only by believing in the truth of atonement hidden in the truth of the water and the Spirit can one attain the righteousness of God. The faith of those who try to sanctify themselves by following the Law is a foolish faith. There is no one who can follow all the requirements of the Law.

By condemning sin in Jesus' flesh

Verse 3 says, *"For what the law could not do in that it was weak through the flesh, God did by sending His own Son in the likeness of sinful flesh, on account of sin: He condemned sin in the flesh."* We can find out from this passage just how detailed Paul's witnessing of the law of the water and the Spirit is. Here, Paul tells us how God the Father placed all the sins of the world onto Jesus: *"By sending His own Son in the likeness of sinful flesh, on account of sin: He condemned sin in the flesh."*

What does it mean when it says that God condemned sin in the flesh? It means that God the Father sent His only begotten Son to this earth, had Him be baptized by John to place all the sins of the world onto His body, and thereby cleansed all the sins of the believers forever. This is why it says that *"what the law could not do... God did."* God blotted out all the sins of the world by placing them on His Son. And by having Him die on the Cross and be resurrected from His death, all the sins disappeared.

This is the gospel of truth that saves you, and this gospel is the gospel of the water and the Spirit. What our Lord said to Nicodemus in John 3:5, *"Unless one is born of water and the Spirit, he cannot enter the kingdom of God,"* is precisely this gospel. This gospel that manifests the righteousness of God was revealed when Jesus was baptized by John, bled on the Cross, and arose from death.

Matthew 3:15 says, *"But Jesus answered and said to him (John the Baptist), 'Permit it to be so now, for thus it is fitting for us to fulfill all righteousness.' Then he allowed Him."* This passage bears witness to the righteousness of God and its manifestation in Jesus. When Jesus came to the Jordan River from Galilee and tried to be baptized by John the Baptist, John refused to do so at first, asking, *"I need to be baptized by You, and are You coming to me?"* But Jesus ordered John in severe tone by the following passage, *"Permit it to be so now, for thus it is fitting for us to fulfill all righteousness."*

What, then, does "to fulfill all righteousness" mean? It means that Jesus took upon Himself all the sins of the world through His baptism received from John. When Jesus came up from the water after His having been baptized, the heavens were opened to Him and the Spirit of God descended like a dove. Then *"a voice came from heaven, saying, 'This is My beloved Son, in whom I am well pleased.'"* God was pleased by Jesus' baptism through which He took upon Himself all the sins of the world. Here we see all three Persons of the Triune God together, the Father, the Son, and the Holy Spirit, who have decided to save the mankind from its sins and to fulfill this promise.

The Scripture tells us that the heavens were opened to Jesus when He was baptized, and that a voice from the heaven declared, *"This is My beloved Son, in whom I am well pleased."* That is to say, God the Father was pleased by the fact that His Son took upon Himself all the sins of the world at once by being baptized by John. Because Jesus was thus baptized, and because by His baptism all the sins of the world were placed on His body, He fulfilled all righteousness by being crucified on the Cross and rising from death again.

In other words, Jesus was baptized by John to fulfill all the righteousness of God. He then died on the Cross. This baptism and this death were meant to fulfill all the righteousness of God. Jesus took upon Himself all the sins of the world with His baptism, and this is how He could bleed on the Cross. And by resurrecting from death, He fulfilled all the wills of God.

"All the righteousness of God" means the act of delivering the mankind from all its sins. To fulfill this righteous act, Jesus took over the sins of all people with His baptism and bled on the Cross. All the righteousness of God was fulfilled by the most just and proper method. The baptism, blood, and the resurrection of Jesus are what fulfilled the righteousness of God, and this righteousness of God has made us sinless, placing in us the very righteousness of God. The Triune God planned this, Jesus fulfilled this, and the Holy Spirit bears witness to its righteousness even as now. You must believe in the Word that God sent *"His own Son in the likeness of sinful flesh, on account of sin: He condemned sin in the flesh."*

Ask yourself. Ask yourself if you think you can really follow all the commands of the Law perfectly for the rest of your life. You will, of course, do your best to follow them, but you will never be able to live by the Law completely. When you break the smallest detail of the Law, you are breaking all of the Law (James 2:10), and this is why everyone without exception ends as a complete sinner under the Law.

You may be sincere in your desire to follow the Law and do your best, but the righteousness of God that He demands from us is never attainable by following the Law. You must realize that the only reason why God gave us His Law is so that we may come to recognize our sins. Because we are weak in our flesh, no one can follow the Law of God to its fullest extent.

This is why God, to deliver us deep from our sins, sent His Son to this earth and had Him be baptized by John to take upon everyone's sins. By having Him baptized in His flesh, in other words, all the sins of the world was placed on His flesh. This is why the Scripture tell us that God *"condemned sin in the flesh"* of Jesus, and this is how God has made us sinless.

We must know and believe in how God has made our sins disappear. By having His Son be baptized by John, the representative of the mankind, God placed all our sins on Jesus. He then had Jesus carry all the sins of the world to the Cross, and, to pay their wages in our stead, bleed and die on it. And by His resurrection from death, He opened the way to redemption for all those who believe in it. God has thus planned and thus carried out our salvation from sin.

We must therefore believe in our hearts that the baptism of Jesus and His blood on the Cross were meant to be our atonement. Those who believe in the righteousness of God must surely believe in Jesus' baptism and His blood on the Cross.

You, too, must believe accordingly, to receive the remission of all your sins and to be perfectly justified and be sinless. You must correctly understand how God has made your sins disappear, and follow His will and believe in it before God, rather than believing in your own efforts. ✉

Who is a Christian?

< Romans 8:9-11 >
"But you are not in the flesh but in the Spirit, if indeed the Spirit of God dwells in you. Now if anyone does not have the Spirit of Christ, he is not His. And if Christ is in you, the body is dead because of sin, but the Spirit is life because of righteousness. But if the Spirit of Him who raised Jesus from the dead dwells in you, He who raised Christ from the dead will also give life to your mortal bodies through His Spirit who dwells in you."

Whether someone is a true Christian or not is distinguished according to whether the Spirit of God dwells within him/her. How can someone be a Christian, whether he/she believes in Jesus or not, if he/she does not have the Holy Spirit within his/her heart? Paul tells us that whether we believe in Jesus is not the most important question, but whether we believe in Him *having discovered the righteousness of God or not*. The true faith required by the saints is the faith that is ready for the Spirit to dwell in them. The presence of the Holy Spirit in you will determine whether you are a Christian or not.

Thus, Paul said, *"Now if anyone does not have the Spirit of Christ, he is not His."* He said "anyone." It does not matter whether the person is a minister, evangelist, or revivalist. If one does not have the Holy Spirit within his/her heart, the person is not His. You must keep in mind that if you do not believe in God's righteousness that leads you to receive the Holy Spirit, you are a sinner who is destined to go to hell. We should thus be all concerned about the gospel of the water and the Spirit that contains the righteousness of God.

If the Holy Spirit dwells in us, this means that we died to sin through our faith in the baptism of Christ. But our spirit is alive because of the newly attained righteousness. Moreover, on the day when our Lord comes again, our mortal bodies will receive life as well. This is why we must think about the One who has given us the Holy Spirit.

If you do not have the faith that believes in God's righteousness, you do not belong to Christ. If, on the other hand, you do have this faith in God's righteousness, the Spirit of God dwells in you. Without this faith, the Holy Spirit would not reign over you. Therefore, if you do not have the Word of redemption that contains the righteousness of God, you do not belong to Christ, even if you were to outwardly confess and recite the Apostles' Creed in every Sunday service. If you do not belong to Christ, your spirit will be cursed and it will lead you to eternal destruction, no matter how much you might have wished to do good. ✉

To be Carnally Minded is Death, but to be Spiritually Minded is Life and Peace

< Romans 8:4-11 >

"That the righteous requirement of the law might be fulfilled in us who do not walk according to the flesh but according to the Spirit. For those who live according to the flesh set their minds on the things of the flesh, but those who live according to the Spirit, the things of the Spirit. For to be carnally minded is death, but to be spiritually minded is life and peace. Because the carnal mind is enmity against God; for it is not subject to the law of God, nor indeed can be. So then, those who are in the flesh cannot please God. But you are not in the flesh but in the Spirit, if indeed the Spirit of God dwells in you. Now if anyone does not have the Spirit of Christ, he is not His. And if Christ is in you, the body is dead because of sin, but the Spirit is life because of righteousness. But if the Spirit of Him who raised Jesus from the dead dwells in you, He who raised Christ from the dead will also give life to your mortal bodies through His Spirit who dwells in you."

Overseas mission is effective when done through literature, which is what we are doing right now. We are blessed when we read the Word of God and our faith grow because we believe in His Word.

People have been suffering for the past five centuries, deceived by such false doctrines as the Doctrine of Incremental Sanctification, the Doctrine of Justification, and others that claim that redemption is possible through prayers of repentance.

Romans 8:3 tells us that God did what the Law could not do in that it was weak through the flesh. God sent His own Son in the likeness of sinful flesh, condemned sin in His flesh, and judged Him to deliver us from all our sins.

Today, we turn to Romans 8:4-12 for God's truth. Romans 8:3-4 says, *"He condemned sin in the flesh, that the righteous requirement of the law might be fulfilled in us who do not walk according to the flesh but according to the Spirit."* The question, of course, is this: what does this mean?

First, what does it mean to not live according to the flesh?

This means to not seek the profits of the flesh. It is to discriminate between the wishes of the Spirit and the lusts of the flesh, and to stay away from those who do not obey the word of God. Verse 5 states, *"For those who live according to the flesh set their minds on the things of the flesh."* What does "the things of the flesh" mean? This means that there are those who, even as they attend church, seek after their own desires.

To put it simply, Christians should not go to church for the purpose of profit-seeking businesses in the world. This is living according to the flesh. These people go to churches with large congregations to introduce and advertise their businesses, in the hopes of acquiring regular and loyal customers. They attend church and believe in Jesus for the sake of their own flesh.

There are others. Those who teach sectarianism within the Christian community, and those who teach their followers to pursue only material blessings are also the ones who live according to the flesh and who have set their minds on the things of the flesh.

We can easily encounter sectarianism in our Christian community. Who are these sectarians then? These are the people who deceive themselves with their misplaced faith in the superiority of their denomination. They say that their sect was established by so-and-so, that they have such-and-such theologians, that they are this big and greatly known over the world and have this strong a tradition, and so on. All these boastings are what make up the vanities of these people and build up their own faith. There are many with such faith in this world.

Sectarians believe in Jesus for the benefits of their own flesh. Those who live according to the flesh still boast of their churches and of having been materially blessed by attending their large churches. Some churches have such common community goals as "love your wife." But this is what "those who live according to the flesh" means. Should churches set their eyes on loving one's wives as their goal? They should not. Am I then saying that we should not love our wives? Of course not! But such goals, however nice and attractive, cannot be the fundamental purpose of our Church.

Those who live according to the flesh set their minds on the things of the flesh. Too many ministers today have turned themselves into such people by being interested only in increasing the size of their church membership, offerings, and building—these have now become the main purpose of their faith. Build a bigger, taller, and larger church has become their greatest goal. Even if they outwardly say that gathering more followers is to lead them to Heaven and offer other such excuses, their ultimate purpose is to raise more money in order to build bigger church buildings.

To make their churches to follow the things of the flesh, they had to turn their followers into religious fanatics. Some pastors have built their success on their ability to turn their congregation into fanatics, half-crazed, delusional, and utterly misguided.

Those who live according to the Spirit of God

However, there are those who really live according to the Spirit of God among the Christians. These who live according to the Spirit live according to the Word of God, believe what is written in the Scriptures while denying their own thoughts, do as God pleases, and preach the gospel of the water and the Spirit.

The Bible states that those who live according to the Spirit set their minds on the things of the Spirit. If we have been forgiven for all our sins by believing in God's righteousness, we should not live thoughtlessly, but live meditating on the work of the Spirit. Those who live by the Spirit think spiritually and set out to do the things of the Spirit by faith. Happy are those who pursue the things of the Spirit. These are the people who please God, save others from the sins of the world, and live by faith. We have been forgiven for our sins and therefore must set our minds on the things of the Spirit and live according to Him.

The goal in our lives is to fulfill the work of the Spirit,

which is to preach the gospel of the water and the Spirit. We should set our minds on the things of the Spirit. How much have you set your mind on the things of the Spirit? We are waging a spiritual warfare and must practice the things of the Spirit by believing in God's righteousness and by preaching it. We must always think of what pleases the Lord and challenge the work of the Spirit by setting our minds on God's work, even if we may be weak and full of shortcomings. When a particular work is done, we must yet strive again for more work that would please the Lord.

We are now preaching the gospel of the water and the Spirit to the whole world through literature. About 200 to 300 persons receive our free Christian books and e-books daily by visiting our website. By striving with faith for the preaching of the gospel of the water and the Spirit to everyone in every country in the world, we are serving the gospel with you in His Church. If we had not set our minds on the things of the Spirit, we would not have been granted these fruits of the Spirit. We should carry out His work one by one with our minds set on the things of the Spirit. Then we will please our spiritual bridegroom, Jesus Christ, like the virtuous wife found in Proverbs chapter 31.

Verse 8 states, *"Those who are in the flesh cannot please God."* This refers to those who have not received the forgiveness of sins. *"The carnal mind is enmity against God; for it is not subject to the law of God, nor indeed can be. So then, those who are in the flesh cannot please God" (Romans 8:6).* As such, sinners who do not have the Spirit in them can neither do God's work nor please Him.

Sinners do not subject themselves to the Law of God. Nor do they subject to the righteousness of God. They cannot please Him. This is because they cannot understand what the will of God is, as the Holy Spirit does not dwell in them. What pleases the Lord is to forgive all the sins of humankind with the gospel of the water and the Spirit. He is not pleased with the praise and worship of sinners.

God is not pleased when sinners praise Him. No matter how much sinners raise their hands to praise Him and shed tears in worship, they cannot please Him. Sinful Christians try to please God by being intoxicated with emotions. They cannot please the Lord. Those who are with sin cannot please the Lord because they are sinners. No matter how much they try, sinners can never please the Lord. It is not a matter of how willing they are to please the Lord; it is a matter of how impossible it is for them to please Him.

Would God be pleased if people built bigger churches? He would not. If it is necessary to move into a bigger church building, by all means a bigger church should be built. But building a bigger church just for the sake of building it does not please God at all.

A church in my town, for instance, recently spent over US$3 million to build a new church building, even when the previous building was standing right next to it and still in excellent shape and accommodations. When the size of the congregation was only 200-300 at most, was it really necessary to build such a church? God's church is not built of bricks. God tells us that we are the temple of God and that the Spirit of God dwells in the hearts of the righteous.

It is right to build a bigger church as a necessity, but does building bigger churches by itself give glory to God? No, it does not. Does gathering more people into a church give more glory to God? No, you cannot please God by just doing that.

Those who are in the flesh cannot please the Lord.

Sometimes, there are even righteous people who pursue only the profits of the flesh. These people cannot please the Lord. Among the righteous, there are some who are still bound by their thoughts of the flesh like sinners. These people cannot please God. They, in reality, are not unable to lead a healthy life of faith in the church, complain, and resent God's church, and eventually leave the church.

Therefore, we who are righteous should lead a life that is righteous and pleasing to God, not a life that seeks only the profits of the flesh. We should think on the works of God and His righteousness, serve the works of His righteousness, and use our bodies, minds, and belongings as the instruments of the righteousness of God. We should lead a life that is pleasing to God.

Those who are in the Spirit of Christ

Let us read verse 9 together. *"But you are not in the flesh but in the Spirit, if indeed the Spirit of God dwells in you. Now if anyone does not have the Spirit of Christ, he is not His."*

This passage, according to Paul, means that if we believe in the gospel of the water and the Spirit—in other words, if we believe in God's righteousness—and have been redeemed from our sins, we are no longer in the flesh but in the Spirit. If anyone has the Spirit in his/her heart, this person is in Christ, and if anyone does not have the Spirit of Christ, this person is not His.

We are, therefore, not in the flesh but in the Spirit. We, who are in the Spirit and have been delivered from sin through the gospel of the water and the Spirit, should not forget that we are the soldiers of righteousness, who have the capacity to please God as the righteous in Christ. We should not despair at the weaknesses of our flesh, but please God with the faith that, although we are weak, we are His and we are in Him, and that therefore we are His workers.

We must know that it is not allowed for us to pursue only the profits of our flesh after we are born again. We should live knowing that the righteous are destined to live only for the righteousness of God. Verse 10 shows us how Christians should live: *"And if Christ is in you, the body is dead because of sin, but the Spirit is life because of righteousness."*

In truth, we, our bodies, were crucified and died with Jesus Christ because of our sins. We have been saved from all our sins through the righteous act of God. Because of this righteousness, the spirits of the righteous thus have eternal life. Eternal life! We should know that those who have been justified are no longer allowed to live only for their own flesh. Those who do not live for the righteousness of God after being born again are far from His blessings.

We were destined to live for God's righteousness. Maybe some of you, after being born again of water and the Spirit, have thought in desperation, "The Bible says that those who are in the flesh cannot please God. I must be one of them." But this is not true. God has regenerated us to live as the soldiers of His righteousness.

Some people think like that probably because they have misunderstood the Bible. Even if some of the righteous think that they cannot live according to God because their bodies live according to the flesh and because they are weak, the truth is that those who have the Holy Spirit in them rejoice by doing God's works. Doing God's works make them happy, glad and well. On the other hand, a life without doing God's works is a life without motivation and purpose, a cursed life.

After we have accepted the gospel of the water and the Spirit and dwell in God's righteousness, the Holy Spirit dwells in us. The Holy Spirit comes upon and dwell in anyone who has received the redemption. What happens to those in whom the Holy Spirit dwells? They are destined to serve the righteousness of God and do His righteous work.

In short, those who have received the forgiveness of sins and have been justified should live only by faith. The righteous can keep their faith only when they live by faith and do God's works. If you think that you will live this world by your flesh despite having been justified, this is because you have not realized that you have received the forgiveness of sins and that your destiny has already changed.

The destiny of the righteous has changed. Before they were born again, they had lived for the world and for their own purposes, and had been happy while living for their carnal desire. However, after being born again, it is impossible to live like that again. We have received the forgiveness of sins. Would we be happy even if we made a six-figure income? When we have to devote ourselves to delivering other souls from this world, how could we be satisfied with only material things?

I am, in other words, asking you to think hard about the things of the flesh and those of the Spirit. You do not have to do those things in order to know them; all that you have to do is to give some serious thought to this matter.

I have so far preached on Romans chapters 1 through 6 in my previous sermon book on Romans, and from chapter 7 to 16 in this book. These two sermon books, the 4th and 5th

volume of my Christian book series, will be delivered to Christians worldwide for their reading. I am sure that many people will get to know God's righteousness through my Christian book series. Through the previous three sermon books of mine, I have talked about the fundamental teachings on God's salvation. The first volume talked about the gospel, the second volume discussed theological issues, and the third volume was on the Holy Spirit and what the correct way to receive the Spirit is. And these fourth and fifth volume on Romans talks in depth about how wrong many of the theological doctrines are, why sins do not disappear even when Christians believe in Jesus, and how the gospel of the water and the Spirit is revealed as the righteousness of God.

I believe that the gospel will spread more widely over the world through this book. There has been a remarkable progress in the preaching of the gospel when we published the third volume compared to the times when we published the first two volumes. Now, after the third volume, more and more people are asking for the first and second volumes of my Christian book series.

After these two books are published, we will know how great the power of the gospel of water and Holy Spirit is. I pray that many blessings will be abundantly bestowed by God to those who come to know His righteousness. They will know how to understand the Book of Romans, that it is to be understood by the faith in the gospel that contains the righteousness of God.

We are all working together for the gospel. Are you not also doing God's work? You are supporting the ministry of preaching the gospel to save sinners from their sins. When we are faithful in our parts and serve the gospel, so many souls all over the world will be delivered from all their sins. How, then, can we forsake this precious work for the sake of worldly work?

I want to make it clear to you that we, the righteous, are destined to no longer live only for our own flesh. Now, our destiny has been set to accomplish the righteousness of God, to save souls, and to live for this righteousness. You must know this and live the rest of your lives for God, for the true gospel, and for the salvation of the souls lost in sin.

This is what the Book of Romans is talking about in this part. Let us look at the verses 10 and 11. *"And if Christ is in you, the body is dead because of sin, but the Spirit is life because of righteousness. But if the Spirit of Him who raised Jesus from the dead dwells in you, He who raised Christ from the dead will also give life to your mortal bodies through His Spirit who dwells in you."*

The above passage means that we, our bodies, have long been dead because of our sins. But our spirits are alive because of the righteousness of God and faith. If anyone believes in God's righteousness, he/she will gain a new life. We have gained new lives by believing in God's righteousness.

Verse 11 says, *"But if the Spirit of Him who raised Jesus from the dead dwells in you, He who raised Christ from the dead will also give life to your mortal bodies through His Spirit who dwells in you."* This means that He will resurrect us at the end of the world. The life with which we had lived long ago only for our flesh and sin has now passed away, and our destiny has changed to live the rest of our lives for God and His righteousness.

You may be bored with the lives of the righteous, thinking, "No doubt the righteous will gather often to say what they say."

However, even hearing the yawn of a born again believer sitting next to you or even listening to their praises and voices will renew your minds if you stay in the church. This is because the Holy Spirit works in God's church and in the hearts of the believers. Your mind will become renewed and you will gain new strengths in your heart, be fed by the spiritual bread of life, and obtain spiritual duties to go out and perform the spiritual works.

You can be refreshed at the gathering of the believers. The fact that you become separated from the world shows that your destiny has changed. That is why those who live according to the flesh have set their minds on the things of the flesh, but those who live according to the Spirit, on the things of the Spirit. We, who have now become justified, no longer live according to the flesh. The righteous no longer want to be slaves to sin. We want to at least live according to the Spirit and set our minds on the things of the Spirit. The righteous do the things of the Spirit, the work of winning souls to Christ.

We must work hard for God's work, deny our own thoughts for it, and set our minds on it. We must now live the rest of our lives in this way. Your destiny has been changed to live only for the righteousness of God, because you have received redemption by believing in the gospel of the water and the Spirit. I hope that you know this truth.

I am sorry, but you can no longer return to the world and become a slave to sin anymore. If you return to the world now, it would mean your own death. To be carnally minded is death. Your spirit will die, your mind will die, and your body will die, if you still remain pursuing your carnal desires. Israelites did not return to Egypt upon their exodus; nor could they be happy in meeting an Egyptian after crossing the Red Sea. Likewise, we who have been justified can no longer return to Egypt, nor be happy in meeting a spiritual Egyptian.

If a righteous, born again person goes out to the world and lives with the sinners of the world, he/she would go crazy for wanting to go back to God's church. He/she would miss God's church. Let us therefore live with our minds set on the things of the Spirit.

What do the things of the Spirit of God mean? Are they not the things of God? Are they not the things of serving the gospel of God? And yet are we not weak and imperfect? You are weak, and so am I. But have you not received the forgiveness of sins even when you were weak and imperfect? Of course you have! Does the Holy Spirit then dwell in you? The answer is an emphatic yes!

Are we, then, capable of setting our minds on the things of the Spirit or not? Of course we are—we are all capable of setting our minds on the things of the Spirit. Do you know that God has changed your destiny so that you would do the things of the Spirit? Do you believe this?

Our minds have now changed. If you do not know that your mind has changed when in fact it has, it spells only trouble for you. You must set your mind steadfast to the righteousness of God. The church of God will then be your home, your fellow believers will be your brothers, sisters, parents—your family, in other words—in the same Spirit. Everyone in your church will become your family. If you have not thought so before, now is time to reconsider and give some serious thought to this teaching.

Do not think that only the family of flesh and blood is your family. Here is your home and every born again person's home. You are all a part of the family of God. That is why we must live according to the Spirit. We must live for God, for to be spiritually minded is to gain peace. ⊠

Walking in
The Righteousness of God

< Romans 8:12-16 >
　　"Therefore, brethren, we are debtors—not to the flesh, to live according to the flesh. For if you live according to the flesh you will die; but if by the Spirit you put to death the deeds of the body, you will live. For as many as are led by the Spirit of God, these are sons of God. For you did not receive the spirit of bondage again to fear, but you received the Spirit of adoption by whom we cry out, 'Abba, Father.' The Spirit Himself bears witness with our spirit that we are children of God,"

　　Paul the Apostle, as a man who received salvation from God, said that the born-again believers should not live according to the flesh, but the Spirit. In particular, Paul said that if we, who have the righteousness of God, live according to the flesh, we will die, but that if we live by the Spirit, we will live. We must thus believe in this truth. What, then, should those who believe in God's righteousness live by? Should they live according to the righteousness of God or the lust of the flesh? They must know what is right and discipline their bodies to devote themselves to the righteous works of God.

The unavoidable obligation

　　Paul claimed that we have an obligation to live according

to the Spirit, not our sinful nature, because we Christians have been saved from God's wrath and led into His righteousness. Before we became aware of the righteousness of God and believed in it, we could not live according to the Spirit. But now that we know and believe in God's righteousness, we can devote our hearts, thoughts, talents, bodies, and time to His righteous works. We should use ourselves as tools in preaching the righteousness of God and doing His righteous works.

Living according to the flesh

If you are in Christ and live by your sinful nature and not by the Spirit, the Bible states that you will perish just like all unbelievers. That is because even though you are a born-again Christian, you do not in fact live according to God's righteousness. If you are to be a true Christian, you should no longer live by the flesh, but by the righteousness of God, for you are destined to serve His righteousness because you believe in it. If you live only according to the flesh in spite of this, your spirit will die. However, if you live according to the righteousness of God, you will live in peace forever.

Sons of God

"For as many as are led by the Spirit of God, these are sons of God" (Romans 8:14).

Those who believe in God's righteousness received the Holy Spirit as a gift, and the Holy Spirit leads them. These are the "sons of God." The "sons of God" have the Holy Spirit dwelling in them. As such, those who do not have the Holy

Spirit dwelling in them are not His. The starting point in following God begins with faith in His righteousness. It starts by believing in the Word of the gospel of the water and the Spirit to become a child of God. In other words, becoming God's child begins by believing in the gospel of His righteousness. It means that you become a family member of God by believing in His righteousness, and that God has given His righteousness to save you from your sins.

When Jesus was visited by Nicodemus, a Jewish leader, Jesus told him that no one could become a child of God unless he/she is born again of water and the Spirit. Nicodemus was marveled by this and asked, *"How can a man be born when he is old?" (John 3:4)*. Jesus answered, *"Most assuredly, I say to you, unless one is born of water and the Spirit, he cannot enter the kingdom of God. That which is born of the flesh is flesh, and that which is born of the Spirit is spirit. Do not marvel that I said to you, 'You must be born again.' The wind blows where it wishes, and you hear the sound of it, but cannot tell where it comes from and where it goes. So is everyone who is born of the Spirit" (John 3:5-8)*.

Jesus said that one who is not born of water and the Spirit cannot understand the meaning of being born again. The faith in the baptism that Jesus received from John the Baptist and the blood that He shed on the Cross enables those who believe in His righteous act to receive the righteousness of God. Those who believe in the Word of the gospel are able to receive the Holy Spirit as a gift. One can reach the righteousness of God by believing in the gospel of the water and the Spirit. Everyone who accepts God's righteousness can become a child of God. Those who become His people are our brothers and sisters.

The Spirit bears witness that we are children of God

"For you did not receive the spirit of bondage again to fear, but you received the Spirit of adoption by whom we cry out, 'Abba, Father.' The Spirit Himself bears witness with our spirit that we are children of God" (Romans 8:15-16).

There are only two ways in which we can bear witness to the fact that we are the children of God. First, the righteousness of God that is revealed in the gospel of the water and the Spirit has made us His children; and second, the Holy Spirit comes to us. The Holy Spirit works within the gospel of the water and the Spirit. God planned all these things. Having faith in the gospel of the water and the Spirit is the witness in ourselves that tells us that we have become the children of God. Those who have become God's children by knowing and believing in the righteousness of God have the right to pray to God as "Abba," our Father.

Let us try to think rationally. How can someone with sin in his/her heart call God his/her Father? God the Father has never kept a sinner as His child, and a sinner has never served God as the Father. You must look inside yourself and see if, by any chance, you are also making a mistake like this. Those who bear witness to becoming the children of God through the Holy Spirit are those who believe in the righteousness of God. We must think deeply about God's righteousness. ⊠

Those Who Inherit God's Kingdom

< Romans 8:16-27 >

"The Spirit Himself bears witness with our spirit that we are children of God, And if children, then heirs—heirs of God and joint heirs with Christ, if indeed we suffer with Him, that we may also be glorified together. For I consider that the sufferings of this present time are not worthy to be compared with the glory which shall be revealed in us. For the earnest expectation of the creation eagerly waits for the revealing of the sons of God. For the creation was subjected to futility, not willingly, but because of Him who subjected it in hope; Because the creation itself also will be delivered from the bondage of corruption into the glorious liberty of the children of God. For we know that the whole creation groans and labors with birth pangs together until now. Not only that, but we also who have the firstfruits of the Spirit, even we ourselves groan within ourselves, eagerly waiting for the adoption, the redemption of our body. For we were saved in this hope, but hope that is seen is not hope; for why does one still hope for what he sees? But if we hope for what we do not see, we eagerly wait for it with perseverance. Likewise the Spirit also helps in our weaknesses. For we do not know what we should pray for as we ought, but the Spirit Himself makes intercession for us with groanings which cannot be uttered. Now He who searches the hearts knows what the mind of the Spirit is, because He makes intercession for the saints according to the will of God."

All the people who have been forgiven of their sins believe in the gospel of the water and the Spirit and have the Holy Spirit in their hearts. It says in 1 John 5:10, *"He who believes in the Son of God has the witness in himself"*. He who has the righteousness of God in his heart has the Holy Spirit dwelling in it, and it is the faith in the gospel of the water and the Spirit that makes it possible for the Holy Spirit to dwell eternally in his heart.

We became God's children by having our sins forgiven through our faith in the gospel of the water and the Spirit. The Holy Spirit has dwelt in our hearts and has become our witness, saying, "You are the children of God and His people." To those who do not have the Holy Spirit in their hearts, on the other hand, the Law bears witness, "You are not God's children, but sinners."

To those who believe in the gospel of the water and the Spirit, the Holy Spirit bears witness, "You are God's children. You are the sinless people of God." God made it clear enough so that we would know that, in order to become God's children, we must believe in the gospel of the water and the Spirit.

You might ask, "I do not feel anything, so does that mean that I am not God's child?" Some people are so infantile in their faith and may not realize that they have the Holy Spirit in their hearts. But the Holy Spirit confirms to us that even though we are in our doubtful selves, the Spirit cheers us up by saying, "Hey! You are God's children! Do you not believe in the gospel of the water and the Spirit? Because you believe, you are God's people." Even when we are doubtful, therefore, if we believe in the gospel of the water and the Spirit, we are God's children. The Holy Spirit witnesses that we are God's children. The Holy Spirit is not something that dwells in our hearts through our feelings and senses. Those who believe in the gospel of the water and the Spirit have no sin in their hearts, and since they have no sin, the Holy Spirit dwells in them. They are surely God's children.

The Holy Spirit tells us in our hearts, "You believe in Jesus' baptism, His Cross, and have been forgiven; therefore you have no sin and are God's children."

However, His proof does not come in the voice like that of a human being. So, do not expect to hear a booming voice! If you desire after listening a voice, then Satan might disguise his voice as a human's and try to tempt you. Satan works by peeking into people's thoughts while the Holy Spirit works according to God's Word.

Those who have God's Righteousness are His children and heirs

Let us read verse 17 together. *"And if children, then heirs—heirs of God and joint heirs with Christ, if indeed we suffer with Him, that we may also be glorified together."*

If we are God's children, we are also His heirs. An heir is someone who receives everything from his parents. In other words, we have the right to share everything God the Father has. If asked, "Who is God the Father's heir?," we can answer, "The people who believe in the gospel of the water and the Spirit and have been forgiven of their sins are His heirs."

People with this kind of faith are blessed and will inherit God's glory in His Kingdom with Christ. It states here that since we are joint heirs with Christ, in order to be glorified together, we also have to suffer with Him. To be joint heirs with Christ means to live in our Father's Kingdom eternally. If you believe in the gospel of the water and the Spirit, then you are a joint heir with Christ. We are heirs because we will inherit everything that our Father has.

From time to time, I can feel God's Kingdom coming near us. Everything happens in its own good time. God's promises in the Bible are also being fulfilled one by one. Now all that is left is for the people of Israel to repent, confess Jesus as their Savior, and be saved from their sins, along with a few other things. Israel is supposed to receive Jesus as their Savior during the Seven Year Tribulation.

The realization of God's Kingdom on earth and in Heaven is linked with the repentance of the Israelites. I believe that the last day will come soon. I believe that the day is near when those who believe in the gospel of the water and the Spirit will dwell eternally with God. The whole world waited for the year 2000 and thought it would be that day, but the year 2000 already passed. The tumultuous worries about the Millennium Bug have passed and we are already half-way through the year 2002, when, in fact, many people in the world had thought that all the changes on earth would happen in the year 2000.

Nevertheless, our long awaited Kingdom of Christ is still approaching each and every one of us. The Holy Spirit also leads those of us who were forgiven of sins to sense the nearing of the Kingdom of God. Now, as before, everything will be fulfilled as God said. Let us wait for that day with faith.

In the future, Israel will become a stumbling block and an obstacle to world peace, and for this it will garner the enmity of many nations. This is what the Bible tells us—that Israel will become the enemy of many and then some of the Israelites will realize that the Messiah whom they have waited for so long was indeed Jesus. They will be forgiven of their sins by believing in the gospel of the water and the Spirit. What God has planned is about to be accomplished. However, all these things will take place in due time, so we must not wait for them to happen by a certain date and time as some misguided eschatologists predict. Those who believe in the gospel of the water and the Spirit will get to see God's prophecies come true. The believers have the hope that God's promised Kingdom on earth and the Kingdom of Heaven are coming. I believe that such a day is near us.

The time will soon arrive when the things that the Lord has promised will come true one by one. I am confident that the day when the Thousand-year Kingdom and the Kingdom of God promised by God will be realized is very near us. Do you also think so, inspired by the Holy Spirit as I am? Do you believe that every prophecy of God will be fulfilled through the Holy Spirit? The Holy Spirit helps us to truly believe God's promises with all our hearts.

Through the Holy Spirit, we are sure in our hearts that the promises of God on the last days will soon come true. We believe through the Holy Spirit that what passes in our minds and our hopes will come true along with all of God's prophecies. This is the true faith.

You and I are the heirs of all of God's promised blessings; therefore, we need to wait within the Holy Spirit. God's Kingdom will come to us shortly. Israelites will soon believe and accept Jesus Christ as their Messiah.

Many people are awaiting Him right now, saying, "Please come Lord Jesus." Paul said that since he was God's heir, the suffering he went through could not be compared to the glory that he would soon receive. It meant that in order to receive glory together with Christ, we would have to suffer with Him too. This is because we believe and wait for God's Kingdom to come. In order to receive the glory with Christ, we also have to suffer with Him.

Paul's hope was for all creation, including all animals and plants, to be freed from their death. That is why all of creation is waiting earnestly for the coming of the sons of God. The hope for the sons of God is that the day will come when all the creatures will be able to live eternally.

Therefore, we must realize that we believers have been blessed with eternal lives. Whether we will see the day our Lord comes in our lifetime, or whether our Lord will wake us up from our sleep to take us away, we will have to wait for Him.

Is God's glory that shall be revealed in us truly great?

The glory that shall soon be revealed to the righteous is an everlasting glory—inheriting the eternal Kingdom and living forever in God's glory. There shall be no more death, nor sorrow, nor crying. There shall be no more pain in the Kingdom, and the Kingdom has no need for the sun or moon to shine on it, for the glory of God illuminates it. The Lamb is its light. It is a place where only Jesus and the born again, sinless believers are found, and it is filled with God's glory. The Kingdom is filled with golden rays. The glory of the Kingdom where we will live forever is such great that words cannot describe it. Because this glory that we are expecting is so great, Paul tells us that our current sufferings are nothing compared to the glory that shall be revealed to us.

Sometimes we can see God's glory in nature while we are working for God in this world. When we look at the multicolored flowers, the bedewed grass, the nature shown in the shining leaves, the warm spring atmosphere, the freshness of the forests, the clear winds, the stars that shine brightly on cold nights; when we think of the four seasons, we cannot help but to think of the Heaven. When seeing these wonders of God's creation, we hope that God's Kingdom would come even sooner.

When the Kingdom of God comes, there shall be no more death, and we will live gloriously. There will be nothing lacking so we will live in abundance and prosperity. Just the thought that I will live with glory in a place where everything is perfect and ready fills my heart with God's glory. The fact that all of those things will become ours, the believers, is like a dream, and makes us be grateful one more time that we have been born again. I thank the Lord who has filled my heart with this hope to the fullest.

Right now, we can only hope for Heaven through our imaginations, but we know that in the future, all of God's promises will come true. Our hope thus becomes more intense and our sense of the nearing glory of God becomes stronger as days go by.

This is why the believers hope for the future. Faith in God and the hope for the future is the glory and faith of those who will inherit the Kingdom of God. Is this glorified faith, then, a blessing given only to those who believe in the gospel of the water and the Spirit? The answer is an emphatic yes! Only time needs to pass before God's glory is given to the righteous, to those who believe in the gospel of the water and the Spirit. In due time, God's promises of all His glories will come true for us. All these glorious things will truly happen to the believers. The glory that awaits us is overwhelmingly splendid and beautiful.

You and I, who have the same faith in the gospel of the water and the Spirit, are the people who will enter God's Kingdom of glory. The confusing and evil world may darken our hearts at times, and we may become discouraged and disoriented. But those who have been born again can overcome these hardships by believing that they have become the heirs of God. Even though there may be all sorts of troubles in the hearts of the sinless believers, they will be able to find strength and live on by reminding themselves of God's promises. I am thankful that the Holy Spirit remains in our hearts, comforts us, and testifies to our spirits that we are God's children.

Those who have recently been redeemed of their sins should also look to the glory of Heaven and live in hope. We equally became the God's people. If you have lived the life of faith in church for a long time, you can see the Holy Spirit inside your souls rejoicing in the riches of your glorious inheritance.

Even the Hearts of the Righteous groan on this earth

Let us read verse 23 together. *"Not only that, but we also who have the firstfruits of the Spirit, even we ourselves groan within ourselves, eagerly waiting for the adoption, the redemption of our body."* Let us ask ourselves, "What do we hope for in living?" We, the believers, live hoping for the redemption of our bodies. When we say that we are God's children, it means that only our spirits are His children. Our bodies have not yet received the glory, so all the believers hope that their bodies will also be changed.

When the believers' bodies wear God's glory, they would be able to pass through a fire and they would not burn, and they would be able to go through any sort of obstacles or walls. Our changed bodies will be free of the limitations of time and space.

But our bodies have not changed yet, so we who have the first fruits of the Spirit groan inside. So, the righteous people who have been born again by believing in the gospel of the water and the Spirit wait for the redemption of the body.

To groan! It is written that even we who receive the first fruits of the Spirit groan. Have you felt the Holy Spirit groaning inside of you? When did He groan? The Holy Spirit groans when we try to chase fleshly desires.

When we look at the world and love what we see, the Holy Spirit in us groans. Our bodies have not changed, so they enjoy and try to pursue the worldly things, but because our souls have been changed already, the Holy Spirit inside us groans. We must thus turn back our hearts that try to pursue worldly pleasures and receive the guidance of the Holy Spirit.

The Holy Spirit groans inside us, who are the heirs of God, because the Holy Spirit is within us. Living in this world we can see how dark the future is and how weak our bodies are; during times like this, we should look up to and long for the blessings of God's heirs because they know that their bodies will also be redeemed. The believers wait for the day that they will have perfect bodies that are completely redeemed.

Living with the glorious hope

Let us read verses 24 and 25 in one voice. *"For we were saved in this hope, but hope that is seen is not hope; for why does one still hope for what he sees? But if we hope for what we do not see, we eagerly wait for it with perseverance."*

"Did we receive the forgiveness of all our sins in hopes of God's Kingdom?" Let us ask this question. We said that we received forgiveness of our sins by believing in the gospel of the water and the Spirit. *"But if we hope for what we do not see, we eagerly wait for it with perseverance,"* God says so.

In order to go to Heaven and be freed from our sins, we must be saved by believing in the Word of the water and the Holy Spirit. After being saved from all of our sins, if we turn our eyes to the world and hope for what can be seen, then this means that we neither know God's glory nor are waiting for it. If we hope for what we see, then that cannot be hope. That is why Paul asked, *"Why does one still hope for what he sees?"* We who have now become the righteous should not hope for what is on earth, but we, according to His promise, should look for new heavens and a new earth in which His righteousness dwells (2 Peter 3:13).

This kind of faith is what the righteous hope for. The righteous live in hope for the new Heaven and earth. What we can see with our bodily eyes is not what we truly hope for. We cannot see with our human eyes, so we wait for God's promised Kingdom of glory with our spiritual eyes. That is why those who are truly righteous place their hopes in the Kingdom of Heaven. The hope is to believe that what God has told us will really come true.

God said, *"And now abide faith, hope, love, these three"* *(1 Corinthians 13:13).* We have received the remission of our sins through our faith and hope for the Kingdom of Heaven. His Kingdom will come to earth and be present in the Heavens, and we hope that we will live eternally in His Kingdom. This is why we believe in God's promised Word and endure our present sufferings.

It is written here, *"But if we hope for what we do not see, we eagerly wait for it with perseverance."* What we persevere for is not something we can see with our eyes. We wait for God's promises that we cannot physically see. God's promises will come true to us believers because we were told that God's glory will soon be revealed, and we believe in this promise. Since we believe that our Lord is coming back again to this earth, we can endure our present sufferings.

God's Kingdom will, without even a trace of doubt, come to this earth. When the gospel is spread to all the nations, God's Kingdom will surely come. The righteous wait for that day with patience. Our Lord will come while we are waiting. This is the truth for you and I who are living in this era.

There is a Ukrainian female co-worker who translates our books into Ukrainian. She recently saw the World Trade Center buildings collapsing from the terrorist attack and said that she felt confused and afraid. She asked if this could be announcing "the era of the pale horse" in Revelations and asked for any books related to this part of the Scripture.

We cannot definitely say that this incident is an omen of the pale horse era, but we cannot deny that it may be related. If things like this happen frequently, then there will be wars, and the nations will fight each other. When wars break out, the world will suffer from famines and 'the pale horse era' could suddenly come true.

So, when I see these incidents that foretell the destruction of the world, I renew my will that we should spread the gospel to the ends of the world. It is true that we are losing hope for this world and that our hearts groan when tragedies strike us.

Nevertheless, as long as we live, we have to wait for God's Kingdom, which we cannot see with our physical eyes but only with our spiritual eyes.

Because we believe in the gospel of the water and the Spirit, we hope for the Kingdom of Heaven and wait for it with perseverance. Because we believe that God's Kingdom is coming closer to us, we can endure all our hardships. This is possible because the Holy Spirit resides in our hearts.

Are you suffering? Endure well and have patience. It is not only you who are suffering but all of us as well. We will have hope that when this is over, everything will turn out all right. Do you not know that you cannot develop hope spiritually when you are not physically suffering hardships? When the body is too comfortable, we do not look for God and seek blessings from Him. We thus drift away from God. We who have been born again should have hope for the coming glory and endure our present hardships.

God said that those who endure troubles with perseverance for the Lord are blessed. The day when God's Kingdom comes to earth will arrive, and we will enter His Kingdom. We have to endure, have patience, and not lose hope for that day. We must endure and wait for that day. No matter how sad and hard it may be right now, we have to wait and persevere until the Kingdom of God comes as a new Heaven and earth.

The Holy Spirit helps those who have God's righteousness

Let us read verse 26. *"Likewise the Spirit also helps in our weaknesses. For we do not know what we should pray for as we ought, but the Spirit Himself makes intercession for us with groanings which cannot be uttered."*

Does the Holy Spirit pray for us? Yes, He does! The Holy Spirit knows our weaknesses and prays for us.

I talked a little about the groanings of the Holy Spirit. To go over it again, the Holy Spirit groans when we head toward the direction that God does not want us to go. When we look at the circumstances of the world and groan with it, when we go in the direction that our Father God does not want us to go to, or when we disregard our Father's will and live indifferently to His will, the Holy Spirit groans.

When the Holy Spirit dwelling in a born-again believer groans what cannot be uttered, we lose the energy in our hearts and become weak. That is when the Holy Spirit makes us pray. The Holy Spirit sometimes makes intercessions for us, or makes us aware of the fact that we need to pray.

The Holy Spirit groans in our hearts and makes us pray before our Father according to His will. "Lord God, You have blotted out our sins through Your baptism and Your blood on the Cross, and thorough this we have become Your children. We hope that Your second coming will come true on earth soon. We pray that Your will may come true." We pray like this.

We ask for spiritual faith. "God, we are poor and lacking in Your eyes, so please give us the faith needed for Your will to come true." God then helps us because He knows our weaknesses. The Holy Spirit does not leave us alone but makes us pray according to God's will and prays for us too, strengthening our hearts.

The Holy Spirit makes us pray according to God's will, and when we ask for help, He lets us know what God's will for us is, and gives us new strength.

"For we do not know what we should pray for as we ought, but the Spirit Himself makes intercession for us with groanings which cannot be uttered."

Do you feel these things? When you think and act differently from what God wants us to do, do you feel the Holy Spirit telling us, the righteous people, that something is wrong? The Holy Spirit says, "Hey, you're wrong!," and our hearts start to groan. Did you know that this is the Holy Spirit groaning? You probably have experienced that when a righteous person's heart is in joy, it is because the Holy Spirit is rejoicing inside. Then you will know that when your heart groans, it is the Holy Spirit groaning.

When we are weak and act wrongly, the Holy Spirit groans and makes intercessions for us, and God our Father gives us strength. The Holy Spirit has made us pray for all things, giving us new spiritual strength. That is why those who have the Holy Spirit in their hearts are very happy. The Holy Spirit gives us strength through God's Word. In other words, the Holy Spirit works with His Word inside our hearts to give us new spiritual strength.

The Holy Spirit does not wish to talk through other means. He gives us strength through the Scripture, God's church, and through our fellowship with our brothers and sisters. That is why God's church is very important, and why the church has a very important role to play in the works of the Holy Spirit.

In the church are the believers, their fellowship, praises, and messages. Regardless of who the preachers are, the Holy Spirit is present and works in them so that they would deliver the appropriate messages that are needed at proper times. The Holy Spirit works among both those who give the message and those who receive it, awakening their minds and giving each of them the blessings that they need. The Holy Spirit does this in God's church where the righteous people are gathered. That is why the church is very important for the believers. When a believer is going through a hard time in his/her heart and yet cannot share his/her pain with others, God's servants will still be able to notice it through the Holy Spirit. If the believers are in a gathering of God's church, the Holy Spirit will be able to touch and comfort their hearts. The Holy Spirit will help them to hold on to the Scripture and give them the strength to recover.

When living our lives of faith, we believe in the gospel of the water and the Spirit, receive forgiveness for our sins, become God's children, and as proof, we receive the Holy Spirit as a gift. Then, God gives us His church. After giving the church, God talks to His servants through the church and makes His servants preach His message. He cures our wounds with the Scripture, gives strength to those who are weak, blesses those who are poor in heart, and gives them the ability to carry out His work. He carries out His will through us. Therefore, believers can never cut themselves off from the church.

Believers can never be cut off from their interactions with other righteous people, or from their growth in God's Scripture. Absolute truth is found only within God's church. Therefore, believers need to unite with each other in the church. Faith without unity is a false faith.

Do you believe that the Holy Spirit resides in your heart? When we unite with God's church, as it says in the Scripture and as the church tells us in its message, the Holy Spirit will help us and open our eyes to the truth, giving us blessings. So, unite with the church with such faith. The Holy Spirit will rejoice then.

We have lived until this hour with the help of the Holy Spirit. We will also live with His help in the future. That is why the Holy Spirit is so important to us, who have received forgiveness of all our sins. We have to know and believe that the Holy Spirit exists. We must know that we have to live by the Holy Spirit and receive His guidance in our hearts. Those who have the Holy Spirit in their hearts have to follow His will. If you are a righteous person, then the Holy Spirit dwells in you, and thus you must follow the law of life as the Holy Spirit guides you.

Let us read verse 27 together. *"Now He who searches the hearts knows what the mind of the Spirit is, because He makes intercession for the saints according to the will of God."* Our God the Father knows the mind of the Spirit that dwells in us. The Holy Spirit knows everything in our minds; therefore, God the Father knows everything that is in our minds. As such, "He, the Holy Spirit makes intercession for the saints according the will of God."

This means that our Father knows what is in the mind of the Holy Spirit, and the Holy Spirit prays according to our Father's will. Believers thus get to live according to God's will. That is why those who are forgiven of their sins find the benefits of their lives of faith through the Holy Spirit. The minds of the righteous are led by the awakenings of the Holy Spirit.

Troubles arise in the church when those who do not have the Holy Spirit in their hearts are found in God's church. Those who do not believe in the gospel of the water and the Spirit do not have the Holy Spirit inside them, and so they cannot communicate with the true believers who do have the Holy Spirit. They bring about many problems in the church. In contrast, when those with the Holy Spirit listen to a sermon by a servant of God who is filled with the Holy Spirit, their hearts are at peace because they can understand what God is trying to tell them through His servant.

Anyone who has been forgiven of his/her sins surely has the Holy Spirit dwelling in him/her. We have the Holy Spirit in us and live according to God's will and by the guidance of the Holy Spirit.

The Holy Spirit guides us in these ways: sometimes through the church, sometimes through the fellowship with the believers, and other times through God's words. He makes us find God's will and allows us to follow His righteous way. The Holy Spirit gives us new strengths to live on God's side until we reach His Kingdom.

You and I, therefore, must realize how important the Holy Spirit is in our lives of faith. When we believe in the gospel of the water and the Spirit, we receive the Holy Spirit as a gift, as it is said in the Scripture, *"Repent, and let every one of you be baptized in the name of Jesus Christ for the remission of sins; and you shall receive the gift of the Holy Spirit" (Acts 2:38).*

God gave us the Holy Spirit as a gift so that He may guide us to live according to His will. This is the will of our God the Father. He tells us that we must live according to His will in order to enter His Kingdom. We have to have the Holy Spirit in order to live according to God's will, and only those who believe in the gospel of the water and the Spirit receive the Holy Spirit. We must thus believe in the gospel of the water and the Spirit so that we may receive the Holy Spirit as a gift and live according to God's will and enter His Kingdom.

We do not receive the Holy Spirit and the redemption separately. People today think that these two blessings are different things. They think that the Holy Spirit will descend on them if they go and pray fervently in mountain caves, saying prayers in strange tongues. They think that the Holy Spirit will then descend on them and directly give them His messages and converse with them. But this, unfortunately, is just not true.

The Holy Spirit and the Scripture cannot be separated, and the Holy Spirit and the believer cannot be separated either. This is why the relationships between the believers and the Holy Spirit, the church and the Triune God—the Father, the Son, and the Holy Spirit—are so close to each other.

We who live in this last era live by the Holy Spirit. We live according to our Father's will and by the Holy Spirit. The Holy Spirit knows all of God's will. Our Father knows everything that is in the mind of the Holy Spirit. The Holy Spirit guides our thoughts and communicates with God. In this way, the Holy Spirit gets to pray according to God's will, and our Father answers those prayers by making us live according to His will.

That is why Paul talked in Romans chapter 8 verses 16 to 27 about the works of the Holy Spirit.

We are able to wait for God's Kingdom through the Holy Spirit. We can endure our present sufferings and live according to our Lord's will, hoping for His Kingdom with the power of the Holy Spirit dwelling in our hearts. We can endure through the Holy Spirit, obey our Lord through the Holy Spirit, and have the ability to serve our Lord through the Holy Spirit. All these things have been given to us through the Holy Spirit. We must realize that we are the people who walk with the Holy Spirit, always studying God's Word, uniting our hearts with the

Word, and listening to and following the Word. We must live our lives so that our Father and the Holy Spirit can rejoice in us, not carnal lives that please only our flesh. This is what Paul says in this passage.

God is always with us in our lives. He keeps our hearts, and wants to help us. May the Lord continue to bless us. When our Lord comes again, everything will be changed to glory. We, who now have the righteousness of God, will inherit all of God's Kingdom and glory. Whoever wants to inherit the Kingdom of God should listen carefully and believe in the gospel of the water and the Spirit.

Hallelujah! I pray that the righteousness of God will be with you and bless you. ✉

The Second Coming of The Lord and The Millennial Kingdom

< Romans 8:18-25 >

"For I consider that the sufferings of this present time are not worthy to be compared with the glory which shall be revealed in us. For the earnest expectation of the creation eagerly waits for the revealing of the sons of God. For the creation was subjected to futility, not willingly, but because of Him who subjected it in hope; because the creation itself also will be delivered from the bondage of corruption into the glorious liberty of the children of God. For we know that the whole creation groans and labors with birth pangs together until now. Not only that, but we also who have the firstfruits of the Spirit, even we ourselves groan within ourselves, eagerly waiting for the adoption, the redemption of our body. For we were saved in this hope, but hope that is seen is not hope; for why does one still hope for what he sees? But if we hope for what we do not see, we eagerly wait for it with perseverance."

Those who are righteous by believing in the in the righteousness of God have received the glory of heaven. This is why they suffer with the gospel of the water and the Spirit of Jesus, to clothe all people with the glory of heaven. Believers dedicate themselves to the gospel of the righteousness of God and suffer on earth because partaking in Christ's sufferings is glorious and righteous.

Is it not honorable for us to suffer for God, whom we deeply honor and respect? It certainly is; it is a glorious suffering. This is why those who believe in God's righteousness suffer for His righteousness. For whom are you suffering right now? Are you suffering for the world and your flesh? What good would it be for your soul to bear the world's suffering? Suffer for the righteousness of God and believe in it. The glory of God will then be upon you.

Inheritance with which we will be blessed in the future

Let us think about the inheritance that we will receive. The inheritance that we will receive in heaven is the reward of reigning with Jesus in the new heaven and earth. The glory we will receive in the Thousand-year Kingdom and the eternal Kingdom of God is so great that it cannot be measured. Only the born-again believers themselves can know and will possess this glory that awaits them.

The incomparable glory

"For I consider that the sufferings of this present time are not worthy to be compared with the glory which shall be revealed in us" (Romans 8:18).

Comparing the glory to be received by the believers to their sufferings of the present time, Paul said that their glory would far surpass their present sufferings. This is absolutely true; the glory that awaits us is most definitely far greater than the suffering that we bear now.

The earnest expectation of the creation

"For the earnest expectation of the creation eagerly waits for the revealing of the sons of God. For the creation was subjected to futility, not willingly, but because of Him who subjected it in hope; because the creation itself also will be delivered from the bondage of corruption into the glorious liberty of the children of God" (Romans 8:19-21).

All of God's creation yearn to be released from the corruption from sin. To be released, the Kingdom of God must be established on this earth. These creations also wait for the children of God to become the masters of the Thousand-year Kingdom. All creations thus wait for the day when the sons of God reign with Him clothed in God's glory, for the Kingdom of God to come.

Waiting for the redemption of our body

"For we know that the whole creation groans and labors with birth pangs together until now. Not only that, but we also who have the firstfruits of the Spirit, even we ourselves groan within ourselves, eagerly waiting for the adoption, the redemption of our body. For we were saved in this hope, but hope that is seen is not hope; for why does one still hope for what he sees? But if we hope for what we do not see, we eagerly wait for it with perseverance" (Romans 8:22-25).

Those who believe in the gospel of the righteousness of

God are saved from all their sins. They wait for the Kingdom of God, for the day when it comes, with perseverance through all their sufferings. They suffer incessantly for the gospel, and, through suffering, their hope for the Kingdom of God becomes even more earnest. This is only natural for them. They do not wait for the kind of hope that is seen through the eyes of the flesh, but instead, the Kingdom of God that is not seen and their own transformation.

People and all other things in today's world live an indescribably exhausting life. As time goes on, the world changes, and as technology and civilization grow, people's hope for the future increases in their hearts. They expect to see a paradise on earth in the future and yet become anxious, nervous, and dreary, wondering why the process takes so long, despite all the progress. Computers, automobiles, and other technological and scientific advancements continue, yet it has become harder and harder to hear people's laughter.

Is there hope for the future of the humanity? The answer is an unfortunate no. According to the Word of Revelations, as well as in the opinion of scientists, disasters await us with the shortage of water, the destruction of the ozone layer, draught and deforestation that will lead many people to die of thirst and heat. Can you feel all these disasters awaiting us in your heart?

Are we living in a pleasant world? It may seem pleasant in some ways. What is there that cannot be bought with money? But we need clean water and a healthy environment. Yet the ozone layer is being destroyed, allowing deadly rays to pierce through the atmosphere, while ultraviolet rays causes plants to mutate and the people's hearts to harden. People increasingly worry, "What will happen to this world?" But unlike the people of the world, we the born-again believers have faith that we will be partake in the first resurrection and reign with Jesus for a thousand years.

The Bible tells us that the Lord Himself will descend again from heaven with a shout, the voice of an archangel, and the trumpet of God (1 Thessalonians 4:16). The question is "when" He is coming. Our Lord promised that He would come down to take those who believe in the gospel of the water, the blood and the Spirit, and so we are waiting for that day.

Those who are born again believe in this gospel. "My sins were passed onto Jesus when He was baptized, and I believe in the Lord as the Savior who was judged for my sins, in my place." God has granted us salvation through His only begotten Son, Jesus Christ. He is coming again to resurrect His people and to let them reign for a thousand years on this earth. The Bible is like a picture puzzle that must be matched together by its readers.

When Jesus first came down, He came to call on the sinners to repent. He bore their sins in His body through His baptism and was judged for them through the blood that He shed on the Cross. When the Lord, who now resides heaven, comes again, He will resurrect all those who believe in God's righteousness to reign with Him for a thousand years.

The Millennial Kingdom

Those who truly love others in this world are the children of God. They are the only people who deliver the gospel of God's righteousness to every lost soul to win them to Christ. Do people of this world reward the children of God? No. Then who does? When Jesus comes again, He will reward them by resurrecting those who are born again and allowing them to reign for a thousand years.

The Thousand-year Kingdom is for us, the born-again believers. Even as the present world is becoming desolated, when our Lord comes again, we will live in a new world. There, the Lord will allow us to reign with Him and live happy and joyful lives for as long as we want.

Paul said in Romans 8:23, *"Not only that, but we also who have the firstfruits of the Spirit, even we ourselves groan within ourselves, eagerly waiting for the adoption, the redemption of our body."* Are you waiting for that day? Even we who have the firstfruits of the Spirit groan within ourselves, eagerly waiting for the redemption of our bodies. God said that He would resurrect us, change our bodies, and allow us to live with Him. We, who have been born again as the righteous, hope and wait for His second advent through the Holy Spirit.

We groan within ourselves. The born-again believers know what this world is going to be like. What the fortunetellers foretell of the future means nothing. The born-again believers know precisely what will happen in the future. Even if the world were to change into what we had exactly predicted, no one would believe us now. But those who believe in the written Word of God just wait without boasting. Even if other people who do not recognize God's Word regard them with contempt, they live with hope.

Those who do not believe, therefore, must receive salvation before their lives come to the end. They must believe that Jesus took upon their sins by His baptism and was judged in our place on the Cross. Only then will they be able to enter the Kingdom of God when the final day comes. We will be rewarded then, and enter His Kingdom to have eternal life.

Are you sad? Are you weary? Or, are you satisfied with your life? We must clearly know and believe how Jesus became our Savior before we pass away. We must also prepare for our lives in Heaven. This world is not everything; knowing this truth, we must prepare to live in Heaven. This is what the wise do. Do you live in pleasure day by day? If so, you are a foolish person. Those who desire the better, that is, a heavenly country, and prepare to make their dreams come true by entering it, on the other hand, are the wise who truly build their house on the rock.

In the Millennial Kingdom

God made us in His own image and wanted us to live with Him forever. That is why the Lord came to this earth, received His baptism, and shed His blood to deliver us from all our sins. Those who believe in the righteousness of God live with the Lord, and the Lord will reward them for it. Our Lord will wipe away the tears from our eyes and reward us for all the hardships and loneliness that we have suffered.

God renews all things. He will allow a new world to come, where a weaned child can put his hand in a viper's den and will not be bitten (Isaiah 11:8). We must believe in and eagerly wait for what is not seen, hoping for that day with perseverance. If we say that we wait for what is seen, we are foolish. If, on the other hand, we wait for what is not seen and believe in the Word of God, we are then wise. After our salvation, we wait for the glory that, though presently unseen by our eyes, is sure to come.

God Himself groans more than we do but still makes us

wait. We are eagerly waiting for our flesh to be changed into spiritual bodies and to reign when our time comes. What does the Holy Spirit who dwells in us say? For what does He make us wait? He is making us wait for the Millennial Kingdom. The Lord is waiting to renew our bodies and live with us. We are also waiting to reign for a thousand years together with God.

Hallelujah! We give thanks to our Lord.

Christians live with their hope for heaven and confidence in their hope. This confidence is based not on our emotional feelings, but on the Word of God, who does not lie. ✉

The Holy Spirit Who Helps The Righteous

< Romans 8:26-28 >
"Likewise the Spirit also helps in our weaknesses. For we do not know what we should pray for as we ought, but the Spirit Himself makes intercession for us with groanings which cannot be uttered. Now He who searches the hearts knows what the mind of the Spirit is, because He makes intercession for the saints according to the will of God. And we know that all things work together for good to them that love God, to them who are the called according to his purpose."

The Holy Spirit is in the hearts of those who believe in the righteousness of God. The Holy Spirit makes them to pray and helps them to do so. He also makes intercessions for them with a groaning that cannot be uttered. This means that the Holy Spirit helps them to pray according to the will of God. That is why those who believe in the righteousness of God are called the children of God. The Lord promises them that He will always be with them to the end of time.

The Holy Spirit is within the righteous, making intercessions according to the will of God. How do you think that you can receive the Holy Spirit? By praying? Do you think that you can receive the Spirit despite all your sins? The Holy Spirit works and dwells only in the hearts of those who believe in God's righteousness.

Christians who wish to pray according to the will of God receive help from the Holy Spirit. They learn and understand what they should pray for. If you have received the Holy Spirit by believing in the righteousness of God, the Holy Spirit will make intercessions for you and lead your way.

All things work together for good

"And we know that all things work together for good to them that love God, to them who are the called according to his purpose" (Romans 8:28).

God is on the side of the believers, causing all things to work together for good to those who love God. God loves the born-again believers. He may sometimes use our enemies for our own sake, but in the end, He punishes them for their sins. Every enemy of ours will thus disappear into His everlasting punishment, as everything that God allows is only for the good of the believers. ✉

All Things Work Together For Good

< Romans 8:28-30 >
"And we know that all things work together for good to those who love God, to those who are the called according to His purpose. For whom He foreknew, He also predestined to be conformed to the image of His Son, that He might be the firstborn among many brethren. Moreover whom He predestined, these He also called; whom He called, these He also justified; and whom He justified, these He also glorified."

Today, we would like to consider the above passage in Romans chapter 8. It is said that God predestined, called, and glorified we who are in Jesus Christ, the Son of God. We will talk about this, and also about how people tend to understand the Doctrine of Incremental Sanctification.

Romans 8:28 says, *"And we know that all things work together for good to those who love God, to those who are the called according to His purpose."* We have to think about who *"those who love God"* are.

Did all things really work together for good? So said God. In the beginning, before God created people, He planned to make us His people according to His purpose and has done so for good in Jesus Christ, His only begotten Son.

We have to remember that in the Garden of Eden was the tree of the knowledge of good and evil. Why did God plant this tree? It would have been better if God had not planted the tree of the knowledge of good and evil in the first place. Many people are curious about this point.

But there were God's profound purpose and plan. God created people to make them in His own image. In fact, mankind was no different from the rest of creation until we received God's righteousness.

Why did God plant the tree of the knowledge of good and evil?

That is why we must know the reason why God commanded Adam and Eve not to eat from the tree of the knowledge of good and evil. What was the reason? It was to keep human beings under the Law of God and to make us His children by redeeming us through Jesus Christ. All the righteousness of God is hidden in the Word, *"All things work together for good to those who love God."* Since God said, *"All things work together for good to those who love God, to those who are the called according to His purpose" (Romans 8:28),* we must find the answer to the question in the gospel of the water and the Spirit given by Jesus Christ.

To do this, we must first acknowledge the gospel of God. We will then realize that everything God plans and does is good. But to understand this truth we must be born again by faith in the gospel of the water and the Spirit. We must look for the answer in the gospel that God has given us.

The reason why God created us, planted the tree of the knowledge of good and evil in the Garden of Eden, allowed Adam and Eve to eat from it, and let us know the Law was to make us His own children. Our Lord, who delivered us all, allowed all these to happen so that He could give us the forgiveness of sins, eternal life, glory and Heaven. God made man from dust, and the mankind was made and born to be weak. The Bible often compares us to the vessels of clay. God, who is the potter, formed man out of clay. He formed man from dust and breathed into him the love of the water and the Spirit. God has given us the truth of the water and the Spirit so as to make us His own children.

Pottery that is made with clay breaks easily. In this way, God first created man's body and spirit to be weak in order to make him His child. His purpose was fulfilled by Jesus, who washed away all the sins of mankind and clothed them in God's holiness, to give them eternal life by making them to be born again with the gospel of water and the Spirit. That was why God made us imperfect and weak from the beginning, rather than flawless.

Why did God create man to be weak in the beginning?

Why did God plant the tree of the knowledge of good and evil in Eden and then command Adam and Eve not to eat from it? The reason behind this must be understood and believed within the gospel of the water and the Spirit. Why did God say that the seed of the woman would bruise Satan's head and that Satan would bruise His heel when Adam and Eve fell and sinned? All these things were to make people His own children. It was His plan for us in Jesus Christ, His only begotten Son.

Who, then, are the "called" according to God's purpose? They are those who acknowledge their sins and iniquities and seek the love and mercy of God. We must realize that the theological claims of the Doctrine of Unconditional Election and the Doctrine of Incremental Sanctification are wrong. The Doctrine of Unconditional Election is wrong because our God is not the kind of God who would just choose someone unconditionally while deserting others for no reason.

Rather, those whom God elects and calls are those who despair over their sins and confess that they have no choice but to go to hell—those on whom God has mercy and whom He calls with His gospel of the water and the Spirit.

Among the countless people that are born into this world and returned to God, not a single one is chosen or abandoned by God without any reason. If God did not choose you for no reason, you would protest against God. It would be nonsense to say that God made you or someone the devil's child without any reason. This is not what God has done.

If you have not been chosen by God, it is because you do not believe in the gospel of the water and the Spirit. If you do not believe in the gospel of the water and the Spirit given by God, then God will abandon you, for our Lord said, *"For I did not come to call the righteous, but sinners, to repentance" (Matthew 9:13).* What the theologians have done, unfortunately, is to turn our God into a bigoted and prejudicial God.

Who are the called according to the will of God?

Those who are called by God are the sinners who are bound to hell. They come to God and confess that they deserve to go to hell because they are weak and have no choice but to disobey His commandments until they die. God called on sinners and purified their sins with the gospel of the water and the Spirit. He called on those who had no choice but to be sent to hell and delivered them from their sins with the gospel of the water and the Spirit.

God did not come to call on those who are good and obedient to the Law. God calls on those who really try hard to live according to His will, but acknowledge that their weaknesses force them to sin, though they put faith in and depend on God. God's purpose is to call on the weak, infirm, and feeble to make them righteous, to make them His children. This is God's call according to His will. All things work together for the good to those who are called according to His purpose.

We must believe in God's call. We must not say that we believe in Jesus for no reason. Such faith is not the proper faith. The proper faith is to believe in the Lord according to God's purpose, not your own purpose. That means to believe that God knows our weaknesses well, that He took away our sins once and for all, and that He thus made us sinless. By setting our faith on God's purpose, the baptism and the blood of Jesus Christ, we can become His children. It is God's will to make us His sinless children when we acknowledge and accept His purpose—these are the people whom God truly loves, and on whom He calls.

Who are the ones chosen by God?

God does not have people stand in two lines and choose everyone to His right saying, "Come and believe in Jesus and go to Heaven," and then turn to the left and tell them, "Just go to hell."

Calvinists claim that God chose certain people without any reason and decided to abandon the rest from the beginning. But God is not like that. God made all things work together for good to those who are called upon according to His purpose. It is nonsense to think that we were chosen unconditionally for no reason.

Is God then an unjust God? Certainly not. Everybody is equal before both God and His Law. Everybody is also equal before the judgment. We have received the grace of salvation from God, which saved us from our sins through Jesus Christ. The chance to believe in this truth is also equal for everybody. He allows those who accept God's purpose and know their weaknesses to realize and believe the gospel of the water and the Spirit.

What, then, are the true divine predestination and election? They are for us to be called according to God's purpose in the gospel of the water and the Spirit that He has given us. It was because God has taken away our sins through Jesus and planned to make us His children that we were born into this world and given a chance to hear the gospel. God has planned all this in Jesus Christ in advance. This was God's plan. When we come to the presence of God, we must therefore first consider whether we are like Jacob or Esau.

The Scripture tells us that God loved Jacob while He hated Esau. It also talks about Cain and Abel, and that God loved Abel but hated Cain. Did God hate Esau and Cain and love Jacob and Abel for no reason? No. It was because Esau and Cain trusted only in their own strength and never asked for God's mercy, while Jacob and Abel knew of their weaknesses, asked for God's mercy, and trusted in His Word.

The Scripture explains God's predestination and election

by using these people as an example. To which side do we belong? Can we meet God if we trust in our own strengths, just as Esau did? No, we cannot! The only way we can meet God is to meet Him through the gospel of the water and the Spirit that is filled with God's mercy. On which of the two sides do we stand before God? We are the ones who want to be blessed in God's presence, but always fail to do so because of our weaknesses. Even though we wish to live according to God's purpose, we are still weak and infirm before God, and so the only thing we can ask for is His mercy.

If we wish to be blessed by God, we have to become like Jacob, and have the faith that Abel had. We have to acknowledge before God the fact that we are weak, infirm, and coward.

Psalm 145:14 says, *"The Lord upholds all who fall, and raise up all who are bowed down."* Truly, everyone bows down in the presence of God. We have no courage. We make compromises for the smallest benefit. We are servile. We may at times seem courageous, but that is only for a mere second. If we look into our lives closely, we can find out easily just how servile we are. We submit to the strong and even to untruthful being that compels us to discard the truth. But God has called the servile to love them and to give them salvation in Jesus Christ, and He has made them His children.

We need to realize just how weak and sinful we are in order to be loved by God. We have to ask whether we can really obey the Law to its complete satisfaction. We must then come to the prompt realization that we just are not capable of keeping the Law, and that as such, we cannot live perfect lives.

If I were perfect, I would never need the Savior. If we were perfect, why would we need God's help and blessings? It is because we are so weak before God that we need His blessings. We need His mercy. God's compassion on us was so strong that He sent His only begotten Son and made Him take upon all our sins to wash them away. And God passed judgment for sin on Jesus instead of us so that we may be delivered from sin. This is what we must believe in.

Only with this faith can we become the beloved children of God. It is because of this mercy that we are clothed in His love, and not because of our own efforts to achieve our own salvation.

Even though many Christians teach and follow the Doctrines of Predestination and Election, they also feel anxious about these doctrines. This is because they constantly wonder whether they were chosen by God or not.

These two doctrines make up about 90% of the Calvinist theology. The question is whether, despite their faith in Jesus, they have really been chosen or not, and this is what makes them anxious. But it is not whether you are chosen or not that is important. Rather, what is important is for you to believe in the gospel of the water and the Spirit to be saved by receiving God's righteousness. Those who have received this righteousness of God by faith are the chosen ones.

There once was a doctor of theology who was considered as one of the masters of conservative theology. He put great value into the teachings of Calvinism, such as the Doctrines of Predestination and Divine Election.

One day, he was giving a lecture about these topics when a student asked, "Well, are you chosen by God? How can you know whom God has chosen?"

The theologian replied, "Who can know it? We will find that out only when we stand before God."

So then, the student asked again, "Then what will you do when you go before God and He says that you are not chosen?"

The professor replied, "What can I do about what God has already decided by Himself? That's why I said that you'll know only when you stand before God."

The students thought, "He is a very humble man. Even a great person like him says that he doesn't know whether he is chosen or not. So it is natural that no one can know whether he/she is chosen or not."

But the truth in which God's righteousness was hidden is now clearly manifested. There had been a few things that God had concealed from man, but He has revealed them in due time. How can evangelists preach the gospel when they do not even know whether they are saved and chosen or not? Those who are called by God are the ones who believe in the righteousness of God.

Romans 8:29 states, *"For whom He foreknew, He also predestined to be conformed to the image of His Son, that He might be the firstborn among many brethren."* God the Father predestined to conform us to the image of His only Son, Jesus Christ, so that He might be the firstborn among many brethren. Here Jesus is called "the firstborn." If we believe in Jesus and in the gospel of the water and the Spirit that He has given us, we are saved from all our sins and become God's children. Then, what would Jesus be in relation to us? He would be our eldest brother. He is God's firstborn and we are His younger brothers and sisters.

A long time ago, when I lived in a prayer house, an old evangelist visited me. He had started believing in Jesus when he was in China and then came over to Korea. I overheard him praying one day, and this is what he said: "Brother Jesus and

God the Father, thank you so much for saving me. Brother Jesus, please help me." Jesus is our brother!

We may ask whether God knows everything about us. The answer is yes, He does know everything about us. God the Father knows everything about us. He had planned to save us from our sins through His only begotten Son even before the creation of this world. This was God's plan. His Son Jesus came to the world, was baptized and crucified to save us from our sins. God had already planned it.

We may say that before the foundation of the world, God called on a "tripartite conference." The Triune God—the Father, the Son, and the Holy Spirit—planned to deliver those who believe in His righteousness. His plan was to create the people and make them His children to live together with them in His perfect Kingdom.

The Father, the Son, and the Holy Spirit all agreed on the plan. Then, in the process of thinking about how He should create man and make the mankind His children, God planned to send the Son, Jesus, to the world and to have Him be baptized and put to death on the Cross, so that they can be conformed to the image of His Son.

What was God's purpose in creating us? It was for us to become His children. Is Jesus the firstborn of God? Yes, He is, and because we have become the Children of God, we are also His brothers.

While living on this earth for 33 years, Jesus experienced all human weaknesses and infirmities. That is why when we pray, we say, "Jesus, I am so weak. This is how I am. Please help me and protect me. Soften peoples' hearts to accept Your Word, watch over, give grace, and help them." The Lord hears and answers our prayers. Praying to Jesus and praying to God are one in the same.

What was God's purpose in creating us? It was to make us His children. God knows everything about us. He made us to be born into this world and saved us from all our sins through the baptism of Jesus and His blood on the Cross, because He predestined us, even before the foundation of the world, to be adopted as His own sons and daughters. He therefore knows not only our lives and deaths, but our every single movement. He knows when we were born, who we were born to, when we got married, when we bore our own children, and what happened to us in our lives. God, who knows everything about our lives, gave us the gospel of the water and the Spirit so that we may believe in Jesus Christ and become God's children.

God foreknew us and predestined us. Romans 8:30 states, *"Moreover whom He predestined, these He also called; whom He called, these He also justified; and whom He justified, these He also glorified."* I cannot emphasize enough just how important it is for us to understand and believe in this passage.

Many people take the above verse to support the Doctrine of Incremental Sanctification. Based on this passage—that God predestined us, called on us, justified us, and glorified us—they claim that this is why even though we have sin in our hearts, God considers us to be without sin, and that after going through a period of sanctification, we will become glorified, as if there were staged through which we become holy.

Did not God predestine all the sinners to call them in Jesus Christ? He called us all, and yet some people do not respond to His calling. They are like Esau and Cain. They are the ones who are sent to hell.

In the mercy of God

God the Father planned to call us in His only begotten Son, Jesus Christ, and predestined us to adoption as His own sons by washing away our sins with the water and the blood. People who still do not go to God even when He called them all are outside God's salvation. Such people are excluded from His grace, bound for hell. But there are also the people who obeyed God's call. They say, "Lord even though I'm weak like this, will you accept someone like me?"

God says, "Of course I will."

"Really? Will you accept me when I am so weak?"

"Of course I will accept you."

"God, I don't have anything special to offer to you and I can't even promise you that I'll be good from now on."

"I will still accept you."

"I am not sure I'll get better and I don't even have the ability to do so."

"Still, I will accept you."

"It's probably because you don't know me. You are going to be disappointed at me."

Do we not usually feel embarrassed, as if we want to hide somewhere, when we know how we are, and yet someone says that he/she really believes in us? Why do we want to hide? We want to hide because we are not able to get better and we can't even maintain what we have done so far.

This is why we keep on asking, "Will you accept me even though I'm so weak? Will you really accept me? Am I even allowed to believe in you? Can someone like me receive the forgiveness of sins? Can someone like me become righteous even when I have be able to be good in the future either?" But our God has the power to turn a wild olive tree into a cultivated olive tree.

We were originally olive trees, which are wild by nature, but we became cultivated olive trees by the gospel that Jesus has given us. He called on us, who cannot help but sin. Did He call us when we were just a little bit weak? He called us even when we were absolutely wanting in ability. He called us in Jesus Christ despite our very serious shortcomings and gaping weaknesses. He called us who were infirm. What did He do after He called us? He took away all our sins and gave us His righteousness so that we may have eternal life.

How did He do all these things? In chapter 3 of Matthew, we are told that Jesus came to the world and was baptized to fulfill all the righteousness that God set for all mankind. Jesus was baptized by John, took upon Himself all the sins of mankind, died on the Cross bearing all their sins, and rose again from the dead the third day to save them from the sins of the world. He gave us new lives, and by doing so, He justified us and washed away all our sins. Jesus called us, washed away our sins with the water and the blood, gave us God's righteousness, made us sinless, and then glorified us whom He justified, making us the children of God.

Jesus glorified us to enter Heaven and to live eternally as God's children. Do you understand this? But the religious doctrines teach that, though you are a sinner, if you believe in Jesus, you will gradually be sanctified in time, and that by the time you die, you will stand before God as a perfect person. This is against the truth. This is not the true faith. That kind of faith is for the Doctrine of Sanctification, not for the truth.

The Lord saved us from our sins and God predestined us, called us, washed away our sins with the water and the blood all at once, made us His children, who are sanctified, and blessed us so that we may enter the Kingdom of God in glory. This is the truth, and this is how He spoke of the truth, by putting all the blessings in Jesus Christ together into one sentence. This passage is not talking about the seven stages of the Doctrine of Incremental Sanctifications. It is not saying that we will gradually become perfect after going through the seven stages to become entirely sanctified.

Romans 8:30 does not say that God will call on us after we believe in Jesus or that we will become sanctified as we get older. It also does not say that we gradually climb up the ladder of sanctification step by step until we finally reach the complete sanctification. When we knew Jesus Christ, and Jesus Christ called on us, He forgave our sins once and for all with the water and the blood. It is when we come to God with this gospel of truth that we will be embraced in His arms.

Some people say, "I didn't even know my own sins before, but after hearing the sermon, I'm beginning to realize it. There are one or two sins I remember from the past and I am probably going to keep on sinning in the future, so I don't think I can believe in God." But that is not right. We should think like this instead, "Ah! That's right. I didn't know my own sins even as I was committing them. All the Word of God is right. I must believe in His Word, but I am not able to live according to It. I am inevitably a grave sinner, who is destined for hell. That's why Jesus came."

We are made sinless by believing in Jesus and receiving the forgiveness of sins. We become sanctified and are made the children of God. Since we have become God's children, we are able to enter Heaven and be glorified. This is God's righteousness and the truth.

God predestined us, called us, justified, and glorified us.

You may think that the Doctrine of Incremental Sanctification is right, saying, "I will gradually change and become a sinless person." But you become justified and sanctified all at once the very moment you believe in the gospel of the water and the Spirit. Your heart does not change in stages. Your heart becomes sinless all at once, and it is your faith that gradually grows as you believe in the Word of God and His church.

Our faith grows gradually as we are fed by the Word of God, to eventually reach a point where we can even teach others. But the assertion that we will become God's children after we become more complete and more sinless is not based on the Bible. We become sanctified and sinless all at once.

Did God call us according to His predestination in Christ Jesus? Yes, He did. He called us in Jesus Christ and made us righteous and sinless. God justified us and made us sinless through Jesus Christ, took us in as His children, and glorified us to enter His Kingdom.

We became righteous at once by believing in the salvation of Jesus Christ, who fulfilled all the righteousness of God. We have been blessed because we obeyed God's call and believed that Jesus washed away all our sins, to make us, in spite of our infirmities, the sinless and righteous children of God, the people of His Kingdom.

That is why the Doctrine of Sanctification is incorrect. It makes no sense. The Bible clearly tells us, *"Whom He predestined, these He also called; whom He called, these He also justified; and whom He justified, these He also glorified."* Faith grows gradually, but the forgiveness of sins, becoming the children of God, and entering Heaven—these all happen once and for all. Do you believe in this?

We were able to become God's children by believing in

the gospel of the water and the Spirit. God has saved our worthless lives from all our sins through the grace of the water and the Spirit. Did we do anything for God in any way for our salvation? Did we contribute in becoming righteous? There is nothing that we planned, and no one decides to believe in Jesus even before he/she is born. Is there anyone who decides to believe in Jesus while he/she is in his/her mother's womb?

We happened to hear the truth from those who preached the gospel of the water and the Spirit, realized that it is the truth, and thought to ourselves, "I have no choice but to believe in it; a sinful person like me must believe in it." From that time on, we started believing in the gospel of the water and the Spirit, received the forgiveness of sins, and became God's children.

Only the righteous are the children of God. God forever glorifies them with the eternal riches and honors of the Kingdom of Heaven. That is what being glorified is all about. God has given these blessings to the believers who accept the gospel of the water and the Spirit.

Praise the Lord! ⊠

The Erroneous Doctrines

< Romans 8:29-30 >

"For whom He foreknew, He also predestined to be conformed to the image of His Son, that He might be the firstborn among many brethren. Moreover whom He predestined, these He also called; whom He called, these He also justified; and whom He justified, these He also glorified."

These passages tell us that God has predestined to save people in Jesus Christ. To do so, God has called them in Christ, justified those whom He called, and glorified those whom He justified. All the basics of the Scripture are planned and worked out within Jesus Christ. This is what the Book of Romans tells us, yet many theologians and false ministers have turned this clear and simple truth into a mere doctrine, consisting of their own thoughts and self-interests, and earnestly spread it. We will now turn our attention to examine how many misunderstand this truth.

Some theologians deduce five major doctrines from this passage: 1) prescience, 2) predestination, 3) effective calling, 4) justification, and 5) glorification. These five doctrines are known as the "Golden Chain of Salvation" and have been spread as the truth to both believers and non-believers alike. But their claims are full of flaws.

All five doctrines speak only of what God has done–that is, "God already knew, already elected, already called, justified, and glorified someone." But the Doctrine of Predestination is a doctrine that claims that God has unconditionally elected those whom He would save even before their births. Yet the Biblical truth of predestination teaches that God has made sinners His children by pouring His love over them. Having thus elected them, God has called them, justified and glorified them.

The Error of the theological doctrines of predestination and election

In Christian theology, we can find the "five great doctrines" of Calvinism proclaimed by John Calvin. Among them are the Doctrine of Predestination and the Doctrine of Election. In the following discussion, I will point out the Biblical errors of these doctrines and bear witness to the gospel of the water and the Spirit.

The Doctrine of Election originated from a theologian named John Calvin. Of course, God spoke of the election in Jesus Christ long before Calvin's time, but his Doctrine of Election has led many to confusion. This false doctrine limits God's love and defines it as discriminatory and unfair. Fundamentally speaking, there are neither limits nor boundaries to God's love, and as such, the Doctrine of Predestination that imposes such limits on God's love cannot be anything but wrong. Yet the reality is that many believers in Jesus today have accepted this doctrine as natural and fatalistic.

The ideas of this Doctrine of Predestination have come to rule over many minds, as the doctrine is fitting for those who like philosophizing, and, as such, dominate their minds, making it believable to them. The doctrine claims that even before Creation, God unconditionally predestined and elected some, while others were predestined to be left out of this election. Were this doctrine true, those souls that were not selected would have grounds to protest against God, and He would turn into an unfair and prejudicial God.

Because of these doctrines, today's Christianity has fallen into great confusion. As a result, many Christians are suffering while wondering, "Have I been elected? If God had reprobated me before Creation, what is the use of believing in Jesus?" They end up being more interested in whether they were included or excluded from God's election. This is why the Doctrine of Predestination has produced so much confusion among the believers in Jesus, as they assign more importance to the question of their elections rather than to the true gospel of the water and the Spirit, given by God.

This doctrine has turned the truth of Christianity into just another world religion. But it is now time for us to cast these wrong doctrines out from the Christendom with the gospel that has born witness to the righteousness of God. As such, you must first see to yourself whether the Doctrine of Predestination is correct or not, and be delivered from all your sins by knowing and believing in the gospel of the water and the Spirit. Those who have truly been selected by God are those who know and believe in His righteousness.

The predestination and election spoken by the Truth

Ephesians 1:3-5 says, *"Blessed be the God and Father of our Lord Jesus Christ, who has blessed us with every spiritual blessing in the heavenly places in Christ, just as He chose us in Him before the foundation of the world, that we should be holy and without blame before Him in love, having predestined us to adoption as sons by Jesus Christ to Himself, according to the good pleasure of His will. "* The election spoken in this passage from Ephesians is an election chosen *"in Him (Christ) before the foundation of the world" (Ephesians 1:4).* It also tells us that Jesus Christ has not excluded a single person from the grace of the salvation from sin.

From this passage, we must ascertain what is exactly wrong with the Doctrine of Predestination. The fundamental error of this doctrine is that it is bias against the standard of God's election–that is, its basis of who is to be saved or not does not depend on the Word of God, but instead on His arbitrary and unconditional decision.

If we were to base our faiths in Jesus on the logic of such unconditional predestination and elections, how could we ever believe in Jesus in our nervous uncertainties and worries? Calvinism preaches of a false doctrine that turns the just God into an unfair and unjust God. The reason why Calvin made such a mistake is because he took out the condition of "in Jesus Christ" from God's predestination, and the error has been grave enough to confuse and mislead many. But the Scripture clearly tells us, *"God chose us in His Son Jesus Christ" (Ephesians 1:4).*

If, as the Calvinists claim, God unconditionally chose some in order to be their God while excluded others without any reason, what could be more absurd than this? Calvin turned God into an unfair God in the minds of many people. But the Bible tells us in Romans 3:29, *"Or is He the God of the Jews only? Is He not also the God of the Gentiles? Yes, of the Gentiles also. "* God is the God of everyone and the Savior of all.

Jesus is the Savior of all. He gave redemption to everyone

by taking upon all the sins of mankind on Himself with His baptism by John and His blood on the Cross (Matthew 3:15). The Scripture tells us that Christ saved every sinner by bearing all the sins of the world with His baptism and carrying these sins to the Cross (John 1:29), being judged for these sins in our place (John 19). Also, John 3:16 tells us, *"For God so loved the world that He gave His only begotten Son, that whoever believes in Him should not perish but have everlasting life."* Jesus Christ took upon everyone's sins with His baptism, died on the Cross, and arose from death for all of humanity in God's righteousness.

Our understanding of whom God has called must be based on His Word. To do so, let us take a look at the passage from Romans 9:10-11. *"And not only this, but when Rebecca also had conceived by one man, even by our father Isaac (for the children not yet being born, nor having done any good or evil, that the purpose of God according to election might stand, not of works but of Him who calls)."*

It says here that the purpose of God might stand "of Him who calls." Whom, then, has God called in Jesus Christ? They are precisely sinners whom God has called. Between Esau and Jacob, whom did God love? He loved Jacob. God did not love people like Esau, who was full of his own righteousness, but He called sinners like Jacob and allowed them to be born again through the gospel of the water and the Spirit. This was the very will of God's righteousness that chose sinners like Jacob to love and call through Jesus Christ.

Because Adam was the forefather to everyone, all were born as the offspring of a sinner. In Psalms 51, David says that he was conceived in sin from when he was in his mother's womb. Because people are born as sinners, they commit sins, regardless of their determinations. Throughout their lives, they continue to bear the fruits of sin until the very end. Mark 7:21-27 tells us that just as apple trees bear apples and pear trees bear pears, humans are bound to live in sin for their entire lives because they were born with sin.

You must have had an experience of committing a sin against your wishes. This is because from the very beginning, you were born a sinner. People are born with evil thoughts including adulteries, fornications, murders, thefts, covetousness, wickedness, deceit, lewdness, and others such sins in their minds. This is why everyone lives his or her life in sin. Sin is inherited. Since we were born with the sins that our forefathers passed on to us, we are fundamentally determined to live in sin. This is the reason why we need to believe in Jesus as our Savior and believe in God's righteousness.

Does this then mean that God's first work, Adam, ended in failure? No, it doesn't. God decided to make mankind His children, so He allowed the first man to fall into sin. He fundamentally permitted us to be sinners in order for God to save us and make us His children with the baptism of Jesus Christ and His blood. So, we must know that we were born as sinners without exception.

However, God decided to send Jesus Christ to this earth before Creation, knowing that mankind would become sinners. He then placed on Jesus, through the baptism of Jesus received from John, all the sins of the world and had Him die on the Cross. In other words, He decided to bestow upon anyone who believed with the blessing of the redemption from sin and of becoming God's children. This is God's plan and His purpose for creating mankind.

Some people might ask in their misunderstandings, "Look

at Jacob and Esau. Was not one selected and the other abandoned by God?" But God did not unconditionally elect those who insisted to be saved outside of Jesus Christ. He clearly chose to make everyone His children through Jesus Christ. When only considering the Old Testament, we may get the impression that God chose only one side, but with the New Testament, we can unmistakably see that He elected people like Jacob to save all sinners through Jesus Christ. We must have a clear understanding and believe in whom God called with His Word.

Of Esau and Jacob, who did God call and love? He called no other than Jacob, a man full of shortcomings, deceit and unrighteousness, to love and save him in God's righteousness. You, too, must believe in this truth, that God the Father has called you through Jesus Christ in His righteousness. You must also believe in the fact that the gospel of the water and the Spirit in Jesus Christ is the very righteousness of God.

Why, then, did God choose such people as Jacob? God chose Jacob because he was a representative of all unrighteous humanities. Jacob's calling by God was a calling congruent to His will; a calling in accordance to the Word of God that "we were chosen in Jesus Christ." This calling is also consistent with the Word of truth that *"the purpose of God according to election might stand, not of works but of Him who calls."*

The way to save sinners through Jesus Christ was to completely fulfill the righteousness of God with His love. This was the law of salvation set by the righteousness of God for sinners. To clothe them in His righteousness, God called people like Jacob, who had no self-righteousness at all, and those who answered His calling through Jesus Christ.

Did God call those who were self-righteous and who

seemed just fine? Or did He call those who had no self-righteousness who were full of shortcomings? Those whom God called were people like Jacob. God called and saved sinners bound for hell because of their sins. You must realize that from your very birth, you, too, have been a sinner who has come short of God's glory, and as such, were bound for hell. You need to know, in other words, your true self. God called all sinners through Jesus Christ and saved them in His righteousness.

The people of God are those who have been justified by believing in His righteousness. God predestined to call all sinners and redeem them in Jesus, and He fulfilled what He had predestined. This is the predestination and the true election in Jesus Christ that God speaks of. To understand the true election of God, we must first understand the background of this truth on election, as described in the Old Testament.

Background to God's election from the Old Testament

Genesis 25:21-26 tells us about the story of Jacob and Esau while still in the womb of their mother, Rebecca. Between the two, God chose Jacob. Calvin based his Doctrine of Election on this passage, but we will soon find out that his understanding departs from the will of God. There was a reason why God loved Jacob more than Esau. This reason is that people like Esau, rather than relying on and trusting in God, live by believing in their own strengths, while people like Jacob live by their reliance on and trust in the righteousness of God. When it says that God loved Jacob more than Esau, it means that God loved people like Jacob. This is why we were *"chosen in Christ" (Ephesians 1:4).*

"Unconditional election" without Jesus and outside of God's righteousness is only a false Christian doctrine. This idea is akin to bringing and believing in a god of fate into Christianity. But the truth tells us that God elected all sinners in Jesus. Because God chose to save all sinners "in Jesus Christ," His election was a just election. Had God chosen Jacob unconditionally and reprobated Esau groundlessly, He would have been an unfair God, but He called us in Jesus Christ. And to save those whom He called, He sent Jesus to this earth to take upon the sins of the world with His baptism, which has fulfilled the righteousness of God, and to shed His precious blood on the Cross. This is how God has chosen and loved us through Christ Jesus.

We need to throw away our human thoughts and believe in the Word of the Scripture, not in a faith of literalism, but in our spiritual faiths. God the Father, in other words, chose all of us through Jesus Christ. But how does Calvin treat God's election? True faith is found when one knows and believes in God's righteousness. To believe in human thought as the truth is the same as worshiping an idol, not God.

Believing in the righteousness of God through Jesus is clearly distinct from believing in the erroneous Doctrine of Predestination. Were we not to know and believe in Jesus according to the written Word of God, we would be no different from mere beasts incapable of reasoning. We have been chosen as God's children by the seal of God's righteousness "in Jesus Christ." We should examine our faiths with the basis of the Word of the Scripture.

One of the five doctrines of Calvinism speaks of "limited atonement." This doctrine claims that among the many people of the world, some have been excluded from God's salvation. But God's love and His righteousness cannot be so unfair. The Scripture tells us that God *"desires all men to be saved and to come to the knowledge of the truth" (1 Timothy 2:4)*. If the blessing of salvation were a limited blessing that is granted to some but not permitted to others, there would be many people who would give up on their faiths in Jesus. Those who believe in such false doctrines must return to the gospel of the water and the Spirit, be saved from their sins and receive eternal lives by knowing and believing in Jesus Christ as their Savior. God has saved everyone through Jesus Christ with His righteousness.

If God had indeed loved some and hated others, people would turn their backs from God. Let us suppose that God is standing right here, right now. Were God to select all those who were standing to His right for salvation and those who were standing to his left for hell without any reason, would this be just? Those who are to His left would have no choice but to turn against God. If God were like this, then who in this world would serve and worship Him as the true God? All those who were unconditionally hated by God would protest and in turn, they, too, would hate God. Even the criminals of this world are said to have their own morals and fairness. How, then, could our Creator be so unfair, and who would believe in such an unfair God?

Our Father decided to save all the sinners with the righteousness of God found in His Son Jesus Christ. This is why the Calvinist Doctrine of Limited Atonement has nothing to do with God's righteousness. Yet because of such erroneous doctrines, many people are unfortunately still going astride, believing in God wrongfully or turning away from Him, all from their own misunderstandings.

An untruthful movie

Stephen King's novel entitled, "The Stand," was made into a TV mini-series some years ago, and was highly acclaimed all over the world. The plot of the novel unfolds like this: In the year 1991, a plague strikes America, leaving only a few thousand people alive, who are "immune" to the epidemic. Of the survivors, those who instinctively serve God meet in Boulder, Colorado, while those who worship the "Dark Man" are drawn to Las Vegas, Nevada. The two groups separately rebuild societies, until one must destroy the other.

Among the survivors, a young man named Stuart repeatedly dreams that the end of the world has come, and an elderly woman named Abigail tells him in his dreams to go to a certain place, reminding him that God elected him already. In this movie, God saved this young man because He predestined him before Creation, even when he did not believe in God or Jesus.

Does God, then, unconditionally save those who do not even believe in Jesus? Of course not. God has predestined everyone in Jesus Christ to save those who believe in His righteousness from their sins.

The storyline of this movie is based on Calvin's Doctrines of Predestination and Election. This movie is merely a story that only tells a part of a theologian's doctrine. How could God arbitrarily decide to send some people to hell and yet elect others for salvation? Because God is just, He has predestined and selected everyone through Jesus Christ, and there is none who is barred from the salvation of His righteousness. God's predestination and election without Jesus Christ are meaningless and unbiblical. It's unfortunate that so many theologians continue to claim that God elected some while He reprobated others.

Even before He created the universe, God planned to save all sinners and make them His children with His righteousness through Jesus Christ. He elected, in other words, all sinners through the gospel of Jesus. How, then, do you believe?

Do you believe that the Buddhist monks meditating deep in the mountains are excluded from God's election? If God's predestination and election were unconditional without Jesus Christ, there would be no need for us to preach His Word, nor believe in it. If, without the Savior Jesus Christ, some people were destined to be saved and others were not, there would absolutely be no need for sinners to believe in Jesus. That Jesus has saved us from our sins through His baptism and His blood on the Cross, in the end, it would also be meaningless. But in the righteousness of God found in Jesus Christ, God allowed salvation to even these Buddhist monks who do not believe in Jesus, only if they repent and turn their minds toward God.

There are many people in this world who live their lives believing in Jesus. Were we to divide them into two groups, one group would be those who are like Esau and the other would be those who are like Jacob. People like Jacob identify themselves as sinners bound for hell, and as such, are saved from their sins by believing in the gospel of the water and the Spirit given by Jesus. The other group is made of people like Esau, who try to enter the gates of heaven by adding their own efforts to their faiths in Jesus.

Who are you like? Jacob or Esau? Do you believe in the righteousness of God? Or do you believe in the erroneous

Doctrine of Predestination? Your choice between these two faiths will decide where you will end up–in heaven or hell. You must throw out these erroneous doctrines and receive the righteousness of God to make peace with Him by believing in the gospel of the water and the Spirit, spoken of by God's righteousness. Only this faith gives us perfect deliverance from our sins and eternal lives. ⊠

The Eternal Love

< Romans 8:31-34 >
"What then shall we say to these things? If God is for us, who can be against us? He who did not spare His own Son, but delivered Him up for us all, how shall He not with Him also freely give us all things? Who shall bring a charge against God's elect? It is God who justifies. Who is he who condemns? It is Christ who died, and furthermore is also risen, who is even at the right hand of God, who also makes intercession for us."

If God had already decided to cover us with His righteousness in Jesus Christ even before the creation, then no one would be able to disturb it. By believing in the righteousness of God, and not through the Doctrine of Justification, those who have become genuinely sinless are the true children of God.

As such, not all religious people are right. Few people get persecuted just for believing in Jesus nowadays, but many of those who know the true righteousness of God have been persecuted. However, the people who became children of God by believing in His righteousness can never be separated from God. When God gave us the gospel of His righteousness, who can be against them?

God has given everything to us as a gift

"He who did not spare His own Son, but delivered Him up for us all, how shall He not with Him also freely give us all things?" (Romans 8:32)

For those who have received God's righteousness by believing in His Son, God gave everything as a gift—the Kingdom of Heaven, the privilege of becoming the children of God, the grace of understanding His Word, the blessing of being able to live as a worker of the righteousness, and the blessing of eternal life.

God gave us His Son in order to make us His children. What else would He not give us? God has given those who receive the true faith through His righteousness all the blessing of the heaven and earth. The believers and the servants of God praise Him forever because of His righteousness.

Who shall bring a charge against God's elect?

"Who shall bring a charge against God's elect? It is God who justifies. Who is he who condemns? It is Christ who died, and furthermore is also rise, who is even at the right hand of God, who also makes intercession for us" (Romans 8:33-34).

No one can bring a charge against the people whom God has chosen with His righteousness in Jesus Christ, for Jesus, with the righteousness of God, has made them free of sin. People who believe in the righteousness of God through Jesus Christ have no sin in their hearts. That is because God, not another, made those who believe in His righteousness sinless.

The Son of God, Jesus Christ, came to the earth in the

flesh of a man, was baptized by John the Baptist, took upon Himself the burden of all the sins of the world, died on the Cross and was resurrected from the dead in three days, and became the Lord to those who believe.

This is why we cannot say that they, who became righteous by believing in God's righteousness, are sinners and wrongdoers. Even now, God acknowledges those who believe in His righteousness. As an evidence of this, the Holy Spirit dwells in their hearts. That is why no one can libel God's righteousness or those whose sins have been forgiven by believing in His righteousness.

The righteousness of God appeared through the baptism of Jesus Christ, the shedding of His blood on the Cross, and His death and resurrection. Jesus Christ, after fulfilling all the righteousness of God, sits on the right hand of God as our Savior and interceder. ✉

Who Would Dare to Stand against Us?

< Romans 8:31-34 >

"What then shall we say to these things? If God is for us, who can be against us? He who did not spare His own Son, but delivered Him up for us all, how shall He not with Him also freely give us all things? Who shall bring a charge against God's elect? It is God who justifies. Who is he who condemns? It is Christ who died, and furthermore is also risen, who is even at the right hand of God, who also makes intercession for us."

In Romans 8:31-34, Paul testifies on Christ's inseparable love of the believers by summarizing the gospel of the water and the Spirit and reaching its final conclusion. This passage proclaims the great joy of salvation reached at the zenith of faith.

Paul said in Romans 8:31, *"What then shall we say to these things? If God is for us, who can be against us?"* Like Paul, we have experienced that the gospel of the water and the Spirit radiates as time goes by and becomes an even greater gospel of salvation as more of our weaknesses are revealed. The more we serve the gospel of the water and the Spirit, the more we are filled with conviction and joy.

Paul called the gospel in which he believed as, *"my gospel" (2 Timothy 2:8)*. The gospel that Paul bore witness to was none other than the faith in the baptism and the blood of

Jesus.

"My gospel" that Paul preached does not refer to the gospel of the Cross that the religious people believe in, but the gospel of the water and the Spirit that proclaims the blessing that Jesus took away all the sins of mankind once and for all.

This gospel made Paul a man of great courage. Since he received the forgiveness of sins, the righteousness of God filled his heart and thus his heart was also filled with the Holy Spirit. He devoted himself to bearing witness to the gospel of the water and the Spirit all his life. The gospel of the water and the Spirit has the power and authority to take away the sins of mankind all at once.

Who, then, can dare to be against the gospel of the water and the Spirit that Paul believed in? No one! Romans 8:31 tells us, *"What then shall we say to these things? If God is for us, who can be against us?"* Who in this world can be against those who believe in the gospel of the water and the Spirit? When God saved the mankind from the sins of the world through the gospel of the water and the Spirit, who can take His power in vain? Neither those who believe in Jesus in name only nor Satan himself can fight against or win over those who believe in the gospel of the water and the Spirit.

He justified us all at once

Romans 8:29-30 states, *"For whom He foreknew, He also predestined to be conformed to the image of His Son, that He might be the firstborn among many brethren. Moreover whom He predestined, these He also called; whom He called, these He also justified; and whom He justified, these He also glorified."*

This tells us that God the Father planned to save all the sinners in Christ and called them through the gospel of the water and the Spirit, washing away their sins all at once to make them His children. When our Lord delivered all the sinners from their sins through the gospel of the water and the Spirit, who could be against what He has done?

Who could possibly be against and win over those who have been justified by believing in the gospel of the water and the Spirit? This is nonsense. You must know that anyone who is against those who have been justified by believing in the gospel of the water and the Spirit is against none other than God Himself. You must believe in the gospel of the water and the Spirit to be saved from all your sins at all costs. If in your mind and heart you are against the gospel of the truth, then you cannot be saved from your sins and you will be condemned to hell.

No one can be against those who have the righteousness of God

"What then shall we say to these things? If God is for us, who can be against us? (Romans 8:31)" That God is for us represents the fact that He has taken away all our sins through the gospel of the water and the Spirit and has saved us. Who, then, could be against those who have been redeemed of their sins by believing in the gospel of the water and the Spirit, and who could possibly say that such faith is wrong? It would be a useless exercise in vain. God has approved the faith of those who believe in the gospel of the water and the Spirit.

How can anyone challenge this? Jesus took away all the sins of the world through His baptism and His blood on the

Cross. Who can say that those who believe in this are wrong? No one!

In Romans 6:3 Paul said, *"Or do you not know that as many of us as were baptized into Christ Jesus were baptized into His death?"* Paul meant that he believed in the baptism of Jesus and His blood on the Cross, through which all his sins were passed onto Jesus and were cleansed, and by which Paul died and was resurrected with Jesus.

Galatians 3:27 also tells us, *"For as many of you as were baptized into Christ have put on Christ."* This passage tells us that Jesus took upon all the sins of the world with His baptism, was crucified on the Cross for these sins, and was resurrected, all to bestow us with the blessing that those who believe in this truth would become the children of God. Paul's faith was grounded in the belief that he was baptized into Jesus, died on the Cross with Him, and was resurrected with Him. Therefore, once you believe in the baptism of Jesus, all your sins are cleansed and you become a child of God by being resurrected with Christ.

"As many of you as were baptized into Christ have put on Christ." In other words, those who believe that Jesus came to this world and was baptized by John the Baptist to take upon all the sins of the world, are baptized into Jesus. Moreover, they also believe that they died on the Cross with Jesus, and that by their faith they were resurrected with Him.

Anyone who believes in the baptism of Jesus and His blood will therefore be saved from his/her sins. Just as surely as Jesus is the Son of God, those who are redeemed of their sins by believing in the baptism and the blood of Christ will become God's children. *"For as many of you as were baptized into Christ have put on Christ."* When we believe in the gospel of the water and the Spirit, we put on the righteousness of Christ to become the children of God.

Paul spoke of Jesus' baptism because he received a great blessing by believing in the gospel of the water and the Spirit. But many are yet to receive such a blessing from God that comes with the gospel of the water and the Spirit. Most people think that the gospel that Paul preached was the gospel of the blood on the Cross, but the truth is that he believed in and spread the gospel of the water and the Spirit, which combines the baptism of Jesus and His blood on the Cross.

Why, then, are the followers of Jesus today unaware of this gospel of the water and the Spirit? It is because the gospel of the water and the Spirit preached in the Early Church period has changed with time. In the Early Church period, all the believers believed in and preached the gospel of the water and the Spirit.

In time, however, the gospel was altered and preached as only the blood of Christ while His baptism was increasingly marginalized. This explains why, even now, many people believe only in the blood on the Cross, which deviates from the true gospel of the Early Church period.

These people still have sin in them. They are ignorant of the gospel of the water and the Spirit, in which the righteousness of God is revealed, and as such, they are still sinners, and they still stand against this righteousness of God, even if they say that they believe in Jesus.

What could a spiritually blind person see? The blind may try to understand an elephant by touching it. A blind person may touch an elephant's leg and say that it is a pillar, and yet another blind person may touch its nose and say that it is something long, for neither has seen an elephant before. Likewise, a spiritually blind person cannot talk of the greatness of the gospel of the water and the Spirit.

Therefore, those who do not know the blessing of the water and the Spirit cannot preach it. Those who have seen can easily understand what someone tries to explain with words, but a blind would never really understand it.

People are born sinners. Because we were spiritually sinners from our very birth, we do not know the truth of the gospel of the water and the Spirit. Those who only believe in the blood on the Cross have made a new version of Christianity on their own. How could their sins be washed away when they claim that they believe in Jesus and yet only believe in the blood on the Cross? Only more and more sins would pile up as time goes by.

Those who believe only in the blood of Jesus as salvation are those who are not yet spiritually awakened. But Jesus tells us clearly in John 3:5, *"Unless one is born of water and the Spirit, he cannot enter the kingdom of God."* We must therefore believe in the gospel of the water and the Spirit in order to be blessed with the glory of becoming the children of God and entering His Kingdom.

Since Paul believed in the gospel of the water and the Spirit, he said by faith, *"If God is for us, who can be against us?" (Romans 8:31)* Can those who do not know the gospel of the water and the Spirit be against the children of God? They could be against God's children, but they could never win over them. Those who only believe in the blood on the Cross cannot win over those who believe in the gospel of the water and the Spirit.

Those who are against the righteousness of God can only become His foe and thus can never receive His blessings. No one can receive salvation or have the faith that takes him/her to heaven without believing in the gospel of the water and the Spirit, the gospel in which the righteousness of God is revealed. Those who believe in the gospel of the water and the Spirit can thus overcome the false gospel and return to the true one. The children of God can overcome the world and the devil himself.

Some do not clearly understand the baptism of Jesus and His blood, and their misunderstanding lead them to false faith. If you believe in the blood on the Cross but do not think much of receiving the forgiveness of sins by believing in the gospel of the baptism of Jesus, then your faith is wrong.

Those who believe in the gospel of the water and the Spirit before God are the ones who will attain His righteousness and have the true faith. God tells us that those who believe only in His Son's blood on the Cross are mistaken. Those who do not believe in His righteousness do not believe or recognize the gospel of the water and the Spirit, but those who believe in His righteousness also believe that both the blood of Christ on the Cross and His baptism took away their sins.

We must throw away our stubbornness. Those who disapprove the gospel of the water and the Spirit insist that their false beliefs are true. Those who believe only in the blood have a half faith in His righteousness. Only those who believe in the gospel of the water and the Spirit have the whole faith, and they alone also believe in the righteousness of God and attain His righteousness (Matthew 3:15, 11:11).

The books written by those who believe only in the blood

are turning paper into waste. The doctrines once discussed by theologians are now ignored by Christians, but the gospel of the water and the Spirit is receiving much attention. This truth has existed since the Apostolic Age and will never change. The Word of God exists forever, but those who believe solely in the blood are being erased from peoples' memories. What is the reason? It is because the blood, which has only half of the righteousness of God, has no effect on sinners by itself.

Frankly speaking, most people today, whether they are Christians or non-Christians, commit so many sins. How could all these sins be forgiven by believing only in the blood? The doctrines that emphasize only the blood on the Cross teach people to pray for forgiveness whenever they sin, but for how long can they pray for their sins to be forgiven? No matter what they say, they cannot receive the forgiveness of sins.

Did Jesus come to this world and simply bleed to death without being baptized? You know that this is not true. Jesus came to this world and took upon all sins by being baptized (Matthew 3:15). He was baptized by John before He bled on the Cross, allowing Him to be crucified on the Cross. This is how Jesus fulfilled all righteousness. There is no need for you to cry for His mercy to be forgiven of your sin everyday if you believe in the baptism that Jesus received from John. Instead, believe in the righteousness of God and receive the complete salvation.

Jesus was baptized to take upon all the sins of the world on His shoulder and was crucified to be judged for the sins of the world once and for all. Redemption can be obtained only by believing in the baptism of Jesus and His blood.

Did Jesus give us a salvation that is greater than the sins we commit?

The redemption given by Jesus is far greater than all the sins that we have committed and will commit. If the baptism of Jesus and His blood were not greater than the sins of the mankind, then we could neither believe in Jesus as the Savior nor receive redemption. However, the goodness of the Lord is so great that He took away the sins of the world all at once through His baptism.

Likewise, the gate to Heaven is wide open, but no one can enter this gate without believing in the gospel of the water and the Spirit. You can be against those who believe in the gospel of the water and the Spirit, but you cannot hide from the dreadful judgment of God. Therefore, do not think that you can win over the faith in the baptism and the blood of Jesus, through which the righteousness of God was fulfilled.

Many of those who were against the gospel of the water and the Spirit were also against Paul the Apostle. But no one could say that the gospel of the water and the Spirit that Paul believed in was wrong. They only did not admit that Jesus was the Son of God and their Savior.

Romans 8:32 tells us, *"He who did not spare His own Son, but delivered Him up for us all, how shall He not with Him also freely give us all things?"* God the Father sent His only begotten Son to the world and made Him bear all its sins through His baptism, die on the Cross, and rise again from the dead in order to deliver us from our sins.

In order to save us from the sins of the world and make us His children, as Jesus was, God the Father gave us His only begotten Son. For God to make all those who believe in the gospel of the water and the Spirit, His children and the blessed and righteous, He sent His only begotten Son to be baptized. God had planned to bestow all mankind with His heavenly blessings and the gospel of the water and the Spirit. One of these blessings is to become His child by believing in the gospel of the water and the Spirit.

"He who did not spare His own Son, but delivered Him up for us all, how shall He not with Him also freely give us all things?" (Romans 8:32) "All things" here refer to God's gifts. What gifts? God gave those who received Jesus and believed in His name the right to become His children—that is, those who believed in the gospel of the water and the Spirit are made the children of God. Those who believe in the gospel of the water and the Spirit are without sin. They are righteous and are truly the sanctified children of God.

Those who become the children of God by believing in all these will be gifted with the Thousand-year Kingdom and the Kingdom of Heaven. The righteous are blessed to inherit all the glories of the Heaven.

"Freely give us all things" has been interpreted by some as the giving of the Holy Spirit. They think, "Does this mean that once we believe in Jesus, the Holy Spirit is given to us separately?" This is not true because when you believe in the gospel of the water and the Spirit, you receive the remission of your sins and the Holy Spirit all at the same time. The Holy Spirit cannot dwell in a sinful heart. The Holy Spirit comes to us at the very moment when all our sins are forgiven.

There is more for the believers than receiving the Holy Spirit. God's gifts do not end until all the heavenly blessings are given to us. In this world, people tend to think that such abilities as healing, speaking in tongues, and prophesizing are gifts, but the gifts mentioned in this passage refer to all the heavenly things that our Father possesses. By gifts, Paul is talking about all the things that God bestows on His children who have the righteousness of God.

God said that He would give all good things as a gift to those who believe in the gospel of the water and the Spirit. God gave the gift of being born again to those believing in the gospel of the water and the Spirit. God gives all things of Heaven as a present to those who believe in the gospel of the water and the Spirit. Christians suffer so much living while in this world but when the Kingdom of God comes, they will be endowed with the glory of Heaven.

Do not say you are the elect for no reason

Romans 8:33-34 states, *"Who shall bring a charge against God's elect? It is God who justifies. Who is he who condemns? It is Christ who died, and furthermore is also risen, who is even at the right hand of God, who also makes intercession for us."*

"Who shall bring a charge against God's elect?" Could you bring a charge against those whom God saved with the gospel of the water and the Spirit? Of course not!

Theologians quote Calvin by saying that some were unconditionally selected while others were not. However, we must never use the term "unconditionally" in the presence of God. By doing so, they prove that they do not know God at all, and that their doctrine is false. Unconditional selection means that God loves some for no reason and hates others for no reason as well. How could we say that God is righteous when He loves some and hates others? This is not our God. Our God loves and cares for all mankind in Christ.

Here, in verse 32 it is said, *"He who did not spare His own Son, but delivered Him up for us all, how shall He not with Him also freely give us all things?"* God gave us His Son in order to save all mankind. Through Him, God made us believe that He has taken away all our sins through the Word of the water and the blood. In verse 33 it is written, *"Who shall bring a charge against God's elect?"* Here, the word "God's elect" does not imply that God selects some unconditionally. God selects those who cannot live without Jesus Christ and those without their own righteousness in order to clothe them with His own righteousness.

Those who are chosen by God's righteousness are the ones who believe and rest in the truth that Jesus came to this earth, was baptized, and sacrificed Himself on the Cross to take away all our sins. They are the ones who believe in God, He who has saved them from the sins of the world and clothed them with His righteousness.

Who, then, could bring a charge against the righteous? No one! No one can say that our faith is wrong. No one can judge those who are saved from their sins and are chosen as the children of God by believing the gospel of the water and the Spirit. Those who believe in only the blood of the Cross can neither say that those who believe the gospel of the water and the Spirit are false, nor bring a charge against them before God.

Some people misjudge those who are clothed with God's righteousness by believing in the gospel of the water and the Spirit. But is that right? No! The faith of those chosen to be righteous in the presence of God can never be wrongly judged by anyone.

Who could say that those who believe in the gospel of the water and the Spirit are sinners and wrongly judge their faiths? We have long been preaching the gospel of the water and the Spirit, in which the righteousness of God revealed, to all the people in the world.

But no one has brought a charge against us for preaching the gospel of the water and the Spirit. There were just a few who asked us to approve the faith of only the blood of the Cross. Even they could not say that having faith in the gospel of the water and the Spirit is wrong.

The true gospel of the water and the Spirit is the gospel that contains the righteousness of God. This is the true gospel, and all other gospels are incomplete. Paul the Apostle, who preached the gospel of the water and the Spirit, said that there could never be another gospel beside this true gospel, and he asserted, *"But even if we, or an angel from heaven, preach any other gospel to you than what we have preached to you, let him be accursed. As we have said before, so now I say again, if anyone preaches any other gospel to you than what you have received, let him be accursed" (Galatians 1:8-9).*

No one can say that the gospel of the water and the Spirit is biblically wrong. Those who do not believe in the gospel of the water and the Spirit are against it. If you believe that the gospel of the water and the Spirit given by God is false, then go ahead and protest to God. We, too, have to and are able to fight against the incomplete false gospels that emphasize only the blood of the Cross. How could Jesus be crucified for our sins without first taking them upon Himself through His baptism?

Do not say that the believers of God's righteousness have sins

To "bring a charge" means to ask for the judgment on a trial. The only one who could bring a charge against those who believe in the gospel of the water and the Spirit is an evildoer. Those who believe in the gospel of the water and the Spirit have faith in God's righteousness, so who could wrongly judge their faith? Who could say that they are wrong? There is none, for it is God who justifies them. No one can accuse the believers of the gospel of the water and the Spirit of having any sin.

"It is God who justifies" (Romans 8:33). Who can declare the believers of the gospel of the water and the Spirit to be sinless? Only God can. He declares by His righteousness that the believers of the gospel of the water and the Spirit are justified.

"Justified" is not applied to those who still have sin, but it is applied to those whose sins were actually forgiven, making them "sinless and justified." When God says that the ones who believe in the gospel of the water and the Spirit are sinless, who can dare to say that they are wrong and do not have the righteousness of God? No theologian in this world can say so.

Christianity of today has been corrupted by the Doctrine of Sanctification that tries to attain religious holiness. A theologian in England, after asking, "Is the church of God holy?," claimed that the church of God, too, had flaws. Clearly, this theologian neither knew about the gospel of the water and the Spirit nor had faith in God's righteousness.

But every believer in the church of God believes in the gospel of the water and the Spirit and is completely sinless.

Although he/she may be weak in the flesh, he/she still has the perfect and the flawless righteousness of God.

Is everyone in the church of God without sin? Yes! The church is a place where the believers who are sanctified and without sin gather together in Christ. If the believers have sin, then they are not God's children. What made them sanctified? It is, of course, the faith in the gospel of the water and the Spirit that made them sinless by receiving the righteousness of God. The theologian said that even the church of God had flaws because he did not believe in or even know the gospel of the water and the Spirit.

Who dares to say that the believers of the gospel of the water and the Spirit are sinners? It is God who 'justified' them. Can we, those who believe in the gospel of the water and the Spirit, be with sins only because we are weak? We certainly cannot! Then does this mean that we have no sin even as we still commit sins? Yes, we have no sin! This is why we need to believe in the gospel of the water and the Spirit. People do not intend to commit sins on purpose, but because of their weaknesses.

There are very few people who actually intend to commit sins; almost all iniquities are caused by the weaknesses of human beings. The ones who believe in the gospel of the water and the Spirit do not have sin in their hearts because they have the righteousness of God. We are without sin because God did away with all our sins with His righteousness. That is why the Bible states, *"It is God who justifies."* It is God who declares that the believers of the gospel of the water and the Spirit are without sin because they have His righteousness. We have been delivered from all our sins by believing in the gospel of the water and the Spirit.

If Jesus had not taken away even our future sins, how could we be redeemed of our sins and how could we say that we are sinners no more? If we, after believing in the righteousness of God, commit sins and live in sin, then does this make us not sanctified enough, or disqualify our redemption, and thus destine us back to hell again? The answer is no! If our salvation comes by self-sanctification, who in the world could ever be saved? No one! No one can live a perfect life in the flesh and be sanctified by keeping the commandments completely. So the Bible states, *"There is no righteous, none at all" (Romans 3:10).*

In nature, human beings cannot receive God's righteousness by their own deeds

God sent His only begotten Son, who was baptized by John the Baptist, and put Him to death on the Cross to save all mankind from the sins of the world. Those who believe in the gospel of the water and the Spirit have become righteous by their faith. This is why there could be the righteous even in this world. Abraham also became the father of faith by believing in the Word of God.

Even though many Christians say that they can receive God's righteousness through the Doctrine of Justification, they in fact are ignorant of it. What is God's righteousness? It is far different from human righteousness. In what gospel is God's righteousness revealed? In the gospel of the water and the Spirit is this righteousness of God revealed. If we reject the gospel of the water and the Spirit without believing in it, that means we are standing against God.

No one can be delivered from sin or receive God's

righteousness without having faith in the gospel of the water and the Spirit. Can anyone be against God's righteousness even a bit? I have long believed in and preached the gospel of the water and the Spirit, but I have never seen anyone who could stand against this gospel. No one can be against the gospel of the water and the Spirit on the basis of God's Word because this gospel of the righteousness of God gives us the perfect and complete redemption of our sins.

Who can condemn those who have the righteousness of God?

Let's read Romans 8:34. *"Who is he who condemns? It is Christ who died, and furthermore is also risen, who is even at the right hand of God, who also makes intercession for us."* Could anyone condemn those who believe in God's righteousness to be sinful? No one can.

Could anyone condemn the believers of the gospel of the water and the Spirit, who have been delivered from their sins by faith, to be sinners? No! *"Who is he who condemns?"* Who can say that the believers of the righteousness of God are sinners?

The wages of sin is death. If you have sin in your heart, you are going to go to hell. God judges people because they have sin. But those whose sins have been taken away by their faith in the righteousness of God are not judged by God, because they no longer have any sin to be judged. When God Himself does not judge those who believe in the righteousness of God, who can dare to condemn them? If a believer in Jesus Christ is with sin, he/she is a sinner and will be judged and condemned by God. Sinners will be judged by God for their sins in their hearts and will be shunned by other people. But if a believer in Christ believes in the gospel of the water and the Spirit and receives the righteousness of God, that person is sinless before God and no one can condemn the person. Nor is there sin in the conscience of such people.

"Who is he who condemns? It is Christ who died, and furthermore is also risen, who is even at the right hand of God, who also makes intercession for us." Jesus, the Son of God, came to the earth to give us God's righteousness, received baptism from John the Baptist to bear all our sins, died on the Cross shedding His blood, and rose again from the dead to become our Savior. He now sits at the right hand of God and makes intercession for us as our Savior.

The Holy Spirit also prays for those who have the righteousness of God. Jesus prays for us in Heaven. The Holy Spirit, too, prays for us to God the Father, but in a different way, with "groanings" that cannot be uttered whenever we are weak in our hearts.

How perfect is the righteousness of God in the hearts of those who believe in the gospel of the water and the Spirit? The perfection of God's righteousness tells us that the gospel of the water and the Spirit is also flawless and perfect. ✉

Who Shall Separate the Righteous from the Love of Christ?

< Romans 8:35-39 >

"Who shall separate us from the love of Christ? Shall tribulation, or distress, or persecution, or famine, or nakedness, or peril, or sword? As it is written:

'For Your sake we are killed all day long;
We are accounted as sheep for the slaughter.'

Yet in all these things we are more than conquerors through Him who loved us. For I am persuaded that neither death nor life, nor angels nor principalities nor powers, nor things present nor things to come, nor height nor depth, nor any other created thing, shall be able to separate us from the love of God which is in Christ Jesus our Lord."

Verse 35 says, *"Who shall separate us from the love of Christ? Shall tribulation, or distress, or persecution, or famine, or nakedness, or peril, or sword?"* Who could separate us from the love of Christ, given to those who believe in the gospel of the water and the Spirit that has the righteousness of God in it? Could persecution and troubles cut off that love? Could the seven-year Great Tribulation separate us from that love? Of course not!

No tribulation or distress in this world can cut us off from the love of our Lord that has saved us from our sins. Even when we wish, in our tiredness, to be left alone, and someone asks us whether Jesus has saved us from our sins or not, we would all respond that Jesus has indeed saved us and that we are without sin. Regardless of how weary and troubled our hearts may be, He has still saved us and is still our eternal Savior. Even if we were too tired or ill to steadily hold up our own bodies, we would still confess our thanks for the righteousness of God. No weariness can separate us from the righteousness of God that has delivered us from our sins.

Neither persecution, nor famine, nor nakedness, nor peril, nor the sword can cut us off from the righteousness of God. That we are sometimes shunned and condemned by religious people is the persecution that we face. Our persecutions consist of our friends, neighbors, relatives, and even our own family members leaving us because of their accusations of us being heretics. Could these persecutions separate us from the salvation of Jesus Christ? They most certainly cannot!

Regardless of how severely we are persecuted, it cannot cut us off from the righteousness of God that has saved us. Because God's righteousness has made us sinless, and because this is the unchanging truth, no one and nothing can separate us from God's love.

Famine, whether spiritual or physical, could not separate us. Because we believe in the gospel of the water and the Spirit, what always remains in our hearts is the righteousness of God—that is, the faith in our Lord that He has made us sinless with the gospel of the water and the Spirit. This faith is the faith and the blessing of believing in the righteousness of God. "Because the Lord has made all my sins disappear, I have no sin! God has made me righteous and sinless, clothing me wholly in His own righteousness!" This is why our faith in the righteousness of God will not disappear, no matter how severe the famine may be.

The righteousness of God by the gospel of the water and the Spirit

Unless one believes in the gospel of the water and the Spirit, there is still sin in his/her heart. But one who believes in the righteousness of God has no sin. This is why our Lord said that we could know a tree by its fruits. Those who do not believe in God's righteousness give up their faiths in Jesus when they face the slightest difficulty, famine, persecution, or tribulation.

There are people who think, "Although Jesus was judged on the Cross on behalf of my sins, only the original sin was removed, and I must daily ask for forgiveness of the other sins I commit everyday." Those who have this kind of faith are actually sinning against God by not believing that Jesus has taken away all their sins, and in the process, they condemn and corrupt themselves. These are the very people who deny Jesus and who do not believe in the righteousness of God.

But those who believe in the gospel of the water and the Spirit are those who believe in God's righteousness, and regardless of the circumstances that they face, they will firmly hold onto their faith, saying, "God has surely saved me from all the sins of the world. I am sinless!" Even if we are to face death in the last days of our spiritual famine, we will never deny that God has made us sinless and that we have become His people. The righteousness of God that has taken away all our sins will still remain in our hearts as our faith. The gospel of the water and the Spirit is that powerful and great. No matter what kind of tribulations we face in our lives, because the righteousness of God is in Christ, we will never be separated from the love of Christ.

What is it meant by "nakedness" in the above passage? Nakedness refers to losing all our possessions. Until the Medieval Ages, when there was trouble in a village or a nation in the European countries, people often engaged in witch-hunts, using scapegoats to blame for all the troubles; people took everything away from them and accused them of being heretics. This is why Paul used the word "nakedness" here.

In those ages, it was possible to accuse someone of heresy, and with only one or two witnesses, to condemn the accused to be burnt at the stake, confiscate all his/her possessions, and wipe out his/her reputation.

Even if we are driven to our nakedness in such a manner, lose everything we own and are put to death, the righteousness of God that has, in His love for us, taken away all our sins, will never disappear from us—this is how complete the gospel of the water and the Spirit is.

Neither peril nor the sword can separate us from the love of Christ. Even if we are put under the sword and are killed by it, we who believe have no sin. Many Christians in the Early Church were falsely accused of having set fire to Rome and were publicly executed in the coliseum by being fed to lions. Even as they were dying, they praised the Lord who had saved them. They were able to praise because they were believers in the gospel of the water and the Spirit. Those who have been redeemed by believing in the truth that God has loved them and has taken away all their sins can praise the Lord, even while they are being killed and eaten by lions.

This strength comes from the faith in God's righteousness that has taken away all our sins and in His love. It is because God is in us, speaks to us, holds us strong, protects us and comforts us that such strength can be found. Neither peril nor the sword, nor threatening, nor martyrdom can separate us from God's love.

Those who believe in the gospel of the water and the Spirit are those who believe in the righteousness of God and who are the people of Christ. Those who believe in the righteousness of God are those who are loved by Christ. But some people turn Christ's perfect love into mere emotional love, looking only at His death on the Cross, saddened by and crying over His sufferings. But human emotions can change overnight.

Though our emotions change every morning and every night, the love with which our Lord has saved us cannot be changed or altered by anything. His love is forever unchanging. This is how powerful the gospel of the water and the Spirit is, and this is how great the righteousness of God is. No one can separate us from our Lord, who has made us whole and has clothed us in His perfect love. This is the power of the gospel of the water and the Spirit and it is also the power of our faith in God's righteousness.

The Greek word for "gospel" is *"euaggelion,"* and it was said to have the *"dunamis"*—this Greek word means strength, power or ability, from which we get the word "dynamite"—of God. A handful of dynamite is enough to bring down a house to its foundation and crumble it to dust. A Tomahawk missile launched from a warship can destroy a large concrete building and turn it into oblivion. No matter how fortified the building may be, it is no match for the missile's destructive power.

Two civilian airplanes brought down the Twin Towers of the World Trade Center in New York. What happened when the planes hit the buildings? Ignited by the explosion of the planes, the fire fed by the jet fuel was so intense that it melted everything in the floors that were penetrated by the planes. Because the floors' steel structures and columns that supported the buildings were all melted down, the floors suddenly collapsed, and the buildings could not bear the weight of these collapsing floors, so finally, they disintegrated in their entirety. Had the floors come down slowly, the buildings would not have collapsed. But because the floors fell suddenly and swiftly, the columns and other supporting structures collapsed, and the whole buildings were, as we all witnessed, brought down in a matter of seconds.

The power of God's gospel is that of the gospel of the water and the Spirit. It is also the power that has His righteousness in it. Perhaps it is not fit to use this tragedy to illustrate the righteousness of God, but the power of the gospel of the water and the Spirit given by the righteousness of God is like dynamite that can completely wipe out all the sins. The righteousness of God is that our Lord has saved us by taking away all our sins by coming to this earth, being baptized, dying on the Cross, and resurrecting from death.

The gospel of the water and the Spirit is the righteousness of God with which Jesus has taken away all the sins that mankind has committed, from the very beginning of the universe to its end. This is why nothing can separate God from those who are loved by Him through their redemption by their faiths in the gospel of the righteousness of God. Paul's faith, too, was one that believed in God's righteousness.

Can we, then, receive God's righteousness by the gospel

of just the blood of the Cross? We cannot. Believing only in the gospel of the blood of the Cross alone cannot give us the righteousness of God. Those who think otherwise will easily give up their faith in Jesus at the slightest provocation.

For instance, when their earthly possessions are taken away, or when they encounter difficulties at work because of their religious orientations, they will easily succumb to renounce their faith. This is an inevitable outcome and is applicable to many Christians. Those who, by not believing in the gospel of the water and the Spirit, do not have the Holy Spirit in their hearts and are not redeemed from their sins, are bound to capitulate at the smallest threat.

The reason why today's Christianity is so weak in this world is because of this faith that is limited to only the blood of the Cross. This kind of faith is one that has not received God's righteousness through the gospel of the water and the Spirit.

A righteous believer who has been redeemed from all his/her sins by receiving the righteousness of God can work for many souls. Since he/she believes in the gospel of the water and the Spirit and has the Holy Spirit, and because God is with him/her in His Word, that person can do many spiritual works and turn many lost souls back to God. This is the faith in the righteousness of God, the faith in the gospel of the water and the Spirit. The gospel of the water and the Spirit is given by God, not by our own works, and thus it is also through God that we can do His works.

Verse 36 says, *"As it is written: 'For Your sake we are killed all day long; We are accounted as sheep for the slaughter.'"* Among those who believe in the gospel of the water and the Spirit are those who are actually treated in this manner while living on this earth. In fact, believers in the gospel of the water and the Spirit are often hated by others, particularly by those with wrong faith, who claim to be Christians themselves.

The born-again Christians are, in other words, hated more by nominal Christians than by Buddhists. This passage, that *"for your sake we are killed all day long; we are accounted as sheep for the slaughter,"* is the Word of God spoken to believers in the gospel of the water and the Spirit. Even our Lord, by following the Father's will with His baptism and death on the Cross, was *"accounted as sheep for the slaughter."* The Lord saved us by coming to and living such a life on this earth.

The righteousness of God has won over all the sins of the world

Verse 37 says, *"Yet in all these things we are more than conquerors through Him who loved us."* How can we win over all these things? We claim our victory by the power of our faith in God's love.

One who believes in the gospel of the water and the Spirit has the power of God. But one who does not believe in the gospel of the water and the Spirit only has sin in his/her heart. The faith and salvation of those who are with sin cannot but have ups and downs because of their emotions, and thus, they have no power. But those who believe in the gospel of the water and the Spirit have the power. They do not have power by themselves, but they have the power of the gospel given by God, and with this power, they can withstand and triumph over all persecutions and tribulations. The righteous must engage in a spiritual battle against sinners and preach the gospel of the water and the Spirit to them. The righteous must also tolerate living and being persecuted for the gospel as their natural lot. A life that lives for the Lord is our lot.

An oriental proverb says, "Were one to miss reading for a single day, he would speak out stinging words." What about us then? We, too, are prone to rush into corruption if we let a day go by without living for God and His gospel. This is how we would live our lives until our deaths. But if we live for Christ, sacrifice ourselves and are persecuted for God, and if we wage a spiritual war against the spiritual forces of evil, our hearts will be filled with spiritual food, from which we will find new strengths to go on.

When Christians fall, it is because they did not live for the Lord. But when we live for the Lord, our spiritual strengths grow even more, and our physical health and strengths also become stronger.

Verse 38-39 says, *"For I am persuaded that neither death nor life, nor angels nor principalities nor powers, nor things present nor things to come, nor height nor depth, nor any other created thing, shall be able to separate us from the love of God which is in Christ Jesus our Lord."* As a believer in the gospel of the water and the Spirit, Paul was convinced of this. The same truth applies to us: neither death nor life can separate us from Christ.

In the old ages, those wielding worldly power, such as Roman emperors, tried to persuade Christians to renounce their faith and report their fellow believers to the authorities by offering all kinds of enticements, from high offices, wives and properties, all in return for their renouncement. But the true believers in the gospel never yielded to the temptation of power, property or honor.

Faith is not something that can be exchanged for what the world can offer. If someone were to show us a blank check and say to us, "I will give you this check, if you stop spreading the gospel," we would be able to reply, because of our hope for the future and our strong faith in God, "You will need it yourself, so spend it; to me, it is nothing but a piece of paper."

Only the gospel of the water and the Spirit is the gospel that has the righteousness of God

There are many people who have said to me, "If you just admit that our faith in just the blood of the Cross is also a right faith, we, too, will then approve your faith. Not only will we stop accusing you of heresy, but we will actually help you." These so-called religious leaders in particular have sought such compromises from me. But the righteousness of God is precise and certain when measured by His Word. What is wrong is wrong, and what is the truth is the truth. Giving recognition to a wrong faith is in itself an act of rebellion against God, and so I am not only unable to approve their faith, but I must also constantly point out its fallacies.

"You believe just in the blood of the Cross? Then you must have sin in your heart. You are bound to hell. I can't help it even if you think that I am too serious and unyielding; what is the truth is the truth." Because of such words, people keep their distance from me—more precisely, they cannot be close to me. Many people used to approach me, thinking that I was like them. But each time, I have told them, "You are false shepherds and swindlers who trade in God's name to elk out a living, merely simple thieves." Who would have liked me when I said such things? But what is not is not, and this is why I have been so firm and unfaltering in my stand.

I have also been tempted by those who say that if I only believed in the blood of the Cross, they will give me such and such authority. But as the above passage says, *"nor things present nor things to come, nor height nor depth, nor any other created thing,"* we have no need for any authority, height or depth. We don't need the healing power that some swindlers claim to have. Those of us who are born again have no need for such things, and we don't even like them.

The passage also tells us that no other created thing can separate us from the love of God in our Lord Jesus Christ. Even if there were aliens in this universe, they wouldn't be able to separate us from the love of God that has saved us.

There are some Christians who believe in the existence of extraterrestrial beings. Even among pastors, many believe in their existence. But there is no such thing as an alien. When I was attending seminary, one of my professors, who taught Greek, believed in the existence of aliens. So I asked him, "Can you support your belief with any evidence from the Scripture?" Of course, He could not come up with any answer to my objection. There are absolutely no aliens. God loved the world so much that He gave us His only begotten Son. If there were indeed aliens, there would have been no need for Jesus to be born only on this earth.

After massive investments and research, we have already been able to reach the moon, and our probes have landed even on Mars, but we have not discovered a single evidence that indicates the existence of life forms outside the earth. I can confidently assert, based on the Scripture, that regardless of how developed mankind's scientific and technological capabilities become, and regardless how extensively we search the universe, we will never find extraterrestrials. The Bible tells us that no other created thing can separate us from the love of God in our Lord Jesus Christ. What, then, is this love of God? This is no other than the gospel of the water and the Spirit. This is God's love. The salvation that has saved us and made us sinless with the gospel of the water and the Spirit is the love of God, and nothing can separate us from this love.

Paul speaks of faith again in chapter 9, but it is in his conclusion of chapter 8 where the apex of faith is reached. Chapters 1 through 8 of the Book of Romans form a theme, and with chapter 8 as its concluding chapter, it is here where the height of faith is reached. As the Word of God in chapter 8 shows us, only those who believe in the gospel of the water and the Spirit can become inseparable from the love of God.

Those who do not believe so, however, will never be so. They may perhaps be able to live for the Lord temporarily, but they cannot defend their faith and live for Him until their deaths. They may live religiously for 10, 20 years, but their faith will eventually decay and die out, rendering them completely separated from and having nothing to do with God. It is not that their works are lacking, but that the love in their hearts for Christ will disappear from them. Since they do not have the Holy Spirit in their minds, they neither have love for the Lord in their hearts. There is, in short, sin in their hearts instead.

As days go by, I realize even more how deep and how perfect the love of salvation is, with which our Lord has saved us through the gospel of the water and the Spirit. When I first met the Lord, my depth of appreciation for Christ's love was quiet and calm, as a stone thrown into a lake causes small, barely perceptible waves. My response was only a quiet realization of the fact that Jesus took away all my sins, and that I had thus become sinless. But while living a life of preaching the gospel since then, the waves in my heart have become unimaginably larger and deeper, as if a bomb had gone off inside my heart.

Who says that we should believe only in the blood of the Cross? Did Paul say this? In the Book of Romans, Paul clearly and unambiguously spoke of the gospel of the water and the Spirit: *"Or do you not know that as many of us as were baptized into Christ Jesus were baptized into His death? Therefore we were buried with Him through baptism into death, that just as Christ was raised from the dead by the glory of the Father, even so we also should walk in newness of life"* (Romans 6:3-4).

Isn't this gospel of the water and the Spirit utterly great and thoroughly perfect? Regardless of how small one's faith is, if one believes in the gospel of the water and the Spirit, then he/she is saved from sin. Regardless of how many shortcomings you have, your faith is made whole by the gospel of the water and the Spirit. Regardless of how weak you are, you are saved by your faith in the gospel of the water and the Spirit. Even though we have no power of our own, if we live for God and with God, all the filth will be removed from our hearts.

But those who do not believe from the start will in the end turn against God and leave Him, even if they heard of this gospel and lived with it for 10 years. Those who have decided to neither see nor hear the truth of God by closing their eyes and shutting their ears are so foolish for rejecting God's blessing with their own hands and heading toward their own deaths. They crucify Christ everyday with their sins, even though there would have been no death on the Cross were it not for the baptism of Jesus.

I realize with every passing day just how great and perfect this gospel is—the weaker I get, the more I realize how awesome and whole the love of our Lord is, shown by this gospel, and I thank Him even more for it. The more I preach this gospel, the louder I become; the more I preach this gospel, the stronger I become; and the more I preach this true gospel, the more convinced I become.

Even if you are born again, if you do not listen to the Word of God and do not serve Him, weeds will start growing in your mind, and because of these weeds, your mind will become desolate. When this happens, sing your songs of praise again and think of Jehovah. By singing praises to God, your mind will be cleansed and you will be able to raise your spirit again.

You should shake your mind to discharge it of everything that is impure, and renew your heart again by filling it with the Word of God. Our hearts are already cleansed, but when the impurities of the world enter our minds and tries to confuse and disorient us, we can worship God and pray to Him again by singing praises of the Lord, renewing and re-raising our hearts.

Regardless of where we may find ourselves, praising God is a joyful and exhilarating experience. There is no sin in the minds of those who have been redeemed, so praising and rejoicing comes naturally from their minds. Our joyful hearts' songs of praise can make the weeds that grow in our minds disappear.

At times, our weaknesses are revealed. Because our thoughts and feelings can easily change through different circumstances, though we may be happy and in a good mood when we are with our brothers in Christ, we may have unclean and impure thoughts when we are by ourselves. This is why Paul cried out, when looking at his own flesh, *"O wretched man that I am! Who will deliver me from this body of death? I thank God–through Jesus Christ our Lord!"*

Paul had become whole by being saved by the gospel of the water and the Spirit, even though he was still weak in his flesh. Was Paul the only person who was like this? I, too, am like Paul. Are you not also like him?

When worldly people gather together, the men usually like to drink, often talking about their jobs and who got promoted and who didn't, and so on, while the women busily boast of their husbands, children, homes, and so forth. But the conversations among the righteous are qualitatively different from those of the worldly people. Even as we share our bread together, we talk about the souls that were saved throughout the world: in India, Japan, Europe, Africa, the United States, and so on, praising God and sharing fellowship with our minds.

When reading the Book of Romans, we can experience and share in our hearts Paul's own faith. We can also find out how great the salvation given by God is. We can feel the awesomeness of the gospel. We can understand the passages and discover the meanings hidden in the text. Because we realize how complete and perfect the salvation of our Lord is, we cannot help but praise His righteousness.

Even if the whole world were to change right now, the gospel of the water and the Spirit that has saved us from our sins would remain unchanged. Because the love of Christ has saved us, and because this love has never left us and still remains in us, all we have to do is turn our hearts away from the world and focus on God again. We are weak, and because of this weakness, we sometimes fall into the ways of the world, but every time this happens, we only have to turn our minds toward God and believe in the truth that our Lord has saved us. Our flesh has yet to change and still lives under the law of sin. We must thus continuously deny our flesh and live our lives by our spiritual thoughts. In order to stop the weeds from growing in our hearts, we must always return to God and praise His righteousness.

Do you now realize how powerful this gospel of the water and the Spirit is? Since the entire Book of Romans is based on the gospel of the water and the Spirit, we cannot unlock the Word of God without first believing in this gospel.

I thank the Lord for allowing us to open and see the secrets of this Word. No one can separate us from the righteousness of God, which is the love of Christ. If you want to believe in the righteousness of God, believe in the baptism of Jesus by John and His blood on the Cross as your redemption and salvation. You, too, will then receive the righteousness of God.

May the blessings of the righteousness of our God be with you. ✉

CHAPTER

9

Introduction to Chapter 9

The gospel of the water and the Spirit to both the Israelites and the Gentiles!

Why did Paul say that he has great sorrow and continual grief in his heart for his own countrymen? It's because Paul had a wish for his fellow brethren, so dear to his heart that he was willing to be accursed and be cut off from Christ for their sake. According to his own flesh, he truly wanted his own countrymen to be saved.

In this last age, we are greatly interested in preaching the gospel of the water and the Spirit to the entire world. Spreading this gospel of truth is of God's greatest concern and at the same time, the most important goal for the born-again believers. Whether or not the Israelis will accept the gospel of the water and the Spirit in the last days is another point that draws our attention. We must continue to pray on behalf of the Israelis so that they may be saved, for when they accept the gospel, we know that the Second Coming of our Lord is imminent.

My prayer topics for this year are to pray for the world evangelization and the acceptance of the true gospel by the Israelis. I am also praying that the Israelis will bear God's servants from their own people. God once gave His Law to the Israelites, and He also made them the kingdom of priests before His eyes. Christ Himself came, according to the flesh, from the Israelites, yet they refused to believe in Him, and are still against God by continuing to turn against His will.

The Lord told us that He would be hard to find faith when He would come again.

It is God's will that the gospel of the water and the Spirit, having originated from Jerusalem, would spread all over the world. However, people's hearts are hardened nowadays. Many people have strayed away from seeking the truth.

Recently, a movie titled "The Last Temptation of Christ" that depicted Jesus as an illegitimate child was released in Korea. It was full of blasphemies and its central message was that Jesus was never God, but only an ordinary man, as Prince Siddhartha of India, better known as Buddha, was. This movie tramples on the truth that Jesus is God and our Savior. This is why God said, *"When the Son of Man comes, will He really find faith on the earth?" (Luke 18:8)*

Jesus Christ, in whom we believe, is God, higher than any of His creations, and worthy of praise for eternity. Born into the Israelites, He took upon all the sins of mankind by being baptized by John, bled and died on the Cross, rose again from death the third day, and became the Savior to all those who believe in Him. The Lord, who became the righteousness of God, delivered us from our sins by justifying those who believe in Him.

Paul told us that regardless of how many Israelites there are, Abraham's descendants, those who can become the children of God are only those who believe in Jesus.

The Israelis will be facing many trials and tribulations in the future. God's will is that some of them will in the end come to believe in our Lord as their Savior. Even though our Lord has taken away all the sins of the world, including those of the Israelis, they still refuse to believe in Jesus as their Savior.

Are you weak? Some of us may be weaker or stronger than others. But before God, we are all full of infirmities. We can become God's children, who are free from sin, only by believing that our Lord came to this earth, took our sins on His shoulders by His baptism, and was judged and punished in our stead by dying on the Cross. We must praise and believe in the power of God that has made us His people, free from sin. Our Lord is truly great.

Some people think that everything exists because of men. For instance, they think that laws are enacted by men, and exist for them. However, we must realize that not everything is originated from men; things are only made possible by God's will. God created this world and the entire universe. Even the man-made laws that govern us are grounded, at their essence, in God's will.

Because God works in everything and everything unfolds according to His will, we must discover His righteousness in all things. When we were weak, when we sinned against God, and when we were cut off from Him because of our sinfulness, God promised to send us Jesus Christ. He fulfilled His promise by the incarnation of Jesus and His baptism, through which He delivered us from the sins of the world.

Now, when the gospel of the water and the Spirit spreads into every corner of the world, God's original plan will be completed. When we look at how the events in the world are unfolding, we can see that the United States and Israel are at the center. I believe that without God's intervention, another world war is very much a possibility.

When the World Trade Centers collapsed, its tremendous impact was felt throughout the world. If the world is engulfed in war again, in this time and age, what will happen to us? We will surely not be able to recover from another world war. Even nature cannot recover from all the damages of total destruction by us. I hope that you will all pray so as to be able to preach the gospel of the water and the Spirit to the entire world in peace. Our worry is that without peace in the world, we may not be able to do so. We should all pray for peace, and strive to eliminate war and terrorism.

No man-made religion can eliminate man's sins. Only Jesus Christ, and He alone, can deliver us from our sins. Only through His baptism by John and His blood on the Cross can our sins be blotted out and judged. This blessing is given to those who believe in the righteousness of God. The only way we can be delivered from our sins is by believing in Christ's baptism and His blood. There is no other way. We are not atoned by ritualistic prayers of repentance, as many religious people prefer to do. Rather, the only way to the atonement of our sins is to believe in the righteousness of God that has delivered us from all our sins, completely and fully, through the incarnation of Jesus, who took away all our sins by His baptism and death on the Cross.

We are saved from all our sins by believing in the truth of the gospel of the water and the Spirit

This truth must be preached to every corner of the world. We must recognize that it is the sin of Israelis as well as of Gentiles to not believe in this truth. Everyone must believe in the gospel of the water and the Spirit.

Both nationalities, Israelis and Gentiles, cannot but continue to sin while living in this world. But our Lord took care of all these sins, once and for all, by His baptism. Could there be any simpler and clearer truth than the truth of Jesus' baptism and His blood on the Cross? Why did John baptize Jesus? He was baptized by John and crucified so that He could at once take away all our sins. By not believing in this truth or accepting it into their hearts, people are heading toward their own destructions because of their sins.

The baptism that Jesus received *"for thus"* (Matthew 3:15) fulfills all righteousness. The word 'for thus' is *'hutos'* in Greek, which means 'in this way,' 'most fitting,' or 'there is no other way besides this.' This word shows that Jesus irreversibly took the sins of humankind onto Him through the baptism He received from John. Because Jesus took upon all the sins of the world by being baptized by John, He was able to carry the Cross and bleed on it on our behalf. We must realize that this is the truth of atonement by which the entire human race can be redeemed of its sins.

Our Lord told us, *"If you abide in My word, you are My disciples indeed. And you shall know the truth, and the truth shall make you free."* Jesus' baptism and His blood are God's truth, which delivers us from our sins; it is completely grounded in God's written word. The truth of atonement is to last, with the gospel of the water and the Spirit, for eternity. That God the Father decided to have sinners atoned by Jesus' baptism and His blood on the Cross is His will. When we believe in His baptism and blood for our redemption, we believe in what God has set for us. Our sins are atoned only when we believe in the truth of the water and the Spirit.

If you believe, at this very moment, in Christ's baptism and His blood on the Cross, the truth of atonement, as your redemption, then you are now justified. If, on the other hand, you do not believe, then you are still a sinner. *"For all have sinned and fall short of the glory of God,"* We can be forgiven from all our sins and become God's children only by believing in Jesus Christ as our Savior. There is no reason why someone should not believe in the truth of this gospel of the water and the Spirit. There is no one who does not need this gospel of redemption. Everyone needs it. Why would anyone not want to believe in it, when the truth of the gospel of the water and the Spirit is so clearly set out before him/her, were it not for his/her unwillingness to be cleansed of his/her sins?

Many throughout the world have accepted the gospel of the water and the Spirit and are preaching it to spread it even further. Some of them have asked to become volunteer distributors of our books. If you could be delivered from your sins by only believing in the blood of the Cross, then everyone in this world would have become justified, free from sin. If one believes only in the blood of the Cross, one would still continue in sin, despite repeated prayers of repentance on a daily basis, as such prayers are routine, going through the motion, and merely an exercise in religious rituals.

If you are trying to wash away your sins by offering prayers of repentance, then you are actually committing a grave sin against God, for your act degrades the righteousness of God, which can be fulfilled not by your own effort, but only by the baptism of Jesus and His sacrifice on the Cross, through which Jesus took away all your sins and was punished in your place.

If you accept Jesus as your Savior, believe that your atonement is through the baptism of Jesus and His crucifixion. Jesus promised to deliver sinners from their sins, and He lived up to His promise by being baptized by John at the Jordan River and bleeding on the Cross to fulfill the righteousness of God. What reason is there for us not to believe in this truth?

You must believe in Jesus' baptism and the shedding of His blood on the Cross as your redemption.

The truth that Jesus took upon all the sins of the world on Himself when He was baptized is found in Matthew 3:13-17. Only those who are not willing to be forgiven for all their sins would refuse to believe in this truth. You can become God's child and receive eternal life only by believing in the truth of the gospel of the water and the Spirit—nothing else will deliver you from your sins. There is nothing more wonderful than believing in this truth, nothing else that is a better gift from God than His forgiveness. Among the many gifts that God has bestowed upon us, the atonement of our sins is the best gift of all.

The second-best gift that God has given to us is the coming Millennium over which we will reign, and the third gift is that we will thereafter live in the Kingdom of Heaven and reign, with God, for eternity. God has allowed, even to this last age, this truth of redemption to be revealed to both the Israelis and the Gentiles.

As prophesized in the Scripture, two servants of God will arise from among the Israelis, and God will perform wondrous miracles of the gospel through them. The Israelis will then hear the gospel of the water and the Spirit through the two servants, whom God will raise from their own people, and many will come to believe in Jesus as their Messiah. We wait for that day, as John had awaited by asking, *"Come, Lord Jesus!" (Revelation 22:20)*

When the time comes for the Lord to come again, you will realize how grateful you are for having believed in this truth, by which you were forgiven and saved. It is my heart's earnest desire that you would be delivered from all your sins by believing in the truth of the gospel of the water and the Spirit. The world may change, but the gospel of the water and the Spirit, by which God has saved us from our sins, is a never-changing and eternal truth. We must believe in this truth to receive the unchanging salvation of atonement. May the truth of God's redemption be yours.

God has delivered us by making us the vessels of mercy

Romans chapter 9 records that God saved Jacob because He loved him more than Esau. As such, Jacob was made a vessel of mercy, while Esau was made a vessel of wrath. This brings the question of why? That is, did God favor Jacob over Esau? Undoubtedly, there will be plenty of people who would argue, "Because God unilaterally and prejudicially chose to love one person while hating the other unconditionally, His predestination and selection were wrong."

When we look at the world created by God, we can see how beautiful and pure His creations are. Plants, animals, and all other things that were created by God seem so perfect. How, then, could God love one person while hating another with bias? But this is not the case.

Because of the disobediences of Adam and Eve, sin entered the world, and because of this sin, all who came after them were destined to continue in sin, and could not avoid being condemned to hell. Just because God saved Jacob from sin and did not deliver Esau, it does not implicate Him in any wrongdoing. Before His eyes, God had every reason to do so.

We can find many who behave like Esau within the Christian community. Typically, such a person would never miss a worship service, no matter when or where it is held, from early-morning service to late-night worship. Some may even spend more time in church than at home, commuting from work to church, not to home. We may call them 'religious runners'. Among them, however, are many who do not take the righteousness of God seriously. This is because they are trying to build their own righteousness, and in doing so, are ignoring God's righteousness.

Even those who ignore God's righteousness still want to go to heaven and have their sins forgiven. But their efforts are in trying to establish their own righteousness before God and other people, not in trying to be saved from their sins. God said to those who do not believe in His righteousness that the faith in God's righteousness is not for everyone.

What kind of people, then, can believe in God's righteousness? These are the people who recognize their sinfulness, who, in their own minds, realize that they are worthy of nothing. They are the kind of people who, when they discover God's righteousness through His atonement manifested in the gospel of the water and the Spirit, immediately believe in it and turn the glory to God. That we believe in God's righteousness and are thus saved means that we are pitiable people who need God's righteousness. Otherwise, we would be doomed to live in sin for the rest of our lives.

But those who seek their own righteousness before God are those who are prideful. Such a person might say, "Lord, I gave you tithe, stayed up all night offering prayers to you, never missed the daily early-morning services for the past ten years, and have done good deeds for you."

However, God would be more pleased if he had

recognized that he/she had no righteousness at all, and thus needed to believe in God's righteousness through the atonement of the water and the Spirit, rather than trying to prove, by his/her own effort, something that he/she does not and cannot have.

Even now, in the Christian community, there are plenty of people who are doing all kinds of things to try to show their own righteousness. Some even faithfully act out their words. But because they do not believe in God's righteousness manifested through the gospel of the water and the Spirit, their sins are not completely washed away. God will determine their ends. We all hope that they would become God's true children through the remission of sins by their faith in our Lord's baptism and blood as the truth of atonement.

On the vessels of salvation, the Apostle Paul said that God has mercy on whomever He has mercy, and has compassion on whomever He has compassion. Who, then, are the people who receive God's mercy? All human beings cannot live by God's Word, even though they really want to do so. They stumble over and over again despite their truthful desire to believe in and live by His Word. They end up feeling sorry before God, are guilt-ridden, and think that they deserve to be condemned to hell. Thus, they ask God to have mercy on them, recognizing that they are pitiable in both this earthly world and in the Kingdom of God. Because they know that they cannot be saved unless God has mercy on them, they desperately ask Him for it.

Deliverance from sin, in other words, is found for those whom God pities, and on whom He has mercy. For these people, God bestowed the gospel of the water and the Spirit by having His only begotten Son take upon all the sins for Himself with His baptism, die on the Cross, and be resurrected from death—all to deliver them from their certain destructions. Our Father has mercy on those who are pitiable.

But there seem to be more people on whom God has wrath, than those on whom He has mercy in this world. God told us that in today's Christian community, there are both the vessels of mercy and the vessels of wrath. There are, in other words, people who are loved by God and people who are not loved by Him.

Romans 9:17 tells us, *"For the Scripture says to the Pharaoh, 'For this very purpose I have raised you up, that I may show My power in you, and that My name may be declared in all the earth.'"* God allowed people like the Pharaoh to arise so that His power may be known. However, to the vessels of mercy He has shown His love, so that His name may be declared throughout the world. Because of our sins and God's wrath, we were all destined for hell. But we were saved from all our sins as God has bestowed on us His love of righteousness, for He had mercy on those of us who believed in Him.

Those who do not believe in the righteousness of God and are only interested in pursuing their own righteousness are turning against God. These are the people that God has left for His wrath; for His powerful wrath to be demonstrated, there must be those who stand against Him, and through this, the justice of God's judgment is shown.

People like the Pharaoh are those who have rejected the love of God's righteousness. To Pharaoh, God gave ten plagues; the last one being death. To those who have rejected God, only the endless lake of fire awaits them. This is the wrath of God's power. There are many powerful people in this world and many who deny God, but God will eventually bring them down, to proclaim the power of His wrath. This is why He leaves the hardened hearts of those who deny Him alone.

What is important for us, then, is how we can become the vessels of mercy, because by becoming this, we can believe in the love of God's righteousness. We have nothing to show for before God; rather, we were born to believe in His righteous love. The Bible tells us a story about a tax collector and a Pharisee praying before God. God had mercy on the former, while He had none for the latter. People who are like the tax collector are those who recognize before God that they have done nothing good and that they have only fallen short of His glory; therefore asking God for His mercy.

These are the kinds of people who would be clothed in God's love of righteousness. But people who are like the Pharisee constantly brag about how much they have done for God—that they gave tithes, that they fasted twice a week, that they prayed, and that they were religiously devout. Depending on where we stand before God, we will be either clothed in the love of God's righteousness or be subjected to the wrath of His punishment. If we harden our hearts before God, our sins will forever remain unforgivable. Without forgiveness, our destiny would be hell.

The gospel of the water and the Spirit has been preached all over the world. The unsaved remain unsaved just because their hearts are hardened. There is nothing righteous in humans, and only by faith can we be clothed in God's righteous love. God hates those who, even though God made them, refuse to recognize His righteousness. But those who believe in the gospel of the water and the Spirit, the righteousness of God, will all be loved by Him and receive eternal lives.

Many Christians in this world today are living as the vessels of wrath before God. This is why we need to learn from the Book of Romans what the righteousness of God is. The reason why God loves some, and not others, is because some believe in His righteousness while others do not believe in it. This is the truth that I wish to speak of. What God did to Jacob and Esau was right. Among those who believe in Jesus, there are many who want to be loved by God without having believed in the gospel of the water and the Spirit. These people are like Esau, and God will judge them for their sins accordingly.

God has sent His Son to be baptized by John in order to take away at once all the sins in the world. Do you believe in this truth? Do you truly believe it deep inside your heart? We will at once be delivered from all our sins when we believe in the truth of the gospel of the water and the Spirit, by which the righteousness of God is shown. Jesus took away all the sins of this world and put them on His shoulder, died on the Cross, and was resurrected from death, all at once, so that we, too, may at once be freed from our sins.

But if we attempt to be atoned without believing in God's righteousness, we would be sinning against Him. If we do not believe in His righteousness, then it would mean that Jesus Christ would have to be baptized and die everyday for our sins. Would God, in His infinite wisdom, choose such a way? To deliver us from our sins, God sent His Son only once, to be baptized, crucified, and resurrected for all our sins only once, so that He may save us completely all at once.

Our God is a righteous God. God planned the remission of our sins within His righteousness. God does not blot our sins out just because we pray for His forgiveness every time we sin.

Instead, He blotted out all the sins of those who were at once redeemed by believing in His righteousness once and for all.

What, then, happens to the daily sins that we commit afterward? These are taken care of when we thankfully worship God for His righteousness and turn all the glory to Him only. From God's viewpoint, Jesus at once took upon Himself all the sins of the world with His baptism, bled on the Cross and was judged in our stead, and thus at once took away all our sins, for our complete salvation. The love of God's righteousness had been completed from His plan to eliminate all the sins of the world at once.

Romans 9:25 states, *"As He says also in Hosea: 'I will call them My people, who were not My people, And her beloved, who was not beloved.'"* Yes, God said that He would call them His people, who were not His people. Because the righteousness of God in which we believe is not a theory, but reality, we are delivered from all our sins by believing in His righteousness. Since it is a reality, those who ignore His righteousness will be hated and judged like Esau. There is no one who can boast of his/her righteousness before God.

To deliver us from all our sins, God saved us with His righteousness. How, then, can we not thank and praise Him? We cannot help but spread the gospel of the righteousness of God in thankfulness and faith. ✉

We Must Know That Predestination was Planned within God's Righteousness

< Romans 9:9-33 >

"For this is the word of promise: 'At this time I will come and Sarah shall have a son.' And not only this, but when Rebecca also had conceived by one man, even by our father Isaac (for the children not yet being born, nor having done any good or evil, that the purpose of God according to election might stand, not of works but of Him who calls), it was said to her, 'The older shall serve the younger.' As it is written, 'Jacob I have loved, but Esau I have hated.' What shall we say then? Is there unrighteousness with God? Certainly not! For He says to Moses, 'I will have mercy on whomever I will have mercy, and I will have compassion on whomever I will have compassion.' So then it is not of him who wills, nor of him who runs, but of God who shows mercy. For the Scripture says to the Pharaoh, 'For this very purpose I have raised you up, that I may show My power in you, and that My name may be declared in all the earth.' Therefore He has mercy on whom He wills, and whom He wills He hardens. You will say to me then, 'Why does He still find fault? For who has resisted His will?' But indeed, O man, who are you to reply against God? Will the thing formed say to him who formed it, 'Why have you made me

like this?' Does not the potter have power over the clay,
from the same lump to make one vessel for honor and
another for dishonor? What if God, wanting to show His
wrath and to make His power known, endured with much
longsuffering the vessels of wrath prepared for destruction,
and that He might make known the riches of His glory on
the vessels of mercy, which He had prepared beforehand
for glory, even us whom He called, not of the Jews only, but
also of the Gentiles? As He says also in Hosea:

'I will call them My people, who were not My people,
And her beloved, who was not beloved.'
'And it shall come to pass in the place where it was
said to them,
'You are not My people,'
There they shall be called sons of the living God.'
Isaiah also cries out concerning Israel:
'Though the number of the children of Israel be as the
sand of the sea,
The remnant will be saved.
For He will finish the work and cut it short in
righteousness,
Because the LORD will make a short work upon the
earth.'
And as Isaiah said before:
'Unless the LORD of Sabaoth had left us a seed,
We would have become like Sodom,
And we would have been made like Gomorrah.'
What shall we say then? That Gentiles, who did not
pursue righteousness, have attained to righteousness, even
the righteousness of faith; but Israel, pursuing the law of
righteousness, has not attained to the law of righteousness.
Why? Because they did not seek it by faith, but as it were,

by the works of the law. For they stumbled at that stumbling stone. As it is written:

'Behold, I lay in Zion a stumbling stone and rock of offense,

And whoever believes on Him will not be put to shame.'"

What is the true predestination planned by God?

Let us now turn our attention to what 'predestination planned by God' is. In order to understand precisely what predestination is, we must regard the written Word as God's Word, and correct ourselves if there is anything wrong in our faiths. For this, we must first understand why God loved Jacob while He hated Esau. We also need to find out whether or not the contemporary Christian understanding of predestination deviates from the Scripture. We must all have an accurate understanding of the predestination established by God.

To receive blessings from God, we Christians need to find out how God's predestination fits into His plan. When thinking of God's plan, many contemporary Christians think that their destinies were predetermined before their births, without any relevance to their faiths, as if the fates of Jacob and Esau were unconditionally and unilaterally determined by God. But this is not the case. Whether we are loved by God or not is determined by whether we believe in His righteousness or not. This is the truth that God has given to us in His plan.

If you want to correctly understand God's predestination, you need to throw away your own thinking and focus on the righteousness of God

Because many people cannot think of and believe in the righteousness of God manifested through Jesus Christ, they tend to think of God's love in whatever way that they may choose, and some even think that God's love is not just. They must realize that this is not the right way to think. We need to cast away our wrongly arrived convictions of faith by not considering God's righteous plan, manifested through Jesus Christ. If you simply think that God loves some while He hates others, you must realize that this is a wrong kind of faith, concocted by your own wrong thinking.

Human minds are plagued by mistaken thoughts. Many contemporary Christians do not have the right faiths because their minds are too often overflowing with wrong thoughts. This is why you need to throw away your worthless thoughts and put your faith on the right path by following the Word of God and believing in His righteousness.

Because predestination is planned within the righteousness of God, it can be correctly understood and believed only when we believe in His righteousness. We must therefore have faith in His plan and in His righteousness. God's plan is to clothe those who believe in His love within His righteousness in righteousness.

Thus, His predestination is that He would make the believers His people by clothing them with the salvation of the remission of sins, paid for by Jesus' baptism and His crucifixion. We must establish the right relationship with God by having faith in the truth planned by Him within His righteousness. God has made those who are like Jacob the

objects of His love, while He has made those who are like Esau
the objects of His wrath.

God's predestination is not that of fatalism.

Predestination within God's plan was established within
His righteousness. God's love is not something set arbitrarily
without any plan. If everyone was unconditionally elected
before his or her birth, as if his/her life was set by fate, how
could one be delivered from sin by believing in the
righteousness of Jesus? If one's fate was set before his/her birth
in such a way that whether or not he/she was to be loved by
God was a preplanned and predetermined outcome, who would
think that God is just, and who would believe in such a God?
No one would want to believe in such an arbitrary and
dictatorial God.

But our God's plan is neither arbitrary nor dictatorial, but
only to deliver us from our sins within His righteousness and to
make us His people. God gave us His righteousness within this
plan, and within this righteousness of love, He gave us His
forgiveness. He has prepared to clothe those who believe in the
love of His righteousness in love, and those who do not believe
in it in wrath.

I would like to say the following to those who are
resentful of God's predestination under a misunderstanding.
God's plan is to make us, who were created by Him, His own
people. We must therefore be thankful for His predestination. It
is better for us to be the thankful people who believe in God's
righteousness than to be the resentful ones who reproach Him.
Everyone who believes in Jesus as his/her Savior must have an

accurate understanding of and faith in God's predestination, planned within His righteousness.

God's true predestination was established by Him who calls

Today's passage says, from Romans 9:9, *"For this is the word of promise: 'At this time I will come and Sarah shall have a son.' And not only this, but when Rebecca also had conceived by one man, even by our father Isaac (for the children not yet being born, nor having done any good or evil, that the purpose of God according to election might stand, not of works but of Him who calls), it was said to her, 'The older shall serve the younger.' As it is written, 'Jacob I have loved, but Esau I have hated.'"*

This passage tells us that God's predestination is that of love, planned within the love of God's righteousness. As shown in Genesis 18:10, although it was humanly impossible for Sarah to bear a child, Abraham believed in God's promise because He had given His word. This is how God justified Abraham: God gave his son Isaac to him because he believed in Him, and God approved his faith.

So when we talk about faith in the righteousness of God, we are talking about faith in the Word of God. Our discussion of God's plan and predestination should also be guided by our faith in His Word. Those who do otherwise—when, for instance, people confuse their pursuit of the righteousness of God with illusions or signs they claim to have seen while praying or dreaming–are making a huge mistake with their faiths.

Paul further adds that, *"Rebecca also had conceived by*

one man, even by our father Isaac (for the children not yet being born, nor having done any good or evil, that the purpose of God according to election might stand, not of works but of Him who calls), it was said to her, 'The older shall serve the younger.'"

The Scripture tells us that Isaac, having no child of his own, prayed to God, and God answered him by giving him twins. We can see that the predestination planned within God's righteousness has a certain relationship with the faiths of those who are loved by Him.

It is worth repeating verse 11 here again: *"for the children not yet being born, nor having done any good or evil, that the purpose of God according to election might stand, not of works but of Him who calls."* The key to understanding the truth of predestination and election within God's plan is that the purpose of God stands "of Him who calls." Between Jacob and Esau, according to the predestination within God's plan, God called and loved Jacob.

When God calls people and loves them, in other words, He calls and loves people who, like Jacob, are far from being righteous. God did not call Esau, who thought of himself as righteous and was full of pride. In God's predestination set within His plan, it is a matter of course that God would call and love people like Jacob. God's purpose in calling people like Jacob was to make sinners into His own children, free from sin. He who calls to clothe the called in love is God, and between Jacob and Esau, he who was called was Jacob.

We must know and believe in the righteousness of God within His plan. Jacob represents the typical figure of a sinner to whom God has shown His mercy within His righteousness, while Esau represents one who turns against God by ignoring

His righteous love and pursuing their own righteousness. This is why the key to disclosing God's Word on predestination set within His plan is to understand that the purpose of God stands "of Him who calls."

We must free ourselves from the illusory faiths created by our own thoughts. God could, within His righteousness, only love Jacob and hate Esau. God's explanation of His plan and predestination is provided to everyone through His declaration that the purpose of God stands "of Him who calls." God's plan is the truth of love fulfilled within His righteousness. When God loved Jacob but hated Esau, the predestination was meant to fulfill the righteousness of God, according to His plan for salvation.

It is not, as claimed by many other religions, by good works that you are loved and saved by God, but only by believing in His plan and His righteousness do you become His children, redeemed from your sins.

Is God wrong?

God loves those who believe and love His righteousness. There is, in other words, nothing wrong with the fact that our Father decided to love and make those who believe in the righteousness of God within Jesus Christ His children. God did not plan to love everyone in Jesus Christ, but to love people like Jacob.

We must, then, ask ourselves whether we are like Jacob or Esau. But even those who are full of their own good deeds and their own righteousness still want to be loved by God, but no one can stop them from rushing down the wrong path. So these two kinds of people are always there, loved or hated by God even as we speak now.

We must give thanks to God and praise His glory by believing in His righteous love and His plan for our salvation. We should also thank Him for the fact that the gospel of the water and the Spirit, in which we believe, wondrously reflects upon the righteousness of God. Everyone must realize that to be clothed in God's love, he/she must first recognize his/her own infirmities and sins before God, and believe in His righteousness.

The problem is that many Christians, unable to believe in Jesus' baptism and the truth of the Cross that fulfilled the righteousness of God, wrongly believe that God loves certain people while others are simply fated to be abandoned by Him.

Even more problematic is the unfortunate fact that this kind of unsound faith is prevailing and being preached to others with great conviction. It is quickly being spread; leading to more and more people who misunderstand God's love, shown by God's predestination planned by Him. What God is trying to tell us with the story of Jacob and Esau is that to become His children, it is not human righteousness that is needed, but only the faith in the love of God's righteousness, predestined according to His plan.

The Scripture tells us that God gave Sarah the son that He promised to Abraham. This tells us, even today, that only those who have faith in the love and the Word of the righteousness of God can become His children. To become such children, we must recognize the truth that was given with our faiths in God's righteousness and His plan, and to believe in this truth, we need to believe in God's love and His righteousness.

Jesus Christ's love toward us and God's plan for us is the absolute truth and love given to all of us. To save us from our sins, Jesus took upon all our sins with His baptism, died on the Cross and was resurrected from death, all to give those of us who believe in Him eternal lives.

This truth does not mean that just by being religious and displaying our own efforts, we can become God's children, but it means that the only way to become God's children is by believing in the Word of love and the righteousness of God, told to us and planned for us by Him. We must all realize that only those who believe in God's love and righteousness are clothed in His love.

What, then, should be our disposition? To have faith in Jesus' baptism and His blood on the Cross. We must ask God to have mercy on us. We must recognize before Him that we do not deserve to be called His people, for we are all sinners. We must understand that it is only through His plan for us— that we may know His righteous love—that we can become His children.

Those who are hated by God are hated because they do not need or believe in His love and righteousness. We must therefore know and believe in the plan of love that God has predestined for us. The clear truth is that those who know and believe in the love of God's righteousness will be loved by Him, while those who reject and repudiate His love will be hated by God.

Who can receive the gospel of the water and the Spirit?

The gospel of the water and the Spirit given to us by God is the only truth that reveals His righteousness. What kind of people, then, are those who receive this truth into their hearts?

These are the people who, recognizing that their destinies lie in eternal damnation and that they are sinners before God and His Word, ask for His mercy. "I am a sinner, Lord, who cannot live by Your laws at all. I give up my heart and surrender to You." These are the people to whom God has granted the remission of sins of His love in His righteousness. The faith in the gospel that manifests God's righteousness is of utmost importance for all sinners.

God did not give us His law so that we would follow each and every clause of them, a fact often misunderstood by many. The purpose of the law, rather, was to lead us to the recognition of our own sinfulness. Why, then, do sinners attempt to follow the law? It's because every sinner's instinct seeks redemption and the absolution of his/her sins.

But no one is capable of following all the laws. The attempts were only imitations, merely instinctive mimicking, trying to cover their sins in desperation—a faith of deception before God. That's why sinners should throw away this faith of deception, turn to the faith in the righteousness of God, and be clothed in His love.

To clothe us in this love, God sent Jesus to the earth, who, in being baptized by John, took upon His shoulders the sins of the world, and by bleeding on the Cross, blotted them all out. God has recognized the faiths of those who believe in the love of His righteousness. When we are delivered from all our sins through our faith in the gospel of water and the Spirit, which is the fulfillment of the righteousness of God, we become clothed in His love. This is the promised truth that God has set out for us in His plan.

God will hate those who rely only on themselves. There are many such people around us. But you must be saved from

all your sins by believing in Jesus' baptism and His blood that
have fulfilled God's love and His righteousness. You will then
surely be clothed in God's love, which has been reserved for
those whom He calls. People often try to do things on their
own for God to win His love and forgiveness, but these efforts
are futile without any faith in the righteousness of God.

God called only Jacob to be clothed in His love, not Esau.
Before God, Jacob was a cunning and deceitful liar, but
because he believed in God's love and His righteousness, he
became one of the fathers of faith. We, too, must receive God's
love by believing in Jesus' baptism and His blood on the Cross,
the fulfillment of the righteousness of God, as our redemption.
Because Esau tried to be blessed by his father with his own
hunting, he became the symbol for those who could not earn
God's blessing. We need to spend some time thinking carefully
over this matter. Who in this world are like Esau? Are we not
like him?

People like Jacob are those who engross God's righteous
love. We know that we, too, are weak and wicked, as Jacob
was. God, who has called us even before we were born to stand
not by our works but by His call, has told us to believe in His
love and righteousness to receive His love. God sent Jesus,
who fulfilled the righteousness of God within His plan, for all
of us.

When God first called us, He came to call the sinners, not
the righteous. Those who are hated by Him are those who think
themselves to be full of their own righteousness and who do
not believe in His merciful love. Those who have such misled
faiths are hated by God and cannot be clothed in His love to be
His people. God has predestined this truth for us in His heart.
So, Paul states definitely, *"What shall we say then? Is there*

unrighteousness with God? Certainly not!"(Romans 9:14)

Those who are loved by God are those who are like Jacob

When God looks at you, are you truly the kind of person on whom He would have mercy? What reason does God need when He has compassion for whomever He has compassion for and hates whomever He hates? How can we say to God that He has done us wrong?

There are a countless number of people living on this earth. While some of them are loved by God, others are not. Does this mean that God has wronged them?

God is also a just God who judges the sins of those who have turned against His righteousness. We should avoid any misunderstandings in this matter by understanding God's plan manifested within His righteousness with our faith in this righteousness. There are many misled Christians whose hearts, like the Pharaoh, are hardened. These are the kind of people who are hated by God, as the verse 17 of this chapter explains: *"For the Scripture says to the Pharaoh, 'For this very purpose I have raised you up, that I may show My power in you, and that My name may be declared in all the earth.'"*

We all are insufficient before God. Then, we should not become like the Pharaoh. Should God hate us, who are as obstinate as the Pharaoh, for not believing in Jesus' baptism and His blood on the Cross as our redemption? Yes. People like the Pharaoh turn against God. Such people boast of and rely on their own righteousness, but their own righteousness cannot redeem them from their own sins.

What did the Pharaoh rely on? He trusted in and relied on

the Nile River. He thought that as long as he had its bountiful supplies of water, everything would be just fine. This is why God hates people like the Pharaoh. Anyone whose heart is hardened like that of the Pharaoh will be hated and accursed by God. You must not be like him. By receiving the merciful love that God has given you so freely, you can instead become His children.

Do you joyfully agree with God's righteous plan?

Is your heart prepared to receive God's righteous love predestined for you in His plan? There are some people who, though they believe in Jesus, suffer in anguish because they have misunderstood God's plan. Such people wonder, "I believe in Jesus, but did God really elect me? If He did not elect me, what use does my faith serve? What should I do then? I can't just stop believing in Jesus; what can I do? I truly believe in Jesus, but what happens if I am not in His election?"

They may then try to comfort themselves by thinking, "Since I believe in Jesus and attend church services, God must have elected me. Surely that's the case! Heaven will certainly have a spot for me!" But when they fall into sin, they wonder again, "God must have not elected me! It might be time for me to quit believing in Jesus!" In other words, they think by themselves, conclude by themselves, and end everything by themselves. These people particularly need to rethink their understanding of God's plan and attain the right comprehension to believe in Jesus as their Savior.

Those who believe more in theologians' teachings than God's own Word, on the other hand, might say, "Didn't God say that the older shall serve the younger, and that He loved

Jacob while He hated Esau, even before they were born? Since we believe in Jesus now, surely we must have been set to be saved even before our own births." But the Apostle Paul tells us that the predestination planned by God is *"to stand, not of works but of Him who calls."*

Following the law does not make one God's child. Only by having faith in the righteousness of God and His mercy and love shown by Jesus' baptism and His blood on the Cross can we become His children.

Because of doctrines set by theologians, many people are unable to believe in Jesus' baptism and His blood, the manifestation of the righteousness of God, as their salvation. Those who have heard the gospel's love, showing His righteousness, yet do not believe in it are just like the Pharaoh. God hates those who, without believing in the righteousness of God revealed in Jesus Christ, try to become God's children by believing in Jesus according to their own tastes.

If you did not believe in God's righteous love shown through Jesus Christ, it is time for you to do so. Then, you will be clothed in God's love. We were all like Esau originally, yet we were at once saved from our sins by believing in the love of the righteousness of God. We have received God's blessed love by believing in His righteousness.

God has made available, to both the Israelites and the Gentiles, the blessing of allowing those who believe in His righteous love to become His children. Just as God said, *"I will call them My people, who were not My people, And her beloved, who was not beloved,"* He has given us the gospel of Jesus' baptism and His blood, and to those of us who believe in it, His righteous love.

The following passage, *"And it shall come to pass in the*

*place where it was said to them, 'You are not My people,' There
they shall be called sons of the living God,"* is God's Word of
love that has been fulfilled for us today. We can thus realize
that because we came so short before God, God saved us by
coming to us in flesh and making the love of His righteousness
available to us.

That you and I are saved from all our sins before God is
the redeeming love that has been planned within the
righteousness of God. To be redeemed from all our sins by
believing in the love of God's righteousness, without hardening
our hearts, can only be possible by the faith in the truth. Except
for this way of faith, there is no other way to receive the
remission of sins. We all are born with stubborn hearts, but the
Word of God can win over our hearts and our obstinacy. Our
hearts would then be ruled by God's peace. If you believe in
God, the righteousness of God will be yours.

If the gospel of the truth that contains the righteousness of
God we are preaching did not exist, everyone in this world
would be facing his or her own destruction. Without those who
are spreading the gospel of the water and the Spirit, all of
mankind would have lost its hope. Were it not for those who
are clothed in God's righteous love, the world would have
already come to its end, with everyone having been judged of
their sins. But God has left on this earth those of us who
believe in the love of His righteousness. We can be only
thankful to God that He works through us, despite our many
weaknesses and shortcomings.

The faith that is clothed in the love of the righteousness of
God is the righteousness that has come from Jesus' baptism
and His blood on the Cross. The faith in the righteousness of
God is found in a heart that believes in Jesus' baptism and His

blood. It is through our faiths in His righteousness that we are delivered from our sins. This truth is the plan, predestination, and election that God has set for us.

God has said that whoever believes in the Word of God, which fulfills His righteousness in Jesus Christ, will be saved from his or her sins. One faces destruction not because the righteousness of God has not eliminated all the sins, but because in his/her hardened heart, he/she did not believe in it.

We must make our hearts meek before the Word of God and believe in the gospel of the water and the Spirit. Our hearts must kneel before Him. We were blessed by believing in the love of the righteousness of God. He saved us from all our sins because He had so much mercy for us. We give thanks to Him. We who believe in the righteousness of God have nothing to be ashamed of. On the contrary, we have every reason to be proud of His righteousness.

That God has save us wholly from our sins is because we have come short before Him—praise the Lord for this salvation! To be loved by God, we must be able to believe in His righteousness.

Do you know this righteousness of God? If so, then believe in it. God's righteous love will then come to your heart. May your faith in the love of the righteousness of God that He has planned for you be free from misunderstanding.

May the love of redemption that God has set for you come to your heart. Hallelujah! I give thanks to the triune God who has made us His children in His righteousness. ✉

Is It Wrong for God to Love Jacob?

< Romans 9:30-33 >

"What shall we say then? That Gentiles, who did not pursue righteousness, have attained to righteousness, even the righteousness of faith; but Israel, pursuing the law of righteousness, has not attained to the law of righteousness. Why? Because they did not seek it by faith, but as it were, by the works of the law. For they stumbled at that stumbling stone. As it is written:

'Behold, I lay in Zion a stumbling stone and rock of offense,

And whoever believes on Him will not be put to shame.'"

In calling upon all of us, our Lord said, *"I did not come to call the righteous, but sinners, to repentance" (Matthew 9:13)*. We should realize that to those who pursue their own righteousness, the gift of salvation is not permitted, and to avoid this, we must instead believe in the righteousness of God.

Romans 9:13 says that God loved Jacob while He hated Esau. To those who receive with thanks the righteousness of God, God has given them the gift of the remission of sins, as well as the blessing that makes them His people. We must all believe in God with the knowledge of His righteousness.

We should learn and understand the Word of the righteousness of God given to us all. When one wants to be delivered from one's sins, one must first know his/her own shortcomings and infirmities, as well as the righteousness of God. We must know and believe in His righteousness. God told us that only those who know that they are bound for hell are in need of His righteousness. It is important that we recognize our own sins and realize that because of our sins, we face God's wrath that will make our punishment in hell unavoidable.

But we can receive into our hearts the gospel of the water and the Spirit through our Lord's baptism, His death on the Cross and His resurrection, because only those who know the righteousness of God can believe in this righteousness. This is because God's grace and love are not something that can be earned even by prayers of repentance or a life of piety, which many religious people engage in. However, the remission of sins given by God is for all those who adore and believe in His righteousness.

We must all be ready to believe in the gospel of the water and the Spirit willingly in our hearts. Do you want to receive the righteousness of God? Then admit before God and by His law your own insufficiencies. Recognize that because of your sins, you are under God's wrath, and that you need His righteousness! When you believe in the gospel of the water and the Spirit and accept it into your heart, the righteousness of God will be yours. You must know this truth.

The minds of those who do not believe in the righteousness of God are confused and locked in void.

God told us that our thoughts were confused from the beginning (Genesis 1:2). Why were man's thoughts confused from the beginning? This is because the fallen angel that turned against God prevented people from believing in the Word of the righteousness of God by making their minds confused and void. This is why sin came to man's heart (Genesis 3:1-8).

The Scripture tells us that an angel created by God turned against Him. This angel tried to take over God's throne with his own strength and scheme, and having failed at the rebellion, was driven out from his privileged position. This Fallen Angel then enticed and deceived mankind, and turned them against God. This angel is called Satan. This prideful angel still works in both believers and non-believers alike in all kinds of boastful and rebellious manners. By deceiving man, he challenged the Word of the righteousness of God and His authority.

The Devil always resorts to lies so that people would not be able to believe in the gospel of the water and the Spirit. Having been deceived by the Devil, many fruitlessly try to establish their own righteousness. He let mankind fall into sin, and as a result, made them live their lives with confused and void minds.

The remission of sins and the righteousness given by God

Deliverance from sin for mankind, which has fallen into sin by Satan's evil temptation, does not depend on one's eagerness or his/her own righteousness. However, so many people try to desperately escape from their sins in vain while turning against God without realizing their own infirmities. God rebuked those who seek their own righteousness, those who try to earn the righteousness of God with their good deeds. Redemption is not for such people; only to those who know that they are sinners, and who believe in the true gospel of the water and the Spirit, has God allowed His righteousness.

The sovereign will of God is in its essence different from human thoughts. Paul told us that regardless of how well a person excels in outward manifestations of religious piety-church attendance, late-night prayers, early-morning prayers, fasting, offerings, repentance prayer, etc-he/she would never be able to cleanse away his/her own sins.

God tells us that the works of the law cannot redeem us from our sins and make the righteousness of God ours. As verses 32-33 of chapter 9 says, *"Why? Because they did not seek it by faith, but as it were, by the works of the law. For they stumbled at that stumbling stone. As it is written: 'Behold, I lay in Zion a stumbling stone and rock of offense, And whoever believes on Him will not be put to shame.'"*

As such, to receive the righteousness of God, we must believe in Jesus' baptism and His blood on the Cross, through which Jesus became the sacrificial offering between God and mankind. It is therefore absolutely critical that you understand that you must throw away your own righteousness in order to obtain the righteousness of God. We should not reject the righteousness of God, given to us freely, while we confess Jesus as our Savior.

Even now, many who confess the Lord Jesus as their Savior still remain as sinners because they do not believe in the gospel that manifests the righteousness of God. People cannot earn the righteousness of God by following His law. Those who believe in the Word of the righteousness of God must cast away the pursuits of their own righteousness. You should remember that Jesus became the stumbling stone to those who pursued their redemption and the righteousness of God by their own works of the law.

The gospel of the water and the Spirit, given to us by God, is the truth that redeems those who believe in Jesus Christ as their Savior, and that must accompany those who pursue the righteousness of God. What is absolutely necessary for redemption and eternal life is the faith in the Word of the righteousness of God, manifested through the baptism of Jesus and His blood on the Cross. This Word reveals to us who among Christians cannot receive the remission of sins, and, at the same time, it teaches us the truth that those who believe in the gospel of the water and the Spirit will receive the righteousness of God.

The correct faith, therefore, requires the understanding that God did not decide to pick a certain group of people unconditionally and send them to hell. If God indeed loved some while He hated others arbitrarily, people would not respect His righteousness.

Through the gospel of the water and the Spirit, God has set the law of the righteousness of redemption to deliver all sinners from their sins, and has given us the great blessing of being clothed in His love. Everyone must throw away his/her own righteousness before the gospel of the water and the Spirit spoken by the righteousness of God. God gave His righteousness only to those who believe in it.

God didn't allow people to be able to save themselves from sin by their own righteousness. Without believing in the gospel of the water and the Spirit as the righteousness of God, no one is to receive this righteousness, even if he/she confesses faith in Jesus (John 3:1-8).

The baptism that Jesus received and the blood that He shed on the Cross have become the righteousness of God. This is why Jesus has become the rock of offense to those who pursue their own righteousness. Believers in Jesus, therefore, must realize and understand that when they pursue their own righteousness, they are trampling on God's righteousness. No sinner can enter the Gates of Heaven without having faith in the righteousness of God. We who believe in Jesus must receive the remission of our sins by believing in God's righteousness.

Jesus Christ, who came to this earth, is the Savior of sinners and the very righteousness of God itself. We must truly believe in this righteousness of God, as Jesus has forgiven our sins with His Word by the water and the Spirit. Believers in Jesus must believe in the baptism that He received from John and His blood on the Cross as the righteousness of God. Only those who believe in the written Word of the water and the Spirit can enter Heaven.

We are told to be divided into the vessels of wrath and the vessels of mercy

The Lord said, *"For what profit is it to a man if he gains the whole world, and loses his own soul? Or what will a man give in exchange for his soul?" (Matthew 16:26)* If one comes to lose his/her eternal life, his/her achievements in this world are useless, no matter what they are. It is of no use even though one has conquered the world or even the entire universe, if he/she has not received the righteousness of God by believing in Jesus' baptism and His blood on the Cross.

No matter how highly theological doctrines are developed, only by believing in the gospel of the water and the Spirit that fulfills the righteousness of God can one receive and believe in this righteousness. Believers in Jesus can be free from their sins only when they receive the righteousness of God by believing in it.

Nowadays, it is common to see believers who, professing to believe in the righteousness of God, anguish over their sins in every early morning prayer meeting. They do not in reality believe in the righteousness of God. We must realize that such faiths professed by those who do not believe in the redemption within His righteousness do not please God, but only angers Him. Because they turned against the righteousness of God, they can only remain as His foes.

John 3:5 tells us that *"Unless one is born of water and the Spirit, he cannot enter the kingdom of God."* This is why you should resolve all your problems of sin by believing in the gospel of the water and the Spirit and in the righteousness of God. The gospel of the water and the Spirit has become the righteousness of God that can give you the remission of sins and His righteousness.

If you want to have the kind of faith that would justify you in God's righteousness, you must follow and believe in the Word of the water and the Spirit that contains this righteousness. You must also realize that, for your heart to be filled with faith in the righteousness of God, you need to cast aside your own righteousness. What Paul is telling both the Israelites and the Gentiles is that they must abandon their pursuits of their own righteousness if they want to obtain the righteousness of God.

God gave Abraham his son as the fruit of his faith in the righteousness of God. The righteousness of God appears in the Word of the water and the Spirit. Anyone who believes in the Word of the righteousness becomes a righteous person.

Rebecca, Isaac's wife, had conceived twins by him, and even before they were born, or doing any good or evil, she was told that "The older shall serve the younger." From this passage, some people conclude that God is not a just God, and that this is a mistaken conclusion.

This is because God already knew the future faiths of Jacob and Esau, even as they were still in Rebecca's womb. The secret of the righteousness of God is hidden in the gospel of the water and the Spirit. Because Esau was someone who was boastful of his own good deeds, God saw him as having nothing to do with faith in His righteousness, and this is why God hated him. Jacob, on the other hand, was someone who believed in the righteousness of God and gave all the glory to Him alone; thus, God could not do anything else but love him.

That God loved Jacob and hated Esau, therefore, is just on the basis of the truth. God does not appreciate people like Esau, who boasted of his own power without believing in the righteousness of God, but He is pleased by and loves people like Jacob, who knew his infirmities and believed only in His righteousness.

People often misunderstand the righteousness of God by asking how God could act in such a way to Isaac. They think that if God loved some while hated others, there must be something wrong with God, and they might even refuse to believe in Jesus because they think of Him as a God of injustice.

But how can God be unjust? If one thinks God as unjust, this is only a reflection of the fact that he/she does not have a correct understanding of the righteousness of God. All the more, it is precisely those who, by not believing in the righteousness of God, cover His righteousness with their own human righteousness that does grave wrong before God. Everyone must throw away their own righteousness before the righteousness of God and believe in the Word of the gospel of the water and the Spirit.

This is the only way to believing in the Word of redemption that contains the righteousness of God. That God is unjust is a fragment of your own imagination, derived from your ignorance of the profound purpose of God, set within His plan and predestination. God's righteous plan was to reveal His righteousness before us. Because God knew of the twins' futures already, God planned accordingly in His righteousness and set to love he who believed.

We must understand and believe in the righteousness of God in His plan. Whom, between Jacob and Esau, would God call upon? Our Lord said that He "did not come to call the righteous, but sinners." The righteousness of God, in other words, calls people like Jacob. As for Esau, not only did he not respond to God's righteous call, but he also boasted in his own righteousness. This is why Esau was to be hated while Jacob became the one who answered the call of the righteousness of God.

All these biblical truths must be understood within the faith that knows and believes in the love of the righteousness of God. If one tries to solve the conundrum of God's predestination without the correct knowledge of God's righteous love, he/she will fall into the very trap that he/she has set, leading to his/her own destruction.

God set predestination to reveal the love of His righteousness. Jacob was a man who came to recognize his shortcomings and believed in the Word of the righteousness of God. That God loved Jacob while He hated Esau is just. In the just sight of God, everyone deserves His wrath, but He provided us with His redemption for all those who believe in His righteousness. Those who are clothed in mercy before God are those who do not boast of their own righteousness, but believe in the righteousness of God as their redemption. These are the people who confess, "I deserve to be condemned to hell for my sins. Lord God, have mercy on me, and teach me your righteousness."

God gives the remission of sins only to those who believe in His righteous love, and this is God's plan for us to become His children that He has already revealed to us. You must not misunderstand God's plan to love Jacob and hate Esau. If, by any chance, you had not correctly understood the righteousness of God, then it is time for you believe again in God's righteous love in His righteousness.

I believe in the righteousness of God. Those who can correctly understand God's righteous love can also correctly believe in God's righteous Providence within His righteousness. But few in this world have the correct understanding of God's righteous plan and believe in it, and many are plagued by their misunderstanding of God.

These people think that, because the Scripture tells us that God hated Esau, some people are set by God to be arbitrarily hated by Him, as if it was their fate to be hated by Him. But our God is not such a despotic God. God is a judge who is right and just in His righteousness. God wants to give each and every one of us His righteous mercy and love.

God wanted to give us His righteousness through Jesus Christ, and He clothed those who believed in His righteousness in His mercy and made them His children.

This truth is revealed in the New Testament in Matthew

9:12-13 where Jesus says, *"Those who are well have no need of a physician, but those who are sick. But go and learn what this means: 'I desire mercy and not sacrifice.' For I did not come to call the righteous, but sinners, to repentance."* Those who are well have no need for physicians may even think of them as bothersome. Just as people do not realize the importance of physicians when they are healthy, they do not realize the importance of receiving the righteousness of God into their hearts by believing in it. Not knowing the righteousness of God, they are busy pursuing their own righteousness.

But sinners must abandon their own righteousness and believe in the righteousness of God. You can be either Jacob or Esau before God. Who do you want to be? God's reward and punishment will depend on your decision to whether or not believe in the redemption of the righteousness of God.

There is nothing wrong with God

Every person is by nature a competitive being. Some of them may be highly intelligent and successful people and some may have done many good deeds for others. But without the understanding of and faith in the righteousness of God, they will not have God's approval. Everyone-you and I, even the Israelites-were to be doomed for hell before God. Despite this, we have been justified, not by our own efforts, works, or strengths, but only by our faith in the very righteousness of God.

Because God has impartially and fairly given everyone His righteous love, all those who believe in it can be delivered from all their sins. God is not an unjust God, as you might have thought Him to be.

Whether or not one receives God's blessing of redemption depends on whether he/she decides to receive or reject it. This is why some people have become vessels of wrath while others have become vessels of mercy. Jacob, to put it differently, became a vessel of mercy, while Esau ended up as a vessel of wrath.

But some theologians and those without the Holy Spirit often slander God. They say, "Look, did not God make the Pharaoh as a vessel of wrath? Look at Jacob and Esau! Look at Rebecca! Look at what the potter has done! Did not God make someone the vessel for honor from the very beginning? This can be only fate!" Their logic is as follows: some people were already elected to become God's children even before their births; and such people who were predestined and elected to be clothed in God's love all become His children, while the others are bound for hell. This is how God's election is attacked. But God gave His righteousness to everyone, and He impartially elects those who believe in it.

We became justified by believing in the righteousness of God, when, in fact, we were not His people prior to this. God can approve our faiths because we became justified by believing in the gospel of the water and the Spirit through His Word. This is the truth of the gospel that shows the amazing power of God.

Originally, we had no God in us, did not know Him, and were all sinners, but by believing in the righteousness of God we have become His people. The gospel of the water and the Spirit, in which we believe, is not an incomplete gospel, but the complete and perfect one. We should praise God for giving us the truth by which we can obtain His righteousness.

Our lives may be full of troubles, but we must not forget

the righteousness of God because God has taught us the greatness of His power. The happiest person in the entire universe is the one who knows the righteousness of God. To those of us who believe in God, the triune God is the Father of mercy. He is our holy God. He put the faith in the righteousness of God in the souls of those of us who believe in it. We were made God's children and the recipients of His grace and blessings by knowing and believing in His righteousness.

Yet many people are still preoccupied by their own efforts to do good works. Giving offerings, volunteering for the church, making large donations to it in competition with others- you may think these are all good deeds, but they alone cannot and will not save you. Focusing on these works alone is not an indication of your faith in the righteousness of God, but it is an indication that you are pursuing your own righteousness. Those who are preoccupied with the efforts of their own flesh are going against God. It is those who do not know the righteousness God that are preoccupied with such things of the flesh.

The Scripture tells us that God's salvation is not given to those who run for it, but only to those who believe in His righteousness. This righteousness can be received only by believing in our merciful God. It is not by our works that we are loved by God, but only by believing in His righteousness do we receive His merciful love. This is why true faith depends entirely on whether or not we know and believe in the righteousness of God.

Were we not useless beings from the very beginning? And yet have we not, because of our faith in the righteousness of God, become so noble? We can keep our faiths until the end by believing in the righteousness of God and priding ourselves in the fact that we have now become His children.

There are many in the world who do evil and claim that there is no God, but God had mercy on us because we believed in His righteousness. We are truly noble before God and our pride in God is well deserved. We may face trials and tribulations while on this earth, but we are all spiritually rich and happy. We must all follow the righteousness of God and exalt Jesus.

God made all sinners His children, sinless, righteous, and perfect before Him. We must realize upon whom the righteousness of God comes. This righteousness of God has met all our shortcomings and cleansed away all our faulty sins. Whether you believe in this truth or not entirely depends on you. You, too, have been completely saved from your sins by the righteousness of God. What, then, will you do? Will you postpone your decision to believe for tomorrow?

May the righteousness of God be with you. ✉

CHAPTER

10

Introduction to Chapter 10

Are there people who do not, while pursuing their own righteousness, believe in the gospel of the water and the Spirit? The Scripture says that such people, by not believing in the righteousness of God and instead pursuing their own righteousness, are those who turn against God. What will these people do?

Did God plan to give all of humanity His salvation, which is the righteousness of God, and send Jesus Christ through the Israelites? Of course He did! Jesus so dearly wanted to save every sinner from his/her sins that He came to this earth, was crucified on the Cross, and was resurrected from death. He came, in other words, to save all those who believe in Him.

God the Father sent Jesus Christ to the Israelites to save them from their sins, and yet the Israelites did not receive Jesus, the righteousness of God. Instead, they were obsessed with the pursuits of their own righteousness. Even still, they are unable to accept Him as the Messiah of their people and the Savior of their souls.

Paul said that there are those who are sent by God, and that it is through them that the beautiful gospel can be heard. The gospel heard from the servants of God sent by Him is the gospel that has the righteousness of God. You cannot miss this chance. Only by hearing this gospel of the water and the Spirit, preached by the servants of God who know and believe in His righteousness, can you believe that God has given you the remission of sins and His righteousness.

The gospel of the water and the Spirit is the best and the

most beautiful news in the world. It is this good and beautiful news that has saved sinners from their sins. This beautiful news replenishes people's souls because the gospel of the water and the Spirit given by God is the true food for souls.

In the beautiful gospel of redemption provided by God is the power to forgive everyone's sins. The gospel of the water and the Spirit has the power of blessing to give us peace in our minds by the remission of our sins.

Centered on the law of God, the Israelites were busy pursuing their own righteousness. Because they thought that their own righteousness was abundant with their obedience to the law, they did not receive Jesus as their Savior. They were so eager in their pursuit of the works of the law that they could not even tolerate the righteousness of God. They failed to receive the Lord as their Savior even now, trying to pursue their own righteousness.

Does the Scripture tell us that the Israelites turned against the righteousness of God to establish their own righteousness? Speaking of the Israelites who were obsessed with the law, Paul rebuked their faiths by saying, *"Christ is the end of the law for righteousness to everyone who believes" (Romans 10:4).*

A legalistic faith that pursues one's own righteousness is not the right faith before God. While the Israelites were preoccupied only with following the laws of the Old Testament, they failed to realize that Jesus, who became the righteousness of God, was to be their Savior, and instead turned against Him. In their zeal to boast that they were the chosen people to whom the Word of God was given and who were to follow it, the Israelites ended up as a nation who turned against the righteousness of God.

Are you obsessed with establishing your own righteousness?

The problem with the Israelites' zeal for the law was that their passions were in establishing their own righteousness. Because of their own righteousness, the righteousness of God established by our Lord was utterly ignored.

The result of the legalistic faith of the Israelites was that they ended up turning against the righteousness of God; thus, they still have not realized how irreversibly devastating this result has been. What good or benefits did their pursuit of the work of the law bring them? Their passions for following the Word of God only ended up as obstacles to knowing and believing in the righteousness of God. Once again, we must realize that the "zeal" of those who do not have the correct understanding of the law will only lead them to turn against the righteousness of God in the end.

The Scripture clearly tells us that, to everyone who believes, Jesus became the end of the law for righteousness. Our Lord completed the righteousness of God by taking upon all the sins of the world with His baptism and bloodshed on the Cross, all to cleanse the sins of both the Israelites and the Gentiles. As such, the gospel of the water and the Spirit that contains the righteousness of God, not the law, has become an oasis in the desert for all sinners. It is the gospel of the water and the Spirit that has blotted out our sins and provided us with true sanction. How else but by the gospel of the water and the Spirit could all the sinners of the world find true sanction in their hearts?

Here in the Book of Romans, Paul tells us that establishing one's own righteousness without believing in the righteousness of God is a grave sin. What kind of gospel would have been a beautiful gospel to us, the Gentiles? It is the gospel that has told us that our Lord Jesus took up all the sins of the world with His baptism.

This gospel is the gospel recorded in Matthew 3:13-17, which bears witness to Jesus taking up the world's sins: *"Then Jesus came from Galilee to John at the Jordan to be baptized by him. And John tried to prevent Him, saying, 'I need to be baptized by You, and are You coming to me?' But Jesus answered and said to him, 'Permit it to be so now, for thus it is fitting for us to fulfill all righteousness.' Then he allowed Him. When He had been baptized, Jesus came up immediately from the water; and behold, the heavens were opened to Him, and He saw the Spirit of God descending like a dove and alighting upon Him. And suddenly a voice came from heaven, saying, 'This is My beloved Son, in whom I am well pleased.'"* This is how Jesus took upon all the sins of the world on Himself with His baptism by John.

Paul rebuked the legalists who did not believe in the righteousness of God by asking, *"Who will ascend into heaven? (That is, to bring Christ down from above)."* Put differently, this question asks, "Who can be saved from his/her sins by only following the law?" The purpose of Paul's question was to underscore the point that following the law will never bring about salvation from sin. He is telling us, in other words, that there is nothing that we can do to rid ourselves of sin.

Paul often spoke of God's righteousness in his epistles. Paul's answer to true faith is found in Romans 10:10, where it is said, *"For with the heart one believes unto righteousness, and with the mouth confession is made unto salvation."* The gospel preached by Paul was the gospel that tells us that we can receive God's righteousness by believing in our Lord's baptism and His blood on the Cross, through which this righteousness of God is revealed. We must believe that the Lord gave us the gospel of the water and the Spirit, and that He allowed those who believe in this gospel a true peace of mind.

True faith comes from hearing the Word of God

What does Paul tell us about true faith? Romans 10:17 says, *"So then faith comes by hearing, and hearing by the word of God."* True faith, in other words, comes when we hear the gospel that His servants, through whom God speaks, preaches with His Word.

Our conviction of true faith comes by hearing the Word of God, and so to be the people of true faith, we must hear and believe in His Word. Only by hearing the Word of God can we have true faiths and only by this can our faiths grow. This is why God has sent us His servants, who preach of His righteousness.

When we believe in the gospel of the water and the Spirit given to mankind by God, we can receive the remission of sins and be at rest in our hearts. Deliverance from sin is possible only by believing in the righteousness of God, from which we will find our peace of mind.

Have we not been told that the righteousness of our Lord will wipe away our tears and deliver us from all our aches and pains? Of course we have. By believing in the righteousness of the gospel of the water and the Spirit given by God, all our pains will be taken away. The gospel of the water and the Spirit is the most beautiful news in the world and the fulfillment of God's righteousness.

God sent our Lord, who fulfilled His righteousness, to the Israelites, but in pursuing their own righteousness, they refused to turn to Him. What, then, did God do? To provoke the Israelites to jealousy, God gave the gospel, the fulfillment of His righteousness, to the Gentiles to believe. Did God, then, allow the Gentiles the chance to believe in the gospel of the water and the Spirit? Indeed, He gave them the chance to believe in the gospel of the water and the Spirit, even when they neither sought Him, nor called Him, and worshipped Him far less than the Israelites.

This is why the Gentiles were able to become God's children-by believing in the beautiful news of the fulfillment of His righteousness. This is also why the Scripture tells us that the righteousness of God was revered and glorified outside of Israel.

How many people actually thank the Lord for giving all of us the gospel of the water and the Spirit that has fulfilled the righteousness of God? Our Lord has taken away all the sins of the world with the beautiful gospel of the water and the Spirit. Yet, there are far too many Christians who do not believe in this truth. Do we, then, have any righteousness in us that we can set before God? No, we don't! Then, why don't we believe? Is it because we do not know what the gospel that has fulfilled the righteousness of God is? But knowing this gospel is simple!

We, too, are the kinds of people who would have pursued our own righteousness, just as the Israelites had done, but God saved us from all our sins by giving us the beautiful gospel of the water and the Spirit. We thank the Lord for giving us the gospel of the water and the Spirit, the fulfillment of the righteousness of God, for us to believe.

Do not say, "Who will ascend into heaven?"

Verse 6 says, "But the righteousness of faith speaks in this way, *"Do not say in your heart, "Who will ascend into heaven?" (That is, to bring Christ down from above)."* Both our redemption and our serving the gospel of truth are made possible by our faith in the gospel of the water and the Spirit, not by our works. Were it not for our faith in the truth that fulfilled the righteousness of God, we would have been nothing but sinners who, as legalists pursuing their own righteousness, only bothered God.

Just as our salvation came by believing in the righteousness of God, we can also live for our Lord by having faith in this righteousness. The strength for us to carry on with our lives comes from our faith in God's righteousness, as our knowledge of this righteousness arose by our faith in the gospel of the water and the Spirit.

Is there any truth other than the faith in the righteousness of God for those who are to be redeemed? There is none. The essence of Christianity is centered on faith, and it is no exaggeration to say that the righteousness of God is all about Christian faith. Those who have become justified can live and preach the gospel by their faiths in this righteousness. Do those who believe in God's righteousness, then, face troubles as well? They do. But by the faith in God's righteousness, they can overcome all troubles, as they believe and trust that God will take care of their problems. Such beliefs originate from the faith in the righteousness of God.

What about other faiths that don't include God's righteousness? Are they all the wrong kinds of faiths, based on human deeds? Indeed, they are. The faiths of those who believe in Jesus, without believing in the righteousness of God, are not true faiths.

Could you and I be redeemed from our sins without first believing in God's righteousness? Could we live by our faiths in God without having faith in His righteousness? Neither would be possible. The strength of the righteous to serve the Lord comes from the power of the Holy Spirit, given to them as a gift for their faith in God's righteousness. Can you live in this world with only your own strengths or your earthly possessions? Can you really find a peace of mind with these things?

We can serve the gospel in peace by believing in the righteousness of God. Those who serve the gospel of the water and the Spirit have faith, courage, strength and peace. The righteous people who do not serve the gospel of the water and the Spirit, the fulfillment of the righteousness of God, have neither peace nor courage. Do the minds of the righteous need peace? They do. They need peace not only to spread the gospel of the water and the Spirit, but also to live their lives to the fullest extent.

Is your mind at peace? If you were to live only for yourself, there would be no reason for the peace in your mind to grow. Why would you need any more peace or faith when you only need to meet the needs of the flesh to live in the flesh? But if you are to serve God, the peace in your mind also needs to grow. To serve the gospel that has fulfilled the righteousness of God, your faith and peace must and will grow.

Those who believe in the gospel of God's righteousness are responsible for spreading their peace all around the world. Because this is not an issue of just individual concerns, but of the need to spread the peace of mind given by Jesus Christ to everyone, we need to preach the gospel of God's righteousness to the entire world. God's peace is still needed for others, as well as for us. We need more requests from God in trying to spread this peace to others. When we live to spread God's righteousness, our peace of mind will only grow, and we will find the clear and precious goal of our lives.

If you want to learn the true peace given by God, you need to know and believe in the gospel that has fulfilled His righteousness. You need to experience for yourself the peace of mind that God has prepared for you.

You have served the Lord well so far, but you need to continue to serve Him well, until you are called to His presence, so that others may share in your peace. When you reach for peace with your faith in the righteousness of God, those believers who are following in your footsteps to redemption can also live for the peace of others.

Those who are young in their faiths are novices in the realm of faith, and are limited in their abilities to understand it. But when we live by our faiths, those behind us will, though it may take some time, eventually come to an understanding of how the redeemed live their lives in peace, by following in our footsteps of faith.

Do you find it difficult to teach those who are following your lead how to live by faith? Such a life of teaching is not reached overnight. It might even take a very long time before you can lead them to the kind of faith needed for living in peace. But in time, those who have been redeemed by believing in God's righteousness will eventually learn to live in peace as the people of faith, just as the earlier believers serving God found their peace of minds from Him, by learning from those of us who are ahead.

You and I, we must all live by faith in the righteousness of God. The righteous must live by their faiths in the Word. Both our present and future lives must be determined by faith. The Scripture asks us, *"And how shall they hear without a preacher?"* Because we believe in the righteousness of God, we must preach the gospel to the world. By faith, we can meet all the challenges that we may face while spreading the gospel.

The lives of the righteous that are not lived by faith are those who have lost their peace of minds. Believing in God's righteousness allows people to attain their peace of minds. When we believe in the Word of God and His righteousness for all things, we will be given our peace.

You must stand firmly in your peace and faith by believing in the righteousness of God. You must also praise God, for the Lord has allowed you to live by the deliverance of His righteousness and peace. May you live your life by preaching the gospel, with faith in God, from whom you have received your peace.

Have we been able to learn from the Book of Romans how perfect the righteousness of God is? Romans explains in detail what this righteousness of God is. The righteousness of God that we speak of is not that of man-made righteousness, but of God, Himself alone.

The righteousness of God is perfect and more than sufficient to save us from all our sins. By taking upon all the sins of the world through His baptism, Jesus took care of them all, in perfection. That we can believe in Jesus Christ is due to the fact that the righteousness of God is perfect. Since this righteousness of God wholly saved us from all our sins, it is absolutely necessary for us to believe in the gospel that has fulfilled His righteousness.

By believing in God's righteousness, we can live our lives admiring, thanking, and praising it. People can dwell in the holiness of God only by believing in His righteousness. By believing in this righteousness, our minds are cleansed, we can praise God, and our lives can be lived for His glory.

Had the righteousness of God not been perfect, we would not have been able to be delivered from our sins. Though our original sin may have been forgiven by believing in Jesus, every sin committed daily on our own thereafter would have required daily prayers of repentance.

But after we were redeemed by believing in the righteousness of God, revealed in the gospel of the water and the Spirit, we could then realize that this righteousness of God was absolute. This is why I came to be infinitely grateful for the fact that the righteousness of God is believable and perfect for eternity. Because God's righteousness has delivered us from all the possible sins that we could commit in our lifetimes, we can be saved from sin by believing in His righteousness.

Those who do not compare the righteousness of God with our human filth cannot believe in His righteousness because they simply don't realize just how big it is. Even the most perfect person is nothing when compared to the righteousness of God, and this is why we believe in His righteousness, and are thereby allowed to dwell in His holiness. We become, in other words, those who glorify God by believing and dwelling in His righteousness.

We need to have a correct understanding of the righteousness of God in our hearts-that is, we must realize that the righteousness of God has wholly and completely delivered us from our sins. Do we not commit innumerable sins throughout our lives? How, then, did God carry out the righteous act that has delivered us from such countless sins? He accomplished it by coming to this earth in the likeness of our flesh, taking up all our sins by being baptized by John, dying on the Cross, and resurrecting from death–by fulfilling, in short, all the righteousness of God.

Everyone, young and old, rich and poor, strong and weak, commit sins. Who, then, saved us from all these sins of the world? It was Jesus Christ who, by fulfilling the righteousness of God, delivered us from all our sins. That God sent Jesus to wholly take upon all our sins and to completely eliminate them is the very righteousness of God.

Nothing other than this is precisely the righteousness of God that has saved us from all our sins. God's righteousness has delivered us from all the sins of the world at once. Is not His righteousness utterly and completely perfect? We call this love that God has given us, which will last not only for our lifetime but also throughout eternity, the righteousness of God.

As John the Baptist proclaimed when he saw Jesus the day after baptizing Him, *"Behold! The Lamb of God who takes away the sin of the world!"* As Jesus told John when he first refused to baptize Him, *"Permit it to be so now, for thus it is fitting for us to fulfill all righteousness" (Matthew 3:15).* What do these passages mean? They mean no less than the truth that Jesus' baptism and His death on the Cross are the very righteousness of God. This righteousness of God does not abandon us when we are weak and come short of His glory.

We can only praise God and glorify Him for this abundant love that has saved us and allowed us to dwell in His righteousness. Those who believe in the righteousness of God come to live for His righteousness for the rest of their lives. It is much better for us to trust in God than in human beings or the world. A beautiful life is a life that preaches this gospel of complete deliverance from sin. This is why we absolutely must know and believe in the righteousness of God.

Those who have received the remission of sins would testify, "Jesus has taken away all my sins by being baptized by John! And He was judged in my place for all the sins of the world!" When we believe in God's righteousness, we can only thank Him for such blessings.

When you stumble because of your weaknesses, fall into sin because of the flesh, or when you are discouraged and embarrassed because of your sins, look toward the righteousness of God that has made you whole. Did not the righteousness of God also make us righteous? Did not Jesus completely take away our sins through His baptism? Did not His redemption save us from *all* our sins, including those sins we'll commit in the future?

Only when we believe that Jesus Christ has saved us completely and wholly do we believe in the righteousness of God. Only when we believe in the righteousness of God do we become justified. Those who believe in God's righteousness can become the instruments for His righteousness. The perfection of God's righteousness is complete. Those who pursue their own righteousness, while being ignorant of the righteousness of God, are only fools sitting on their own destruction, to be accursed by God.

Pay attention to Paul's saying, "They have a zeal for God, but not according to knowledge"

How can we live a life of faith, be redeemed, and become God's people if we remain ignorant of His righteousness?

Those who follow the law must know that their sins will lead to their destruction and be thankful that the righteousness of God has saved them completely. That Jesus has become our Savior, that we believe in Him, and that we glorify Him are because we know and believe in the righteousness of God. Only by believing in His righteousness do we become His children, sinless, and receive eternal lives. Those who profess to believe in Jesus and live faithful lives, yet remain ignorant of the righteousness of God are to be accursed.

Paul bore witness in Romans that the Israelites, while being ignorant of the righteousness of God, sought to establish their own righteousness, and by doing so, disobeyed God's righteousness. They too must believe in the righteousness of God.

We must believe that God has delivered us from the sins of the world. All our sins are included in these sins of the world. All of them have disappeared with the fulfillment of the righteousness of God. Do you believe in this truth?

"For Christ is the end of the Law for righteousness to everyone who believes"

The righteousness of God is the end of the law. The reason is because Jesus Christ answered all the requirements of the law by taking upon all the sins of the world with His baptism and crucifixion.

Surely the result of sin is death, yet it is written that the righteousness of God is the end of the law. Why? This is because God the Father has saved us wholly by sending His only begotten Son to the earth to be baptized to take up all the sins of mankind, die on the Cross, and be raised from death.

Believing in the righteousness of God with your heart and following the righteousness of the law are two different things. Did you receive the remission of sins by your deeds? Did you receive your salvation by your own good deeds? All other religions in this world teach that the way to deal with your sins is by doing good deeds. The Buddhist understanding of sin, for instance, teaches that you can redeem the sins of your past life by doing good deeds in your present life. Does this make any sense to you?

A person is born only once and dies only once, and judgment will come afterward. Because everyone is born in this world only once and returns to God thereafter, no one can return to the earth in another cycle of life. This is why people must be redeemed by believing in God's righteousness while on this earth. What kind of nonsense is this Buddhist teaching of karma?

Believing that we are redeemed from our sins is to believe in the righteousness of God. Believing in the righteousness of God is to believe only in His righteousness alone, not in our own acts. How, then, does God's righteousness of faith speak? As is recorded in the Book of Romans, it speaks in this way, *"Do not say in your heart, Who will ascend into heaven?"* This is because the righteousness of God is found by believing in one's heart, not by some kind of physical strength.

We become God's children and sinless people who receive eternal lives by believing in the righteousness of God. Because we cannot resolve our sins by ourselves, no matter how many good deeds we do, our efforts only end up as more sins before God. This is why we should abandon such faiths in ourselves and believe instead in the righteous God to pursue His righteousness. Some people ask, "Can we not be saved just by believing in Jesus even if we are ignorant of God's righteousness? Is it not written that whosoever called the name of the Lord will be saved?" But salvation does not come just by calling on the name of Jesus, but by knowing and completely believing in the righteousness of God.

Whoever believes in the righteousness of God has no shame

Verse 11 says, *"Whoever believes on Him will not be put to shame."* What is the meaning of this passage? Whoever believes on Him is not put to shame because he/she believes in the righteousness of God. *"Whoever believes on Him"* refers to the believer in His righteousness.

What about the passage, "Whoever calls on the name of the LORD shall be saved"? This means that those who know and believe in the gospel of the water and the Spirit call on Jesus, as they believe in Him as the Savior God. As we received our salvation through God's righteousness, we believe that our redemption is given by believing in this truth.

Without this faith, in other words, no matter how many times we call the name of Jesus in vain, we will not be saved from our sins. Because the Scripture as a whole speaks of the righteousness of God in Jesus, calling on the name of the Lord alone will not give us our redemption.

The Bible tells us of the righteousness of God from the very beginning. As is written in the Book of Genesis, God put the tree of life and the tree of the knowledge of good and evil in the Garden of Eden, and told Adam and Eve not to eat from the tree of knowledge. What God did was to demand from them their faith in His Word. God, to put it differently, told them to eat from the tree of life for obtaining eternal lives.

The Word of God says, *"The just shall live by faith."* We, too, live by our faith in the righteousness of God throughout our lifetime—from when we first believed in Him to be saved to when we receive our salvation, and finally, until we reach the Kingdom of God.

Many Christians in this world say that salvation from sin is given by believing in Jesus, but in reality, too many of them are not delivered from their sins because they remain ignorant of the righteousness of God. What will result when people believe in Jesus without knowing the righteousness of God? Such people may show outward indications that they are devout believers through their worships and prayers. But because they are ignorant of God's righteousness, they will remain only as practitioners of religion, as well as undelivered sinners.

Many from both the Christian community and the Israelis remain ignorant of the righteousness of God, and are thus not obeying His righteousness. Those who believe in Jesus, yet do not believe in God's righteousness, stamp on this very righteousness. It is not by doing good deeds, giving large offerings, or other acts of their own before God that the believers in Jesus, so long as they remain ignorant of the righteousness of God, receive this righteousness.

Those who believe in the righteousness of God believe in it, regardless of what circumstances they find themselves in, and thus live lives of praise and thanks for God's glory. To those of us who believe in God's righteousness, the more our shortcomings are revealed, the more His righteousness brilliantly shines before our souls. I pray that you too can have such an awakening.

Can we receive the righteousness of God because we somehow had some justness in our flesh? Of course not! There is nothing that is just in us, other than the righteousness of God. Because God has completely saved us from our sins with His righteousness, we believe and praise in this righteousness. His righteousness has saved us wholly from our sins.

Do not fall into the deed-oriented faith when you are facing dark corners in your life, but always believe in the righteousness of God, regardless of your circumstances. God's righteousness is perfect for eternity. Everyone in this world must know His righteousness, and they must believe in it by obeying the gospel of the water and the Spirit. Since many who profess to have faith in Jesus still live only by the righteousness of the law, they must make sure that they know the righteousness of God.

Paul concludes by saying that the gospel of God fulfills His righteousness. Without the knowledge in the true gospel of God, no one can explain what His righteousness is. Such people might say, when asked to discuss what the meaning of the righteousness of God is, "Jesus is my Savior who died on the Cross, was raised from death, and saved me from my sins." But they will add that they must offer prayers of repentance for their everyday sins, and that to become perfect, they must be sanctified incrementally.

You must know yourself first to know the righteousness of God. If you know both yourself and the righteousness of God, you will have no choice but to believe in His righteousness, because you would realize how high, big, and expansive the righteousness of God is when compared to yourself. But if you do not know His righteousness, you would be obsessed with pursuing your own righteousness. Those who are obsessed with their own righteousness do not obey the righteousness of God, as they only wish to pursue their own justifications.

We must know God's righteousness before we can believe in it and give thanks for it. By knowing the righteousness of God, we can believe that Jesus took away all the sins of the world by taking them up on Himself with His baptism and dying on the Cross. If we can be justified by our own good deeds, we wouldn't need salvation by the righteousness of God. But when we realize that this is not possible, we can appreciate His righteousness even more because God saved us, who could not live our lives based on good deeds.

Are your thoughts and deeds all good? Of course not. It is because we have many shortcomings that God has saved us wholly by His righteousness. Since believing in the righteousness of God saved us, we desire to preach His righteousness to all those in this world who do not know it.

One who does not know oneself finds faults with others and speaks ill of them. But if he/she were a believer in the righteousness of God, he/she must proudly proclaim this righteousness, and must not boast of his/her own righteousness. But those who do not believe in God's righteousness commit the sin of slandering His righteousness. God will judge them for their sins.

God sent His Son to this earth and has given you His righteousness. As we approach the last day, we should not be arguing with each other over whose righteousness of the law is better or worse. Those who believe in the righteousness of God should not concern themselves with their flesh, but should only be thankful to God by believing in His righteousness.

Let us thank our God who has wholly saved us by His

righteousness. Because the righteousness of God has forgiven all your sins, you must not become like those who turn against God by pursuing their own righteousness. ✉

True Faith Comes by Hearing

< Romans 10:16-21 >
"But they have not all obeyed the gospel. For Isaiah says, 'LORD, who has believed our report?' So then faith comes by hearing, and hearing by the word of God. But I say, have they not heard? Yes indeed:

'Their sound has gone out to all the earth,
And their words to the ends of the world.'

But I say, did Israel not know? First Moses says:

'I will provoke you to jealousy by those who are not a nation,
I will move you to anger by a foolish nation.'

But Isaiah is very bold and says:

'I was found by those who did not seek Me;
I was made manifest to those who did not ask for Me.'

But to Israel he says:

'All day long I have stretched out My hands
To a disobedient and contrary people.'"

Verse 17 says, *"So then faith comes by hearing, and hearing by the word of God."* Where does the faith that delivers a person from all his/her sins come from? True faith comes by hearing the Word of God.

I would like to continue bearing witness to the gospel of the righteousness of God through the His Word. Let us begin by taking a look at Romans 3:10-20:

"As it is written: 'There is none righteous, no, not one;
There is none who understands;
There is none who seeks after God.
They have all turned aside;
They have together become unprofitable;
There is none who does good, no, not one.'
'Their throat is an open tomb;
With their tongues they have practiced deceit';
'The poison of asps is under their lips';
'Whose mouth is full of cursing and bitterness.'
'Their feet are swift to shed blood;
Destruction and misery are in their ways;
And the way of peace they have not known.'
'There is no fear of God before their eyes.'
Now we know that whatever the law says, it says to those
who are under the law, that every mouth may be stopped, and
all the world may become guilty before God. Therefore by the
deeds of the law no flesh will be justified in His sight, for by the
law is the knowledge of sin."

How should we understand and believe in these passages to receive salvation? From the very beginning, there were neither the righteous nor those who sought God, but all were sinners. Their throats were open tombs; their tongues were like the venom of a poisonous snake, deceitful and full of cursing and bitterness. Their feet were quick to draw blood. They knew not the way of peace, or the fear of God before their eyes, and only walked in the path to their own destructions and misery. Everyone was a sinner before knowing and believing in the righteousness of God, and the way they found out that they were sinners before God was by the law.

How could we, without the law, know our sins? How

could we know God? Did we ever fear God? Romans 3:18 says, *"There is no fear of God before their eyes."* Did our eyes of the flesh ever see Him? We may perhaps have been slightly conscious of the existence of God, but we neither saw nor feared Him. How, then, did we find out that we were sinners? We came to know the existence of God by hearing His written Word. This is why hearing comes from God's Word.

We know that God created the world because it is thus written in the Scripture, *"In the beginning God created the heavens and the earth" (Genesis 1:1).* It is by hearing this Word of God that we came to know and believe in His existence, and to believe that He is the Creator of the whole universe. If it weren't for the Word of God, there would have been no one who knew of Him, nor feared Him. Neither could we have known of our sins without the Word of God—not a single person.

In other words, we were fundamentally ignorant of God, worshipping futile things, and unaware of our own sins. But God gave us the law, and this is how we came to know of our sins before God. It was by hearing His Word of the law as the Ten Commandments and the 613 detailed articles of the law that we came to know our shortcomings and sins.

No one can know even one's own sins without the Word of the law. Almost every convict behind bars would claim that he/she does not know what his/her crime was, or why he/she had been locked away. Many of them claim to be innocent; that they were sent to prison wrongfully and unjustly. Without knowing the law of God, we cannot know of our own sins, saying, "I have always acted in this way. Everyone does it. How can this be sin?"

Only by seeing and hearing the law of God have we come

to realize our sins. We have come to know that our worship of
other gods, our calling of God's name in vain, our failure to
observe the Sabbath, our killing, our adultery, our theft, our
lying, our envy-our failure to live by the Word of God, in short-
are all acts of sin because the law of God says so. This is how
we have realized and recognized that we were sinners before
God, by the Word of the law. Before this law, we did not even
know our own sins.

Having realized that we are sinners, what, then, should we
do before God? We need to ask how our sins can be forgiven. It
is by hearing the Word of God that we come to know our sins,
and realize our need for salvation. Just as the hungry feels the
need for food, those who recognize that they have broken
God's law and know that they are grave sinners realize their
need for salvation. This is how we come to look for God and
recognize our need to believe in His righteousness through
Jesus Christ, whom He sent for us. As "faith comes by
hearing," we know our sins by hearing the Word of God.

We now know that we are sinners. What should we do to be delivered from our sins then?

Salvation comes by faith in His Word that stands in the
center of our hearts, just as we came to realize our sins by
hearing and learning the Word of God. As Romans 3:21-22
says, *"But now the righteousness of God apart from the law is
revealed, being witnessed by the law and the Prophets, even the
righteousness of God, through faith in Jesus Christ, to all and
on all who believe."*

By giving us His law, Got let us know that we are sinners
before Him, as we have failed to live by His Word. We

consequently have two different needs: we want to live by the law, but at the same time, we desperately seek our salvation from sin. But because *"...now the righteousness of God apart from the law is revealed,"* those who are to be delivered from their sins must find redemption by their faiths in this righteousness of God, not in the law. We know that this deliverance does not come by obeying the law of God, but by believing in the salvation given by God, in the very righteousness of God that has saved us through Jesus Christ.

What, then, is this righteousness of God and His salvation? This is the gospel of the water and the Spirit, spoken of in both the Old and the New Testaments. The gospel of the water and the Spirit appears in the Old Testament as salvation by faith in the sacrificial system, and in the New Testament as faith in the baptism of Jesus and His Cross. Roman 3:21-22 says, *"Being witnessed by the law and the Prophets, even the righteousness of God, through faith in Jesus Christ, to all and on all who believe."*

How can we then receive the righteousness of God? We can receive the righteousness of God by knowing, through the Word of God witnessed by the law and the prophets, that Jesus is God and our Savior, and by being saved from all our sins through our faiths in Him.

In other words, we receive the righteousness of God by believing in His Word, witnessed by the law and the prophets of the Old Testament. That the law and the prophets witnessed God's Word is shown also in the very first chapters of Hebrews and Romans.

That Jesus came to deliver us is the salvation promised to us by God. This promise to save the sinners, who were under the law and bound for their destruction, had been made thousands of years ago by God. He had repeatedly reiterated this promise and revealed just how He intends to keep it through many of His servants who came before us.

Let's see a passage for example. Leviticus 16:21 says, *"Aaron shall lay both his hands on the head of the live goat, confess over it all the iniquities of the children of Israel, and all their transgressions, concerning all their sins, putting them on the head of the goat, and shall send it away into the wilderness by the hand of a suitable man."* The passages from Romans 3:21-22, that the righteousness of God was witnessed by the law and the prophets, means that the complete salvation of Jesus was revealed through the Old Testament's sacrifices of the tabernacle and through such prophets as Isaiah, Ezekiel, Jeremiah and Daniel.

In other words, God had already revealed, through the Word of the Old Testament, just how He would keep His promise of salvation—that He would do so by sending Jesus Christ, having Him take up all the sins of the world with His baptism, die on the Cross in our place, and thereby pay the wages of all our sins with His own body, all for our deliverance from sin through the righteousness of God. Our salvation is thus not by the law, but by our faith in the righteousness of God, Jesus Christ Himself, as witnessed by both the law and the prophets.

God tells us that we are saved from our sins by believing in His righteousness, which was fulfilled by Jesus Christ. Our faith comes by hearing this Word of God, the Word of Jesus Christ. How can we know and believe that Jesus is our Savior? We know and believe that Jesus is our Savior by hearing the Word of God spoken to His servants, that He had promised to save us according to His plan, and that Jesus came to save us according to this promise and plan. As is written in Daniel 9:24, *"Seventy weeks are determined For your people and for your holy city, To finish the transgression, To make an end of sins, To make reconciliation for iniquity, To bring in everlasting righteousness, To seal up vision and prophecy, And to anoint the Most Holy."*

God has set seventy weeks for our people

We continue with the above passage from the Book of Daniel. What the passage describes is the fall of Israel by Babylon, when God determined that the Israelites, because of their idolatry, would be taken to Babylon as prisoners and live there for seventy years as slaves. As determined by God, Israel was attacked and overwhelmed by Babylon, and unable to withstand the devastation, ended up surrendering to the invaders, who took many of the Israelites as prisoners and turned them into their slaves. Among the prisoners taken were also the wise, such as Daniel, whom the Babylonian king made his advisor.

So God punished the Israelites in this way for their sins, but because He was merciful, He did not keep His wrath forever, but instead planned to free them in 70 years.

When Daniel, repenting before God on behalf of his people, prayed for His mercy and deliverance, God sent an angel who spoke the above passage: *"Seventy weeks are determined For your people and for your holy city, To finish the transgression, To make an end of sins, To make reconciliation for iniquity, To bring in everlasting righteousness, To seal up vision and prophecy, And to anoint the Most Holy."* This passage is God's promise to Daniel that He would forgive all the sins of His people in 70 years when their transgressions were finished. It also reveals to us God's promised deliverance through Jesus Christ.

Because the Israelites committed many sins, God had to punish them, and for the price of 70 years of slavery, God forgave all their past sins. When the transgression is redeemed and an end of sins is made, all the sins of the Israelites would no longer be there. When the reconciliation for iniquity is made, the everlasting righteousness is brought, and the vision and prophecy are sealed up, all of God's Words spoken to Jeremiah would be fulfilled. Through the 70 years of slavery, all these would come to bear, and on the 70th year, the Israelites would return to their homeland.

This is what God told Daniel through His angel. This promise was a promise made to the Israelites, but it also has a spiritual significance—just as God set 70 weeks for the people of Israel and their holy city, God has prepared for all of us who believe in Him our Holy City of Heaven, our Kingdom of God.

In Romans, it is said, *"But now the righteousness of God apart from the law is revealed, being witnessed by the law and the Prophets, even the righteousness of God, through faith in Jesus Christ, to all and on all who believe."* When Jesus came to this earth, was baptized, and died on the Cross, all our transgressions were eliminated, our sins ended, the everlasting righteousness was revealed, and the vision and prophecy was sealed up. The passage from Daniel ends with, *"To anoint the Most Holy."* What does this mean? The Most Holy refers to none other than Jesus Christ, who would come to this earth to be anointed.

What does it mean to be anointed? That Jesus would take

upon the three positions of the King, the High Priest of the Kingdom of God, and the Prophet. As our King, High Priest and Prophet, Jesus would fulfill the will of God to deliver us from all our sins. Just as prophesized by the angel who spoke to Daniel, Jesus Christ took upon all our sins on Himself and was judged in our stead by coming to this earth and being baptized.

"Faith comes by hearing." How, then, can we hear and believe in this gospel of the righteousness of God? How can we believe that Jesus Christ is our Savior? We can hear and believe by the Word of God spoken in the Old and New Testaments-by the words spoken by the prophets of God and His servants. This is why Paul said that faith comes by hearing, and this faith comes by hearing the Word of Christ.

The prophets of the Old Testament, such as Daniel and Isaiah, had prophesized about the coming of Jesus Christ. Isaiah, in particular, prophesized, *"Surely He has borne our griefs and carried our sorrows"* and *"He was led as a lamb to the slaughter, and as a sheep before its shearers is silent, so He opened not His mouth"(Isaiah 53:4,6).*

Who in Isaiah's time would have believed that Jesus Christ would be born of a virgin to come to this earth as the commonest of all commons, live for 33 years, be baptized, crucified, and raised from death on the third day? Yet Isaiah saw and prophesized, about 700 years before the coming of Jesus, that all these things would come to pass. He bore witness to the fact that Christ would bear our grief and all our sins.

This is why Paul used the Word of the Old Testament frequently when writing the Book of Romans, to explain how the servants of God bore witness to how Jesus became our Savior-by coming to this earth, taking away all our sins, and saving us with the righteousness of God.

For all have sinned

Romans 3:23-24 says, *"For all have sinned and fall short of the glory of God, being justified freely by His grace through the redemption that is in Christ Jesus."* Because we were born into sin and have all sinned against God, we have come short before His glory and His Kingdom. But we were justified freely by God's grace through the redemption in Jesus Christ. Our justification was for free, without a price. We did not have to pay the wages for our sins because Jesus took upon all our sins and paid these wages with His own life on the Cross, all to deliver those of us who would hear and believe in Him.

What do we mean by faith in the salvation from all sins? We simply mean faith in the righteousness of God. Believing in the righteousness of God has nothing to do with works, but everything to do with our hearts. We become justified by hearing the Word of our Lord and believing in it with our hearts. To save us from our sins, our Lord came to this earth, became the Lamb of God, who carried all the sins of the world by being baptized by John the Baptist, and died on the Cross. On the third day, He arose from death, and now sits at the right hand of God the Father.

Jesus took upon all the sins of the world onto Himself, paid the price for the punishment of our sins with His own life, and arose from death; all to save us from our own certain deaths. We are saved by believing in this. Our salvation comes by faith, and our faiths come by hearing the written Word of God, and our hearings come by the Word of Christ.

"Faith comes by hearing." We believe with our hearts.

Our intellects are for knowledge, while our bodies are for working, and it is in our hearts that we believe. What, then, should we believe in our hearts, and how? By hearing the Word of God, we can hear His gospel, and by hearing His gospel, we can have faith, and by having faith, we can be saved. When we believe, we believe by the Word of God-that is, we believe in the written Word that proclaims that Christ took upon all our sins with His baptism, carried them, died on the Cross and rose again from death.

To have faith in God's Word is to have faith in His righteousness. So, faith without hearing God's Word is futile and useless. Such claims—that God was revealed through one's dreams and whatnot—are all lies.

We are saved by faith and faith alone. Let us read, one more time, Romans 3:24-26: *"Being justified freely by His grace through the redemption that is in Christ Jesus, whom God set forth as a propitiation by His blood, through faith, to demonstrate His righteousness, because in His forbearance God had passed over the sins that were previously committed, to demonstrate at the present time His righteousness, that He might be just and the justifier of the one who has faith in Jesus."* Amen. Our Lord was made the propitiation for our sins. Because of our sins, we were made God's enemies, but Jesus reestablished our relationship with God by becoming the propitiation for our sins with His baptism, death and resurrection.

In the middle of Romans 3:25 is the passage, *"Because in His forbearance God had passed over the sins that were previously committed, to demonstrate at the present time His righteousness."* This passage tells us that God had waited in patience for a very long time, and that He will wait until the

Day of Judgment. Those who believe in Jesus Christ, those who believe in the salvation through the water and the blood, those who believe in the salvation of the Son, who became the propitiation to God the Father–all their sins are passed over by God. 'To have passed over the sins' means that God has passed over the sins of those who hear and believe in the Word of God and His gospel, the very people who believe in the baptism of Jesus and His blood on the Cross.

We may falter from time to time in our lives, but this is because of the weakness of our flesh and minds, and as long as we do not deny the salvation of Jesus, God will not see all these sins as sins. God does not, in other words, look at the sins of those who are saved by believing in the water and the blood of Jesus Christ in their hearts, but passes over them.

Why, then, does God pass over our sins? How can He ignore such sins, when He is the holy and just God? This is because Christ came to this world and was baptized. It is because Jesus blotted out all the sins of the world with His baptism and crucifixion that God passes over our previously committed sins. Do the sins previously committed refer to only our original sin? No, they don't, because while they may appear as our original sin, to our everlasting God the Father, everything is in the past.

In the viewpoint of eternity, time in this world always appears as the past. This world has its beginning and end, but God is eternal, and so when we compare His time with our worldly time, all the sins of the world appear as committed in the past before Him. *"God had passed over the sins that were previously committed, to demonstrate at the present time His righteousness."* This is why God does not see our sins. It is not because He does not have eyes to see our sins, but He does not see them because His Son Jesus Christ has paid the wages of our sins. Because Christ's baptism and crucifixion cleansed away our sins, we actually appear before God as sinless people.

How could God see our sins when Jesus Christ, whose fulfillment of God's righteousness redeemed all those who believe in it, already took them away from us? This is how God demonstrates His righteousness now by passing over the sins that were previously committed, sins that have already been paid by Jesus Christ.

Faith in the righteousness of God comes by the Word of Christ because the Word of Christ itself contains the very righteousness of God. By demonstrating His righteousness, God showed not only His righteousness, but also the righteousness of those who believe in Jesus Christ. God rid us of all our sins, and we, too, believe in our hearts that Jesus has taken away all our sins. This is why we have become as sinless and as justified, as we have put on the same righteousness of Christ (Galatians 3:27). Because both God and we are righteous, together we are all family, and you and I are His children. Do you believe in this beautiful news?

Does this mean that we have something of our own that we can boast of? Of course not! What is there of ours to boast about when in fact, our salvation is possible only by hearing and believing in the Word of Christ? Were we saved because of our own works? What is there to boast of? Nothing! Were you saved because you had attended early-morning church services? Were you saved because you had never missed a Sunday church service? Were you saved because you had made sure to offer tithes? Of course not.

These are all works, and the faiths based on works and/or the faiths supplemented with works are wrong faiths. We were saved from our sins only by believing in the righteousness of God in our hearts. Faith comes by hearing, and salvation comes by faith in the Word of Christ.

Trying to receive the remission of sins through prayers of repentance, after believing in Jesus, is also a false faith, for true faith comes only by believing in the righteousness of God, not by the deeds of the law. As the Word of God says, *"Where is boasting then? It is excluded. By what law? Of works? No, but by the law of faith. Therefore we conclude that a man is justified by faith apart from the deeds of the law. Or is He the God of the Jews only? Is He not also the God of the Gentiles? Yes, of the Gentiles also."*

Salvation comes, for both the Israelites and the Gentiles, by hearing and believing in their hearts that Jesus Christ has saved them with His water and blood. We are saved from our sins when we believe in the righteousness of God. When we believe in this righteousness, which is Jesus Christ, we are saved from our sins. God becomes our Father and we become His children. This is the salvation by faith in the righteousness of God, by hearing and believing in the Word of Christ. Our faiths come by believing in the righteousness of God.

Our salvation comes by our faith in the Word of Christ. Do you, then, believe that Christ came to this earth as your Savior, that with His baptism, He took upon all the sins of the world as a propitiation to God, and that he died on the Cross, arose from death on the third day, and sits at the right hand of God the Father? Do you truly believe in this salvation, in this atonement of our Lord Jesus Christ?

There are many people who ask God to appear in their dreams, who say that they will believe if they can only see Him once with their own eyes. Some even claim to have seen Jesus in their dreams, that He told them to do such and such things-build a church here, a prayer center there, etc., but usually something requiring money-and being deceived by such false claims, many are misled and go astray. There are too many sad happenings in this Christian world. You must realize that all these are not the work of our Lord, but of the Devil himself.

If, by any chance, you see Jesus in your dream, don't take it too seriously. Dreams are only dreams. Jesus is not someone who would appear before you in such a manner-otherwise, there would be no need for the Bible. If Jesus appears before us even once, then we must close the Bible, for there is no need for it any longer. But this will have a devastating effect on Christ's work of salvation.

If we were to believe in Jesus without the Bible, He would have to appear before everyone. But there is no need for this, for our Lord has already fulfilled all the requirements of salvation. This is why faith comes by hearing and believing in the Word of Christ. Have all the people, then, heard of Jesus Christ? They may have heard of the name Jesus Christ, but not all of them have heard the true gospel. This is why Paul asked, *"And how shall they hear without a preacher?"*

We must, therefore, preach this gospel that contains the righteousness of God. But with what and how? By what method or how the gospel is preached is not important; all methods of spreading the good news, through spoken words or printed materials, should be used. Faith comes by hearing, and hearing comes by the Word of Christ. Printed materials preaching the gospel, too, can lead readers to true faith. Regardless of the method, you must remember that faith can come only by hearing, and hearing only by preaching the good news.

If you really have faith in the Word of God in your heart, then you will know that you are a true Christian. I hope and pray that you know this; that you have been saved from your sins. I also hope and pray that you will hold onto the Word of the water and the Spirit dearly. Let us, then, conclude our discussion by reading Romans 10:17 together.

"So then faith comes by hearing, and hearing by the word of God." Amen. Those who believe in their hearts by hearing this written Word of God are those who have the true faiths. Do you have this true faith? Our Lord has delivered us from all our sins.

How thankful and happy we are that the Lord has taken away all our sins! Without the gospel, people are always discouraged, but just by hearing that Jesus took upon all our sins with His baptism, our hearts can be filled with joy and our faiths can begin to grow.

I thank the Lord for saving us. ✉

CHAPTER

11

Will Israel be Saved?

Romans 11:1 says, *"I say then, has God cast away His people? Certainly not! For I also am an Israelite, of the seed of Abraham, of the tribe of Benjamin."* God did not, in other words, abandon the Israelites, for Paul himself was also an Israelite.

God says in Romans 11:2-5, *"God has not cast away His people whom He foreknew. Or do you not know what the Scripture says of Elijah, how he pleads with God against Israel, saying, "LORD, they have killed Your prophets and torn down Your altars, and I alone am left, and they seek my life"? But what does the divine response say to him? "I have reserved for Myself seven thousand men who have not bowed the knee to Baal." Even so then, at this present time there is a remnant according to the election of grace."*

As God told us that there would be many Israelites coming back to Him by believing in Jesus, many Jews will be saved from their sins. We must believe that when the end of time comes, a great number of Gentiles will be redeemed of their sins by believing in the righteousness of God and coming to Jesus Christ.

Paul asked, *"Do you not know what the Scripture says of Elijah?"* Here, Paul is referring to the fact that there will eventually be many Israelites who will trust in the righteousness of God that would take away their sins. With the Word of God spoken to Elijah, the Scripture tells us that many among the Israelis will accept Jesus Christ as their Savior. We believe in this Word.

In the Scripture, the number "7" symbolizes completeness. God created this world in six days and rested on the seventh day. God promised to have reserved seven thousand people who would not kneel down to Baal. This meant that there would be many Israelites who would receive salvation from their sins by accepting Jesus Christ as their Savior.

In explaining the relationship between the Israelites and the Gentiles, Paul believed that many among the people of Israel would be saved.

Did they stumble to fall?

Paul said in Romans 11:6-12 that if the Israelites had fully accepted the fact that Jesus was their Savior, there would not have been the era of the Gentiles' salvation. Because the Israelites did not accept Jesus as their Savior, God allowed the Gentiles to have a chance to be saved by the gospel of the water and the Spirit. By this, God intended for the Israelites to be jealous of the Gentiles, who believed in Jesus and became His children. The Israelites would then begin to accept Jesus Christ as their Savior and eventually accept the fact that Jesus Christ is indeed their Messiah.

The root is sacred thus the branches are sacred

Romans 11:13 states, *"For I speak to you Gentiles; inasmuch as I am an apostle to the Gentiles, I magnify my ministry."* Paul said that he magnified his ministry as an apostle of the Gentiles. He wanted to save the people of his own flesh and blood by provoking them to be jealous of the born-again Gentiles.

"For if their being cast away is the reconciling of the world, what will their acceptance be but life from the dead? For if the firstfruit is holy, the lump is also holy; and if the root is holy, so are the branches"(Romans 11:15-16). This passage means that if Abraham, the root of the Israelites, was saved and earned the righteousness of God by believing in His Word, then it was still possible that the Israelites, the branches of Abraham, would be saved.

At the same time, Paul warned the born-again Gentiles that they should be not boastful because they became the holy people of God as broken branches of a wild olive tree are given new life by being grafted into a cultivated olive tree. As Romans 11:18 states, *"Do not boast against the branches. But if you do boast, remember that you do not support the root, but the root supports you."*

We became God's people because we were saved from our sins by believing in the righteousness of God, but if we abandon God's righteousness, we will also be abandoned. We cannot do this because Jesus Christ has fulfilled all the righteousness of God to save us from all our sins, and because we indeed have been saved from all our sins. We have been saved by our faith in the absolute righteousness of God, not by our own works. We, the Gentiles, became His people through our faith in His righteousness, being substituted for the broken branches of the Israelites.

We can stand firm because we believe in God's righteousness

Therefore, by believing in God's righteousness, both

Christians and Jews can be grafted into Jesus as His people. If we do not believe in God's righteousness, we will surely die because of our sins by His just judgment. Paul warned this to the Israelites first, but we are not exempt from the warning either.

God took pity on us, the Gentiles, and completely saved us with His righteousness. Those who know and believe in God's righteousness are saved from all their sins. All of today's Christians will be put to destruction if they do not believe in the righteousness of God that has saved them perfectly, even if they confess that Jesus is their Savior.

Romans 11:23-24 says, *"And they also, if they do not continue in unbelief, will be grafted in, for God is able to graft them in again. For if you were cut out of the olive tree which is wild by nature, and were grafted contrary to nature into a cultivated olive tree, how much more will these, who are natural branches, be grafted into their own olive tree?"* God, in other words, has the power to lead everyone to have faith in His righteousness. That power is promised in the righteousness of God through the gospel of the water and the Spirit.

For both the Israelites and the Gentiles, their deeds do not lead them to become God's children. Rather, they can become God's children by believing in His righteousness and His promise to make them His people. The righteousness of God completely excludes the righteousness of the Law. Through the righteousness of God, both the Israelites and the Gentiles throughout the world will be saved by their faith. This is the blessing of the great salvation of God that will be fulfilled through the gospel spread by us. This power of God is His promise of faith made in His righteousness.

Let us take a look at Romans 11:26-27, *"And so all Israel will be saved, as it is written:*
'The Deliverer will come out of Zion,
And He will turn away ungodliness from Jacob;
For this is My covenant with them,
When I take away their sins.'"

God has promised that He will eventually save the Israelites at the end of time. As such, God Himself promised to rid the evil and filth from the minds of the Israelites and to make them believe in Jesus Christ as their Savior. Although they had faithful ancestors, the Israelites themselves have not received salvation. But God has willed them to be saved in near future by touching their hearts and making them believe in His righteousness.

God has committed us all to disobedience, so that he might have mercy on us all!

Let us read verse 32, which is a very profound verse. *"For God has committed them all to disobedience, that He might have mercy on all."* Everyone rebels and stands against God. None can completely obey Him, but the reason that God has committed us all to disobedience is so that He could give us compassion and love. This is a very surprising and amazing truth.

Through this passage, we can understand why God had confined humans into disobedience. How amazing His Providence is! God has placed us as disobeyers in order to clothe us in His perfect righteousness and merciful love. We can only believe and thank Him for His amazing purpose. God even committed the Israelites to disobedience to grant them the love of His righteousness. The Israelites still look down on Jesus, regarding Him as a low-life from Nazareth, while many of the Gentile Christians use Him as a means of making money.

Those who disobey God's merciful love have no choice but to be sent to hell. God has already prepared the burning hell for them, but He cannot bear to see people going to hell, for He has great pity on them. "How can I send you to hell?" After the full number of the Gentiles has come into His salvation, many of the Israelites will believe in Jesus as their Savior, when the anti-Christ persecutes them during the last half of the seven-year tribulation. In the future, a countless number of believers who confess Jesus as the righteousness of God will rise among the Israelites.

"For God has committed them all to disobedience, that He might have mercy on all." This amazing passage explains that God has allowed all sinners to be saved by believing in His righteousness.

God told Paul that He would make the Israelites repent and believe in Christ when a sufficient number of the Gentiles became martyrs during the tribulation. As Paul says in Romans 11:33, *"Oh, the depth of the riches both of the wisdom and knowledge of God! How unsearchable are His judgments and His ways past finding out!"*

All true wisdom and divine providence come from God. He made all humans insufficient beings from the beginning. This shows God's wisdom, which allows us to receive His salvation. Because of this, believing in Him during the last days will save even the Israelites. All of us had no choice but to be thrown into the trash and the fire, but God saved us from all our sins with His righteousness planned and accomplished by Him. God has willed for all sinners to be saved by Jesus' baptism and blood, according to the sacrificial system of the tabernacle in the Old Testament, when all of humanity became sinners by being tempted by Satan and breaking the Law of God.

How, then, can anyone dare to stand against God's wisdom? *"For of Him and through Him and to Him are all things, to whom be glory forever. Amen."* Who can comprehend this truth, that God has confined us to disobedience in order to give us His mercy? How dare anyone say that He is wrong for doing that? No one! All glory and divine providence is His forever and ever.

The Apostle Paul, being filled by the Holy Spirit, wrote, *"For who has known the mind of the LORD? Or who has become His counselor? Or who has first given to Him And it shall be repaid to him? For of Him and through Him and to Him are all things, to whom be glory forever. Amen" (Romans 11:34-36).*

Although we are full of shortcomings, we live to spread the gospel of the righteousness of God. Those who stand against this gospel of the righteousness of God are His foes. That's right! Such people can rise even among us, and so we should pray and be aware so that none of us would fall into such temptation. Not under any circumstances should we ever stand against the gospel. We must never turn against the gospel of the water and the Spirit with unbelieving hearts. Those who turn against it will be destroyed in this world and the next.

The time for the Israelites to believe in Jesus is near. How wonderful would it be if the six billion people on this earth would come back to God and received salvation? The righteous, who believe in God's righteousness, should not only look at the present situation, but also look at the work of God planned for the Israelites and prepare their faith to enter and live on a new heaven and a new earth. The righteous should always live by faith and hope.

I thank God, for I know that the day the Israelites will believe in Christ as their Savior is near.

Come soon, Lord Jesus! ⊠

CHAPTER

12

Renew Your Mind Before God

"I beseech you therefore, brethren, by the mercies of God, that you present your bodies a living sacrifice, holy, acceptable to God, which is your reasonable service" (Romans 12:1).

What is this "reasonable service," which in translated as a "spiritual act of worship" in the New International Version (NIV), that we must give to God? Giving reasonable service to God means to offer our bodies to Him to do His righteous work. Since we are saved, we need to present our bodies and be acceptable to God for the spreading of the righteous gospel. The reasonable service that we must give God is to set our bodies apart in holiness to give them to Him.

In chapter 12, Paul talks about what our spiritual service is. It is not to be conformed to this world, but to be transformed by the renewal of our minds, that we may prove what the good, pleasing, and perfect will of God is.

Reasonable service is to dedicate all our bodies and hearts to God. How, then, can the righteous live such a life before God? Paul says that we should not conform to this world, but be transformed by the renewal of our minds, and that we should offer our bodies for God's righteous works. Believing in the righteousness of God, while offering our hearts and bodies, is also a reasonable service to God.

This passage is very important because it tells us that we should not conform to this world, and that instead, we should serve God's works and be transformed by the renewal of our

374   Renew Your Mind before God

minds.

We cannot give spiritual worship without first renewing our hearts. Even the righteous cannot give their bodies or hearts to God if they cease to believe in His righteousness.

We may be influenced by this generation, as the same happened in Paul's generation. Because we live in the middle of the drifting flow of this sinful generation, had we not believed in the righteousness of God we would inevitably be following the current of this age. Even the justified who believe in the righteousness of God cannot entirely avoid being influenced by the secular flow, as they live their lives with the worldly people. This is why the Bible tells us not to be conformed to this world.

How, then, can the righteous offer a reasonable worship, a holy sacrifice to God with their whole hearts and bodies, while being exposed to this world? This is possible only by believing in the gospel of the water and the Spirit that renews our minds ceaselessly. The righteous can know and follow the good and perfect will of God when they renew their minds and be transformed by His righteousness.

Paul is not saying this because of his ignorance of worldly affairs. Nor is he giving religious lessons to the believers by saying, "Let's be good," while remaining ignorant of their circumstances and abilities. The reason why Paul is encouraging us to renew our hearts to serve God is because he very well knows that the believers, too, can be swept away by the ways of this world.

Whether born again or not, physical bodies are not very different from each other. But there is one great difference between those who are born again and those who are not—this is the faith in the righteousness of God. Only the righteous can follow the Lord by incessantly renewing their minds while believing in the gospel of the water and the Spirit.

What, then, can renew our hearts? Faith in the Word of gospel that proclaims our complete deliverance from sin is what renews our hearts. The Lord has forgiven all the sins that we committed with our bodies and minds in our weaknesses and infirmities of the flesh. The minds of the righteous can be renewed because our Lord has forgiven all the sins of the world with His baptism and His blood on the Cross. Our minds, in other words, have been renewed because we believed in God's righteousness.

Now, we need to have a correct understanding of what we do before God. We must discern what His perfect will is, what He wants from us, what missions He has given us, and what the born-again righteous must do. We must renew our hearts in these areas and serve Him. God's will is for us to offer our bodies and minds, dedicating ourselves as holy sacrifices to Him. We can give ourselves as sacrifices to Him when we renew our minds. Renewing our minds comes from believing that God has taken away all our sins.

There is a difference between those who are born again and those who are not. Only the righteous can renew their minds by believing in God's righteousness. We, the righteous, can always do the things that please God in faith by cleansing and renewing our hearts, and denying the worldly lusts of flesh. The righteous are different from the sinners because they can renew their hearts and always serve and walk with the Lord.

You must renew your heart with faith

There are many celebrities on TV. The people of this world are busy trying to imitate the styles and fashions of these celebrities. We can easily come across the latest trends by watching TV. We can open up the world with a remote control. Has not your life conformed to this world?

I feel that this world is rapidly changing. Although we carry bills now, we will eventually carry electronic money and electronic cards. If losing these electronic cards becomes a nuisance, we will be told to receive bar codes in our hands or foreheads for better convenience. I also think that there will be many natural disasters at that time. Let us set our hearts in renewing our minds and spreading God's gospel before such time comes so that we, the righteous, are not conformed to this world.

I think about serving God during every waking moment. I wish to diligently spread the gospel that contains His righteousness now, since it will not be possible to spread His Word when the time comes to put bar codes in our hands and foreheads. I am tirelessly working to follow God's will. Perhaps I will be able to rest only when the day that I can no longer work come. I may even give away all my possessions to the needy when that moment comes.

But as of now, I can only follow God's will, set apart from and not conforming to the world. Many of the righteous in Rome who were saved by the gospel preached by Paul were, with passing times, conforming to the world and drifting away from our Lord. We must take heed not to follow in their footsteps.

Paul wrote this passage out of anxiety, which the believers

in Rome were conforming to this world. "Your bodies are conforming to this world, but there is one precious thing that you can do. Renew your minds. Has not the Lord redeemed all your sins? Remember the righteous gospel of God and think about what pleases Him. Renew your minds and do whole and acceptable deeds, by pondering spiritually, not carnally." This is what Paul admonished to the believers in Rome, as well as to us today.

Although we pretend not to outwardly conform to this world, we in fact do conform. Even so, we can still serve the Lord by renewing our minds. Though in our weakness we find it hard not to conform to this world, we still believe that our Lord has taken away all our sins by the righteousness of God. This is how we can always serve the righteous works of God with our faith in His righteousness. We can wholly follow God's good and perfect will by believing in Him.

We must renew our minds every moment. Because the righteous, who are dead to this world, are purer than the worldly people, they face more risk of degenerating into wrong thoughts, minds, and bodies than the secular people. This is why we must always guard our hearts with our faith in God's righteousness.

Since Christ has taken away all our sins, we only need to stand firm in faith reassuring ourselves of the fact that our faith has been made perfect. Do you believe that our Lord has taken away all your sins by the righteousness of God? If you do, then you can do the works of our Lord in faith, regardless of all the unrighteousness of your past, since the Lord has taken away from you all judgment and condemnation of your sins.

We must renew our minds by believing in the gospel of the water and the Spirit. This is very important. We will all eventually leave the church and die if we do not renew our minds by believing in the gospel of the water and the Spirit in this last era.

Living a life of faith of continuous renewal is like riding uphill on a bicycle. Not renewing one's mind is like stopping on the way uphill and not pressing on the pedals. If you do not press the pedals, not only will you stop, but you will actually slip back and crash downhill.

The same principle applies to our faith in the righteousness of God. We are riding uphill on bicycles. It is difficult to reach the top just by our strength and will. We need to hold steadfast to God's righteousness, as we are still in our flesh. Not a moment passes by without carnal thoughts.

Our will in the flesh is apt to give up easily whenever we run out of our strength. "I can't do this. I can't adapt to this. My willpower is so weak, but that brother's willpower is really strong. I do not have the power, but that sister has great power. I am so weak compared to those brothers and sisters. They seem to be fit to serve God, but I'm not." Anyone who does not believe and hold onto God's righteousness will eventually stop pressing on the pedals and crash downhill.

Does this apply to only a handful of people? Of course not. This applies to everyone. A well-trained cyclist can bike uphill with ease, but a weak person would have a hard time. However, the problem for the righteous does not lie in their physical strength—it is holding steadfast to their faith in the gospel of the water and the Spirit. It is impossible to reach the spiritual top with only physical strength. Being physically weak or strong has nothing to do with it.

Remember that no one can lead a life of faith just because he/she has a strong willpower. You must not compare yourself to others and be discouraged. Hold onto the Lord's righteousness alone. The Lord will pull us through if we incessantly renew our minds with faith in the righteousness of God. The gospel of salvation that we received will be planted in our hearts and the Lord will hold onto us if we examine our hearts daily. We must cleanse our unclean minds by believing in God's righteousness and doing the Lord's work.

I thank our Lord for His grace that has let us serve Him by renewing our minds. By having us renew our minds, our God has allowed us to always run before Him with our faith.

For I know that in me nothing good dwells

Paul says in Romans 7:18, *"For I know that in me (that is, in my flesh) nothing good dwells; for to will is present with me, but how to perform what is good I do not find."* Paul very well knew that there was nothing good in his flesh. That nothing good dwells in the flesh is the rule.

Paul acknowledged that nothing good dwelt in his flesh. He knew that no matter how much he loved the Law and how hard he tried to live by it, he just could not do it. The heart wants to renew itself to follow the Lord, but the flesh ceaselessly wants to retreat from the spiritual battlefields.

This is why Paul lamented in Romans 7:21-24, *"I find then a law, that evil is present with me, the one who wills to do good. For I delight in the law of God according to the inward man. But I see another law in my members, warring against the law of my mind, and bringing me into captivity to the law of sin which is in my members. O wretched man that I am! Who will deliver me from this body of death?"*

How did Paul define his body? He defined it as the "body

of death." What about your body? Is it not also the body of death? Of course it is! The body itself is a body of death. It only wants to commit sin and go wherever sins abound. *"O wretched man that I am! Who will deliver me from this body of death?"* And this is why Paul said, *"I thank God—through Jesus Christ our Lord! So then, with the mind I myself serve the law of God, but with the flesh the law of sin" (Romans 7:25).*

Paul points out that there are two laws. The first is the law of the flesh. It only seeks to follow the desires of the flesh and dwells in the thoughts of the flesh that are completely opposite from what pleases God.

The second is the law of the Spirit of life. The law of the Spirit wants to lead us to the right path that God wants us to follow. The law of the Spirit desires what is contrary to the law of the flesh. We Christians are caught in the middle of the two, trying to decide where to go.

We sometimes keep on following what our flesh wants, but when we renew our minds, we follow God's work desired by the Spirit. The reason why we do this—that is, to offer our bodies as sacrifices to God and then immediately do the things of the flesh—is because we all have the flesh. We must, as such, always renew our minds by the Holy Spirit.

Although saved, we conform to this world easily because we are still in the flesh. Because everyone else in this world live their lives conforming to the world, we are easily influenced by them. There is, as such, only one way with which we can follow God, and that is to renew our minds. We can live by always renewing our minds in faith. This is how we can always follow our Lord, until He comes again.

Looking only at our flesh, none of us can follow the Lord's righteous works and we are all doomed to destruction.

But we can follow the Lord by renewing our minds and holding onto His righteousness with our whole hearts. We must renew our minds and follow Him. This is why Paul said in Romans 8:2, *"For the law of the Spirit of life in Christ Jesus has made me free from the law of sin and death."*

What the Law could not do in that it was weak through the flesh, Christ has done by God's righteousness. As Romans 8:3 states, *"For what the law could not do in that it was weak through the flesh, God did by sending His own Son in the likeness of sinful flesh, on account of sin: He condemned sin in the flesh."*

God sent His only Son Jesus Christ to this world and condemned our sins in His flesh. That *"He condemned sin in the flesh"* means that all our sins were taken away and that we were thus made sinless. We were delivered from our sins by believing in the righteousness of God. In order to meet the demands of the justice of the Law, God sent His Son to take away all our sins through His baptism and blood on the Cross and to save us from all the sins of the world.

After receiving this salvation, two kinds of people appear: those who live according to the flesh and set their minds on the things of the flesh, and those who live according to the Spirit and set their minds on the things of the Spirit. You must understand that the thoughts of the flesh lead you to death, but the thoughts of the Spirit lead you to life and peace. Carnal minds are enmity against God.

We do not subject to the Law of God, nor can we ever do this (Romans 8:7). Even the born-again righteous will fall into the thoughts of the flesh if they do not renew their minds. If we do not believe that God has taken away all our sins, and thus do not renew our minds, we can easily fall into the works of the flesh and cannot follow the Lord. This is why we must always renew our minds.

Paul said that we, the born-again righteous, can either fall into the flesh by following the thoughts of the flesh, or follow the thoughts of the Spirit by renewing our minds. We are swinging between the two. But Paul still said, *"But you are not in the flesh but in the Spirit, if indeed the Spirit of God dwells in you. Now if anyone does not have the Spirit of Christ, he is not His" (Romans 8:9).*

We are the spiritual people of God. We are, in other words, His people. Even though we follow the lusts of the world and conform to them in our weakness, we are still the born-again. We fall into the flesh when we set our minds on the things of the flesh, but because we have the Holy Spirit dwelling in us, we are the people of Christ. Put differently, we became the righteous, the people of God.

Paul said, "Our bodies have become dead by Christ." And he added, *"And if Christ is in you, the body is dead because of sin, but the Spirit is life because of righteousness" (Romans 8:10).* Our spiritual thoughts must be awakened. We are still weak, and our bodies will easily go astray until the time of our deaths. But our minds and thoughts must always be renewed by believing in the righteousness of God.

Let us set our eyes on God's righteousness whenever we come to realize the desire for sin inside us. We can then know that the Lord's righteousness has taken away all our sins. Look onto the righteousness of God and believe. Give thanks to Him for taking away all our sins and think of God's works. Think about what is the will of God, perfect and pleasing to Him. Your mind then will always be renewed.

We must renew our minds by faith and set our minds to

the things that please God. This is how the righteous should live. Only by doing this can we follow the Lord until His return. I know that we are all tired from our daily lives. It is hard to work, and it is hard to come to the church. Everyone is facing difficulties. At times, I even envy Jesus when He cried out on His death, *"It is finished."* I am confident that we, too, will be able to say, "It is finished," and be free from all these hardships.

The second coming of our Lord is near. Until then, let us renew our minds without conforming to this world. Because to follow the Lord our hearts need to hold onto the righteousness of God, our minds must be continuously renewed. This is how we can follow the Lord until His return. The time is near.

I recently read a newspaper article that reported that the Antarctic ozone hole was three times larger than the size of the continental United States. I also read another article about the missile defense initiative. This system aims to shoot down ballistic missiles mid-air, and preliminary experiments have been successful. The implications of these developments are clear: the environment will be increasingly destroyed even as the destructive capacity of the military power multiplies by many folds.

If a country increases its military power, would not its rivals also increase their military strength to match this increase? All the nations of the world will not just stand idle to see one country growing in its power. What would happen if war broke out among these great powers?

When some nations tried to develop nuclear weapons, the great powers tried hard to prevent them from acquiring nuclear capabilities. But let us say that such preventive efforts had failed and that the country in question was able to acquire weapons of mass destruction and threatened to use them. Then, the rest of the world would surely try to develop new weapons to cope with this situation.

Such new weapons will devastate this world with forces much greater than nuclear weapons. War is no longer fought with guns as in the past. Killing humans will be nothing; whole cities or entire countries will be wiped out in an instant. Nuclear war will not be localized, but will lead to a world war. Already devastated by such a war, even greater destruction will await the world in the form of natural disasters. The ozone layer will be destroyed more rapidly, and tidal waves and storms will continually rise from deforestation. Then the anti-Christ will appear with great power and conquer this world.

You may say that I am taking this scenario to the extreme, but the human nature is at its fundamentals evil. Nations build armies and develop new weapons, which can never be used for good purposes. Nuclear weapons can be matched only by the same breed of the weapons of mass destruction. Countries will strike each other so that they themselves will survive. Other nations will attempt to balance against any single country that seeks world-domination. No matter what the intentions were, once made, nuclear weapons and military capabilities can only be used for evil purposes.

Long ago, Paul told the believers in Rome not to conform to this world but to follow the Lord by renewing their hearts. This is a very suitable passage for us who live in this age. In these last days, we must discern what the good, pleasing, and perfect will of God is, and follow the Lord with our faith.

Although we have many shortcomings, our Lord is the

Almighty God. The Almighty dwells in us as the Holy Spirit. Although our physical bodies may be weak, the Holy Spirit in us is very strong. This Holy Spirit renews our minds by faith in the Word so that we may be able to follow the Lord.

Let us all depend on the power of the Holy Spirit, renew our minds, and serve the Lord. If the Lord returns to us while we are serving Him, let us then go with Him. Until this day of Christ's return, we will live to spread the righteousness of God. Renew your mind by believing in God's righteousness. ⊠

CHAPTER

13

Live for
The Righteousness of God

Romans 13:1 states, *"Let every soul be subject to the governing authorities. For there is no authority except from God, and the authorities that exist are appointed by God."*

We must live within the boundaries of social norms. God commanded us to fear and respect those who have authority in both our spiritual and carnal lives. God gives authority to the government officials for a reason, and we therefore must not ignore them. We must remember Paul's saying, *"Owe no one anything except to love one another" (Romans 13:8).*

This is why we have been publishing free books and delivering this beautiful gospel to people all over the world.

The Lord said, *"Love is the fulfillment of the law."* People are obsessed with the illusion that they are faithfully keeping the Law in their religious lives.

God gave us the gospel of the water and the Spirit that reveals His righteousness to save us from sin. We need to believe in God's righteousness, shown in the gospel of the water and the Spirit.

Spreading this beautiful gospel that our Lord has given us is truly granting lives to others, since it saves people from all their sins. We must not owe any debt, other than the debt of love received by the love of Jesus Christ.

It's time for us to wake up

Verse 11 says, *"And do this, knowing the time, that now it is high time to awake out of sleep; for now our salvation is nearer than when we first believed."* We will reign with Christ for a thousand years when our infirm bodies are changed—that is, when our bodies are also redeemed.

We can see the similarity between our generation and Noah's generation. A new wave of homosexuality has stirred up in universities. How wicked is this world when a man stabs and kills another man for just using the payphone for too long? Many such cruel and evil deeds are occurring in this generation.

We must realize that it is now time for us to wake up. The time for our Lord's second coming is very near. We should be keen and be able to discern what this age is like and realize that the Lord's second coming is very near. But at the same time, remember that there are so many people who are not really aware of this age.

"But as the days of Noah were, so also will the coming of the Son of Man be" (Matthew 24:37). Even in Noah's time, people built houses, got married, committed all kinds of sins, and went about their daily businesses until the judgment of God was suddenly poured on them one day. No one but Noah expected the heavy rain and the flood that wiped out all but the few who found refugee in his ark. Those who perished met God's devastating judgment while freely eating and drinking, without any anticipation.

This world is exposed not only to the dangers of war, but also to the tremendous natural disasters that are happening throughout the world with the climatic changes. There is a serious danger lurking even in what we eat, and we can no longer enjoy even our own meals without worrying about them. This is why we must live wisely in this era, and remember that the salvation of our bodies is much nearer than when we first began to believe.

Have you clothed yourself with Christ's salvation?

You may think that the destruction of this world has nothing to do with the realm of faith, and that it has everything to do with secular politics and the economy. But global disasters are warning signs for the destruction of the world. This world will soon face extreme economical and environmental hardships. The Bible tells us that as the Lord's second coming draws nearer, we must *"owe no one anything except to love one another"*—helping, protecting, leading, and cooperating with each other in love. And we must realize that our hopes are nearer than when we first began to believe.

We are living in an era in which we need to live in hope, waiting for the return of Jesus Christ.

Where is our hope? Our hope is found in waiting for the return of Christ who will resurrect us and reward us to reign with Him in the Millennial Kingdom, proceeded by the seven years of the Great Tribulation. As the time draws nearer, we must live with hope, having the righteousness of Christ. We must stand firmer and firmer in the gospel of the water and the Spirit, and serve it with our whole hearts. We must expand our ministry to share the gospel with every soul in the entire world.

We must not owe anything except to love one another

I know that there will be much suffering from natural disasters, like earthquakes and volcanoes. Many movies are being made nowadays with the theme of global destruction. I think that this is because the world will possibly turn out as the Hollywood writers have imagined, and this is the evidence that people unconsciously feel the imminent destruction of the world.

Therefore, we should not concern ourselves with the works of the flesh, but concern ourselves with the works of the Spirit.

We must believe that a life spreading the gospel of the water and the Spirit is the most beautiful life. People throughout the world are astonished at our ministry. Countless people have told us how challenged they have been by our ministry. They cannot believe how we, a group of God's servants from Korea, a small country, can spread the righteousness of God so powerfully. Yes, we are indeed small and weak, but we still spread the gospel through out the world because we believe in the gospel of the water and the Spirit, that is, in the righteousness of God.

Romans chapter 14:8 says, *"For if we live, we live to the Lord; and if we die, we die to the Lord. Therefore, whether we live or die, we are the Lord's."* Paul also said in the previous verse, *"None of us lives to himself, and no one dies to himself."* We exist only because of our Lord.

Since we were born into this world by our Lord and became righteous by His righteousness, we belong to Christ whether we live or die. We will live and leave this world as Christ's, having lived our lives for God's righteousness. God is pleased by us, and has elected to use us as His instruments to spread the joyful news all over the world. He has thus opened the great door of evangelism for us. He has allowed us to spread the gospel through books, without actually going to every nation by foot.

A series of books containing the gospel of God's righteousness have been translated and sent to the English-speaking world, the Spanish-speaking countries, as well as to every country in Asia, Africa, and Europe. I am sure that this new series of books entitled *Our Lord Who Becomes the Righteousness of God* will give great spiritual blessings to every soul in the world. It is amazing how God works to complete His will through the believers in His righteousness.

The world will eventually be covered with this beautiful gospel, and once the gospel that contains God's righteousness is spread all over the world, God will fulfill each and every plan that He has in store for us.

This era is on the eve of windstorms. Oil crises and global financial panic can strike the world once more. We must be more faithful in what we are assigned to do. We must spread the gospel of the water and the Spirit until the end of this world comes. Let us diligently spread the gospel of the water and the Spirit so that no one in this world is left without hearing this gospel. We must cooperate and work for the same purpose. We must work like Gideon's three hundred warriors. Although we are few in number, we are the brave soldiers of Heaven, and God is with us.

Whoever receives the forgiveness of sins and is thankful to God can be qualified to spread the righteousness of God. We will be victorious by faith because we have God's righteousness. Those who believe in this righteousness of God always pursue the works of the Spirit and set their goals on spiritual works.

I pray that God's righteousness will be upon you. ✉

CHAPTER

14

Do Not Judge Each Other

Romans 14:1 states, *"Receive one who is weak in the faith, but not to disputes over doubtful things."*

Paul warned the saints in Rome not to judge or criticize each other's faith. At that time, since there were both those who were very faithful and those not so faithful in the church in Rome, they came to criticize each other's faith. If this happens to you, you must respect each other's faith and do away with any critical stances against God's servants. It is up to God, not us, to raise and build His servants.

Even within God's church, many problems arise among the believers. If we take a look at their faith, we can find all sorts of faith. Some had been bound to the Law before their redemption, and thus, they still have the vestige of their old legalistic faith.

Some Christians take great importance in selective eating. For example, such people may believe that they must not eat pork. Others may believe that they must keep the Sabbath under any circumstances. But we must resolve these difference in our faith in the righteousness of God and not criticize each other over such small matters. This is the gist of what Paul was talking about.

Paul teaches in chapter 14 that we should not criticize our fellow believers' weakness if they have faith in the righteousness of God. Why not? Because although weak, they also believe in God's righteousness.

The Bible regards those who have been redeemed of their sins by believing in God's righteousness as the precious people of God. While they may seem insufficient in each other's eyes, God has nevertheless ordered us not to criticize other believers' faith. This is because although they may be insufficient in the flesh, they still became the children of God by faith.

Everyone's faith differs from each other

Verses 2-3 state, *"For one believes he may eat all things, but he who is weak eats only vegetables. Let not him who eats despise him who does not eat, and let not him who does not eat judge him who eats; for God has received him."*

There can be diversity among the servants of God in believing in His righteousness and following Him. The faith in salvation is the same, but the amount of faith in His Word may differ.

If someone had been a legalist before being born again by the faith in the gospel of the righteousness of God, he/she would need time to abandon his/her own righteousness by wholly believing in God's righteousness. These people tend to take great importance in observing the Sabbath, but you should not criticize them because they, too, believe in God's righteousness.

God is pleased by the faith of those who know and believe in His righteousness. He has taken them as His people. Therefore, those who truly believe in the righteousness of God should make every effort to nourish their fellow believers with God's righteousness, instead of criticizing the weakness of the faith of them.

We must not judge the servants of God

Verse 4 says, *"Who are you to judge another's servant? To his own master he stands or falls. Indeed, he will be made to stand, for God is able to make him stand."*

We must acknowledge God's servants, whom God has approved, and also their faiths. Do you criticize and judge God's servants while living your Christian life? Then God will rebuke your faith even more. If you condemn the faith of those whom God approves just because you do not like them, you are climbing yourself into the judgment seat of God and judging His servants. This is not right. Rather, you should gratefully receive even those servants of God whom you dislike, and obey their guidance while lifting up God's righteousness.

God must approve our faith. We should have the true faith that merits God's commendation and reward. Because God has allowed us to devote our lives to Jesus Christ, we thank Him for His righteousness. We must approve those whom God approves, and disapprove of those whom God disapproves. I hope that you would glorify God by having faith in His righteousness, instead of lifting up your own righteousness. I hope that God would approve your faith. You will then be lifted up because of your faith in His righteousness.

If they also believe in God's Righteousness...

"One person esteems one day above another; another esteems every day alike. Let each be fully convinced in his own mind. He who observes the day, observes it to the Lord; and he who does not observe the day, to the Lord he does not observe it. He who eats, eats to the Lord, for he gives God thanks; and

he who does not eat, to the Lord he does not eat, and gives God thanks" (Romans 14:5-6).

Among the Jews were those who were saved by believing in Christ, our Lord of the gospel of the water and the Spirit. Many of them, though they believed in Jesus, were still bound by the Law. But they were already the servants of God's righteousness because whatever they did to keep the Law, they did to spread God's righteousness.

That is why Paul said, *"To those who are under the law, as under the law, that I might win those who are under the law; to those who are without law, as without law (not being without law toward God, but under law toward Christ), that I might win those who are without law" (1 Corinthians 9:20-21).*

We must neither ignore nor reject the faith of those who believe in the righteousness of God. If they believe in God's righteousness and serve Him, we must acknowledge them as the servants of God.

The righteous shall live for the Lord

Verses 7-9 state, *"For none of us lives to himself, and no one dies to himself. For if we live, we live to the Lord; and if we die, we die to the Lord. Therefore, whether we live or die, we are the Lord's. For to this end Christ died and rose and lived again, that He might be Lord of both the dead and the living."*

We live with Christ and die with Him because we have been saved from all our sins and received new lives by believing in the righteousness of God revealed in the gospel. All the old things have passed away in Christ, and we became new creatures. To truly believe in God's righteousness means to know and believe in the truth that you are Christ's. Thus, those who believe in the righteousness of God have no more to do with this world and have become the servants of God instead.

If you become God's servant, you will lift Him up high, love Him, live for His glory, and be thankful to Him for allowing you to live your life in this way.

Do you truly belong to Christ? Those who believe in the gospel of the water and the Spirit have been crucified with Christ and were brought back to life again with Him. Whether we live or die, we belong to Christ by God's righteousness. The Lord has become the Lord of the saved.

We should not judge our fellow believers

It is written in verses 10-12, *"But why do you judge your brother? Or why do you show contempt for your brother? For we shall all stand before the judgment seat of Christ. For it is written: "As I live, says the LORD, Every knee shall bow to Me, And every tongue shall confess to God." So then each of us shall give account of himself to God."*

Because Christ our God lives, we will one day kneel before Him and confess everything. We must therefore not seat on the judgment seat and judge our brothers and sisters, but stand before God with modesty. It is much more important to live for God's will than to judge and condemn one another in His church. If we judge and condemn our brothers and sisters' weaknesses, we will be judged for our own weaknesses before God. This is why we must realize how good it is to live for God's will, together in His church.

True faith edifies the fellow believers and pursues the

righteousness of God. Remember that a false faith will abandon God's righteousness and only build its own righteousness. What about you? Are you pursuing God's righteousness with faith? Or are you pursuing the righteousness of your own flesh?

We must edify the others' faith

Verses 13-14, *"Therefore let us not judge one another anymore, but rather resolve this, not to put a stumbling block or a cause to fall in our brother's way. I know and am convinced by the Lord Jesus that there is nothing unclean of itself; but to him who considers anything to be unclean, to him it is unclean."*

Because there are differences in the amount of faith among those who believe in the righteousness of God, we should work to build each other's faith by edifying one another. This brings growth to the believers of God's righteousness. If we truly live for God and His righteousness, we are all His people.

If you are a Christian who believes in the righteousness of God, you can do anything with your faith in the Word of God. If you cannot, it is because you are pursuing your own righteousness instead of God's righteousness. Pursuing your own righteousness in the righteousness of God is like pursuing the world and having a wrong faith.

Those who seek their own righteousness, although saved by believing in God's righteousness, are living as God's foes. God wants those who are saved by believing in His righteousness to keep on following His righteousness throughout their lives.

Walk in love

Verses 15-18 says, *"Yet if your brother is grieved because of your food, you are no longer walking in love. Do not destroy with your food the one for whom Christ died. Therefore do not let your good be spoken of as evil; for the kingdom of God is not eating and drinking, but righteousness and peace and joy in the Holy Spirit. For he who serves Christ in these things is acceptable to God and approved by men."*

Those who have been saved by believing in God's righteousness and are living to spread it do not despise His people for the sake of food. We sometimes bring food to share and have fellowship in love. But Paul is warning us against excluding the poor brothers and sisters and sharing only among the wealthy, because that could make our fellow Christians to stumble.

The blessings that God has bestowed on those who believe in His righteousness are allowing us to follow God's righteousness, our peace of mind given by the gospel of the water and the Spirit, and being able to serve the Lord together, sharing in each other's joy that He has given. Those who are wealthy should therefore realize that all their riches are from God, and share them with others to serve the gospel and follow God's righteousness together. God is pleased with and loves those who live such lives.

Seek to edify others

Verses 19-21 says, *"Therefore let us pursue the things which make for peace and the things by which one may edify another. Do not destroy the work of God for the sake of food.*

All things indeed are pure, but it is evil for the man who eats with offense. It is good neither to eat meat nor drink wine nor do anything by which your brother stumbles or is offended or is made weak."

Long ago, in such ancient cities as Rome and Corinth, people sold food that were once offered as sacrifices to idols. Some of the believers in God's righteousness used to buy such meat and eat them. Then, some of the fellow believers who were of weak faith in God's church thought that eating such meat was sinful. This is why Paul said, *"Do not destroy the work of God for the sake of food" (verse 20).*

The same applied to wine. There were some believers who did not worry much about drinking. But Paul admonished that if such behaviors were to weaken the faith of their fellow believers, it would be good for them to stop offending their fellow believers with their drinking. This also happens among us. Therefore, we must live our Christian lives in a way that edifies others, and seek God's righteousness. Issues can rise today concerning the food used as offerings to ancestors, and it is better not to eat that kind of food for the sake of those who are weak in faith.

Have faith in God's Righteousness

Verse 22-23 states, *"Do you have faith? Have it to yourself before God. Happy is he who does not condemn himself in what he approves. But he who doubts is condemned if he eats, because he does not eat from faith; for whatever is not from faith is sin."*

Those who believe in the righteousness of God are the ones who have the correct faith. Faith in God's righteousness is the God-given faith that cleanses away all our sins. Christians therefore must believe in God's righteousness and have the conviction of their faith in His righteousness.

The Scripture tells us that following God without believing in His righteousness is a sin. Anything done without faith is a sin. Knowing that anything done without faith in God's righteousness is a sin, we must have more faith in His righteousness.

The Bible says, *"He who doubts is condemned if he eats."* Everything is clean if you eat with faith in God's righteousness, because God created every plant and animal.

We must understand just how important it is for us to know and believe in God's righteousness. We must also edify our fellow born-again believers and respect their faith. ✉

CHAPTER

15

Let Us Spread the Gospel Throughout the Entire World

"We then who are strong ought to bear with the scruples of the weak, and not to please ourselves. Let each of us please his neighbor for his good, leading to edification" (Romans 15:1-2).

Those who believe in God's righteousness must not seek their own righteousness, since Jesus Christ did not seek His either. The righteous live for the Kingdom of God and spread the gospel for the good of others. Paul said that the strong ought to bear the infirmities of the weak instead of pleasing themselves.

Believers of God's righteousness must preach the gospel so that they can cleanse the sins of others with the baptism and blood of Jesus Christ. This is the reason why God hates those who are lazy and do not spread the gospel to save sinners. We must therefore not seek our own righteousness, but spread God's righteousness to others. We must deliver the gospel of the water and the Spirit so that sinners can be saved through faith. We must also edify each other.

Do not build the house of faith on another man's foundation

Verse 20 states, *"And so I have made it my aim to preach*

the gospel, not where Christ was named, lest I should build on another man's foundation."

There was something peculiar in the gospel that Paul preached. It is that he strived to spread only the gospel of the water and the Spirit. Believers of God's righteousness must strive to spread the gospel of the water and the Spirit, just as Paul did. In order to make this happen, we must seek the good of others, instead of our own. People who seek the good of others do so because they have been crucified with Christ and resurrected with Him. Those who believe in Christ are not dead, but alive.

"For this reason I also have been much hindered from coming to you. But now no longer having a place in these parts, and having a great desire these many years to come to you, whenever I journey to Spain, I shall come to you. For I hope to see you on my journey, and to be helped on my way there by you, if first I may enjoy your company for a while. But now I am going to Jerusalem to minister to the saints. For it pleased those from Macedonia and Achaia to make a certain contribution for the poor among the saints in Jerusalem. It pleased them indeed, and they are their debtors. For if the Gentiles have been partakers of their spiritual things, their duty is also to minister to them in material things. Therefore, when I have performed this and have sealed to them this fruit, I shall go by way of you to Spain. But I know that when I come to you, I shall come in the fullness of the blessing of the gospel of Christ" (Romans 15:22-29).

Paul was an itinerant preacher and overseer of God's church

While Paul was on his way to the Jerusalem Church to serve its Christians, he delivered the contributions from Macedonia and Achaia to them. Paul added that if the Gentiles have been made partakers of their spiritual things, their duty is also to minister to them in material things. The saints in the Jerusalem Church were in the midst of persecution at that time, and could not free themselves from their material deficiencies. The Jerusalem Church, which was suffering great persecution for believing in Jesus Christ, was greatly consoled by the Gentile brothers and sisters.

In the present as in the past, it has become a tradition for God's churches to share their wealth with the needy instead of enjoying it by themselves. The Spirit-filled believers especially cannot live for themselves alone. Why? Because the Holy Spirit dwells in them! They are the born-again who are led by the Holy Spirit who resides in them.

It is wonderful that the Gentile churches supported and funded the Jerusalem Church. This was the work of the Holy Spirit. The Holy Spirit supported the Jerusalem Church for the gospel of the water and the Spirit, not for any individuals, and granted it material relief as well. At that time in Israel, many were beaten, thrown in jail, even killed for their faith in Christ as their Savior.

On TV documentaries, we can often see the remains of the Catacomb martyrs and their hideouts in mountain caves. This was what the Jerusalem Church had to go through at that time. We, too, must give a helping hand to God's churches when they are facing difficulties.

We may brush off the importance of the mutual help that the Early Churches extended to each other, but this was a time when the believers had to live in hiding to flee from persecution. Only the Holy Spirit could make the sharing possible in these circumstances. Because the Jerusalem Church was under persecution, it was natural for other churches to help it. Because this was the work of the Holy Spirit, it was fitting and beautiful.

You, a believer of God's righteousness, should take part in such works as well. The member churches of The New Life Mission raise fund and invest it in spreading the gospel to the entire world. All of them have some type of financial difficulty to cope with, but they are still eager to spread the gospel to save souls.

Paul worked as a tent-maker to preach the gospel of the water and the Spirit. When there was someone who could care for the church that he founded, he entrusted the church to him, and went on his way to another region to preach the gospel— all the while earning his living through tent-making.

Just as you do not live for yourself alone, our ministers do not live for themselves. Those who have the Holy Spirit dwelling in them devote themselves to God's works—that is, to saving the lost from all their sins. Both the ministers and the lay members of our mission serve the gospel through "tent-making ministry," where they hold their own jobs to support themselves and at the same time contribute to the spreading of the gospel, both financially and by volunteering.

Like this, we can find many similarities between Paul's ministry and that of God's church today. We have the same frame of minds, and live lives that please the Holy Spirit. What is on our minds when it is bitterly cold? We surely think of our fellow Christians and servants of God, and wonder if they are suffering from the cold. We, the born-again Christians, care and watch out for one another. All the righteous in the Bible needed one another and served God's righteousness together. This life of faith is the real lives of the righteous.

We have lived with such mind-sets. When we first started to preach the gospel of the water and the Spirit, we had to begin from scratch, as we had nothing. We were so financially strapped that we often had a hard time trying to come up with a few hundred dollars to pay the rent and the bills for the church building. But we still devoted ourselves to our literature ministry throughout this country.

When we were faced with financial difficulties, it was God who solved them for us allowed us to see the fruits of our ministry. Because the Holy Spirit abides in our hearts, our desire to spread the gospel is burning in our hearts, no matter what difficulties are ahead of us. We want to share God's love with all the lost souls by preaching the gospel of the water and the Spirit, just as God's churches and the righteous written in the Bible did.

We can find that the born-again Christians of the Early Church looked after one another and that we, too, do so. This is not possible without the guidance of the Holy Spirit. The Holy Spirit has been spreading the righteousness of God throughout the earth through the devotions of the born again, and will continue to do the same.

Even if we are faced with the end of days!

People say that we are now living in the last age, when all the difficulties prophesized in the Bible will come to be fulfilled.

Catastrophe and disaster will engulf the whole in the last days. As believers, we must stand more firmly in our faith in the righteousness of God and preach the gospel of the water and the Spirit even more diligently. Those who believe in God's righteousness must have the heart to look after and love one another in this last age. Our own hearts may be hardened as the hearts of the world harden, but we can overcome this world in the end, because we have the Holy Spirit in us. No matter what the circumstances, we need to look after God's churches and souls. We must look after those who require our assistance, love them, think of our fellow brothers and sisters, and spread the gospel till the end.

We must devote ourselves to the salvation of others rather than seeking our own righteousness. There are still so many souls, out there all over the world, who have not heard the gospel of the water and the Spirit. People in many countries have never heard the gospel of the water and the Spirit, nor had a chance to know God's righteousness. We must set our minds like the soldiers who are fighting to win the lost souls and nations with the gospel of the water and the Spirit. This mission comes not from coercion, as if we are compelled by force, but it naturally arises in the hearts of those of us in whom the Holy Spirit dwells.

The Great Commission to spread the gospel of the water and the Spirit to the ends of the earth is active in our hearts today. What I want to tell you is that the more difficult this world becomes, the more sufficiently God pours His Holy Spirit on us. We are spreading the gospel through our printed and electronic books offered to those who thirst for the truth, free of charge. We will constantly carry on our ministry worldwide through the Internet.

Although we are not any wealthier than the Americans or the Europeans, we can still give them the gospel that contains the righteousness of God. We have the same mind-set as Peter who said, *"Silver and gold I do not have, but what I do have I give you: In the name of Jesus Christ of Nazareth, rise up and walk" (Acts 3:6).*

We can freely give them the gospel that has fulfilled the righteousness of God, which they had not known. Even though we are no better off than anyone else when measured by the worldly scales, we are the servants of God who can give the gospel that contains the righteousness of God. Those who, having come across this gospel through our ministry, come to know and believe in this gospel will be greatly blessed.

This is the Internet era, and with it God has provided us a way to open the whole world. We have seen how grateful and joyful people were when we gave them the gospel that has fulfilled God's righteousness. The gloomier the world becomes, the more thankful and powerful we will become while preaching the gospel of God's righteousness to the lost. Would the world end like this, or would God give us more chances to spread His gospel? This is what we should think and pray about. Everything will be perfectly fulfilled by the Holy Spirit.

I also used to be selfish, and only cared about my flesh before I was born again. Not only I, but we all were like this. Those who live only for the pleasures of the flesh may claim that they have love, but in truth they cannot actually love others. This is the difference between those who have the Holy Spirit and those who do not. Sinners can only live for themselves, but those with the Holy Spirit has the power to live for someone else, and do actually live for others. The Triune God gives His believers the power to live for other souls. Because God dwells in their hearts and leads them on, they can do His righteous works.

No matter how many churches there are in this world, almost all of them have now become merely secular enterprises. They spare no money to build their extravagant churches and they have huge budgets that are in the millions of dollars, and yet only a tiny fraction of their wealth, if at all, is given for charitable works. They have gone mad to gain more wealth from this earth, discarding their real mission of saving souls from sin as secondary and unimportant. They cannot be a part of the church of God, for His church does not pursue its own interests over those of God.

The true church of God uses its resources to save the lost souls in transparency and honesty. As the Bible says, *"Blessed are the merciful, for they shall obtain mercy (Matthew 5:7),"* God has given us the heart to look after the souls of this world and lead them to redemption, and He has made all these things possible. The gospel of the water and the Spirit has now been put together into publications that have been translated into almost 40 languages and over 60 titles, each of them testifying God's righteousness to those who are facing their spiritual death.

How pleased would God be if we prayed more earnestly and spread the gospel of the water and the Spirit to more sinners to save them, before this world is engulfed in the Great Tribulation and comes to its end? Let us not be discouraged, but be faithful until the very end.

In the past, the poor could survive by helping each other. But we have now entered an era of limitless competition in which only the strong can survive. Whenever we look at this generation, we are convinced of our duty that we must spread the gospel of the water and the Spirit to those who still have not heard it. We all have the heart to deliver the gospel that will bring peace to those who are tired and weary from their unending struggles in this harsh world. Let us deliver the spiritual blessing of the gospel of the water and the Spirit to them. We can live for Christ with our faiths in God's righteousness, for He has taken away all our sins.

The gospel that contains God's righteousness will spread tenfold, a hundredfold, a thousand fold, and a million fold more swiftly now. We will have so much work to do, so let us be faithful. Those who are talented should give their talents to the Lord and spread the gospel to each and every soul. We must all work to spread the gospel according to our God-given talents. We have no power of our own, but I believe that if we pray to God according to the Holy Spirit that stirs in us, God will grant all our wishes.

Christ has given us His true love that loves the sinners. We have been saved from the sins of this world by our faith in the righteousness of God. This is why we must work harder to spread the gospel, even as it become more difficult to live in this world. We have the duty to give the gospel to those who have not heard it yet.

God said, *"I have reserved for Myself seven thousand men who have not bowed the knee to Baal" (Romans 11:4)*. There are still so many in this world who need to receive the gospel of the water and the Spirit. So many souls, whether pastors', theologians', or the laymen's, are rising up.

That we are able to work for the gospel is because of the love of Christ. We still have so much work to do, and at times we feel overwhelmed by them. But we should be more faithful and spread the gospel even more diligently as we face more difficulties. This is the heart of Christ. I pray that you, a righteous, do not think of only yourself. If you think of only yourself, there is no need for faith or prayers because you are just trying to live for yourself and have nothing to do with the lost souls. But if you have to earn your wages to support yourself and other souls as well, what would happen? You would pray to God for help because you are weak.

This is how our faith and prayers grow. This is why God says,

"There is one who scatters, yet increases more;
And there is one who withholds more than is right,
But it leads to poverty" (Proverbs 11:24).

Sharing the gospel of the water and the Spirit with others is the most righteous life of Christians. A spiritual life is one that spreads the true gospel that leads people to Christ. Let us look after our neighbors and their souls, and spread the gospel throughout the entire world. May the blessing of God's righteousness always be with you.

Hallelujah! Let us praise our Lord! I thank Him for allowing us to do His righteous and good works, and for delivering us from the power of the darkness and leading us into the Kingdom of the Son. ⊠

CHAPTER

16

Greet One Another

Paul the Apostle told the saints in Rome and us to greet one another in his epilogue. Whom can we greet whole-heartedly in the Lord even in this age? We can joyfully greet the ministers and believers who are preaching the Word of God all over this world. We can have fellowship with those who are saved by reading the books of the gospel of the water and the Spirit. We, too, have the churches, the believers, and the servants of God whom we can greet in Christ.

Since not everyone believes in the gospel of the water and the Spirit, the righteous cannot greet everyone. There aren't too many people in this world whom we can greet with joy. It is only regrettable that there aren't that many people who believe in the gospel of the water and the Spirit, whom we can greet and have fellowship in the same faith. We cannot have fellowship with the sinners who pretend to be God's servants in worldly churches.

Just as sin and the Holy Spirit cannot dwell together, the sinners and the righteous cannot greet one another. Those who believe in the gospel of the water and the Spirit can offer spiritual worships to God and work for spiritual things. But the sinners, who have not yet received the remission of their sins, attempt to be saved by keeping the Law of God, and thus they cannot have spiritual fellowship with the righteous. Just as a beast and a human cannot converse with each other, the righteous cannot have spiritual fellowship with the sinners.

We can see that the only people with whom Paul had spiritual fellowship were those who had the same faith as his.

We know that if someone had fellowship with Paul, it means that Paul approved his/her faith. So, I thought, "If I were to head to a particular region today, whom should I visit and greet?" I am sure I will visit Sokcho Church if I go to Sokcho, and Gangneung Church if I go to Gangneung. I can meet God's servants and believers, and have fellowship and break bread with them. I can also visit the houses of my brothers and sisters there and greet them. But the people whom I can greet are only those who believe in the gospel of the water and the Spirit, and those with whom I can share the same faith in the Holy Spirit.

We can see how blessed those whose faith is approved by Paul are. How great is it that we have the gospel of the water and the Spirit to confirm each other's faith and greet one another. Do you have the faith in the gospel of the water and the Spirit that lets you greet one another? Can you faithfully confess, without a doubt, to God that you do not have any sin?

I had a chance to greet the fellow believers in China when I visited there. I visited a brother who lived on the banks of the Heran River. As soon as we woke up the next morning, he prepared us a big breakfast. We sat at a huge round table, the kind that we used to use to sit everyone in the extended family, and had a lovely fellowship with the believers there. There also was an evangelist in a nearby city who was so eager to see us. So, we visited and had fellowship with him, too. We can greet whoever believes in the gospel of the water and the Spirit.

Where would I go to if I visited the United States? I'd visit Pastor Samuel Kim and his wife in Flushing, New York. I'd also visit The New Life Church to meet our brothers and sisters there. In Russia, too, there is a born-again church that I visited a few years ago. In Japan, I'd love to visit the house of Deaconess Soon-Ok Park in Tokyo.

We are the righteous who are saved by our faith in the gospel of the water and the Spirit. We were not saved because of any accomplishments of our flesh, but because of the righteousness of God that we received through our faith in the gospel of the water and the Spirit.

As you can see, there are people set aside for the righteous to greet, just as Paul had a list of people to greet in Romans chapter 16. Just as Paul did, we cannot greet every Christian because not all of them have the right faith, but only those who know and believe in the righteousness of God. We cannot help but praise God for giving us the faith in which we can greet and be greeted.

Paul warned us to stay away from these people

Starting from verse 17, the second admonition that Paul makes to us is to stay away from those who only serve their own bellies. *"Now I urge you, brethren, note those who cause divisions and offenses, contrary to the doctrine which you learned, and avoid them. For those who are such do not serve our Lord Jesus Christ, but their own belly, and by smooth words and flattering speech deceive the hearts of the simple" (Romans 16:17-18).* There are those who do not serve Christ, but their own bellies. They are the ones who cause strife among believers and deceive the naïve with smooth words and flattering speeches. We must not greet such people, but stay away from them.

Paul warned us to stay away from such people, for they only enjoy causing distresses in church, disrupt those who truthfully believe in God, and gather the naïve only to feed their own greed. Such swindling Christian leaders try to confine

424 Greet One Another

people under sin by teaching their followers to completely obey the Law. They only fill up their own bellies in the name of Jesus and deceive the innocent. There is no need for us to greet them, for they are in the ministry only to serve their own bellies.

The gospel of the water and the Spirit must be spread to all nations!

Thirdly, Paul talked about the need to spread the gospel to all nations. Verse 26 says, *"But now made manifest, and by the prophetic Scriptures made known to all nations, according to the commandment of the everlasting God, for obedience to the faith..."* The gospel of the water and the Spirit that Paul preached is truly the gospel that all nations must believe and obey. It is only too unfortunate that most of the regions in which Paul planted churches with those who believed in the gospel of the water and the Spirit have now become Islamic regions.

At the time, Paul went to these regions and established church leaders there among the believers of the gospel of the water and the Spirit that contains the righteousness of God. It was similar to the way we send workers to our church after training them in our mission school. Although the churches at that time kept their faith in *"one Lord, one faith, one baptism" (Ephesians 4:5)*, they failed to maintain their faith in the gospel, as they did not record the gospel in writing.

Right now we are in the process of translating our books into Turkish. Someone from Turkey was touched by our English editions and volunteered to translate them. We are now starting to spread the gospel of the water and the Spirit to where Paul himself once preached the gospel and planted God's churches.

We are preaching the same gospel that Paul preached throughout the same region that he had visited. The gospel Paul preached was the gospel of the water and the Spirit that can save all nations just by believing and obeying it.

In the last chapter of Romans, Paul told the saints in Rome to greet one another, to stay away from those who only fill their bellies, and to spread the gospel of the water and the Spirit to all nations.

The Gospel of the water and the Spirit will strengthen us

The fourth thing Paul mentioned was that this gospel of the water and the Spirit is the wisdom of God that will establish us. *"Now to Him who is able to establish you according to my gospel and the preaching of Jesus Christ, according to the revelation of the mystery kept secret since the world began but now made manifest, and by the prophetic Scriptures made known to all nations, according to the commandment of the everlasting God, for obedience to the faith—to God, alone wise, be glory through Jesus Christ forever. Amen" (Romans 16:25-27).* What could establish the saints in Rome? It was Paul's gospel of the water and the Spirit that could and did establish the saints in Rome. This gospel is also the wisdom of God.

In the gospel that God gave us is His wisdom. This gospel has the power to take away all the sins of even those who are full of shortcomings. Those who believe in the gospel of the water and the Spirit are made not only sinless but the preachers of this gospel, no matter how weak and full of shortcomings that they may be. Only the wisdom of God and the gospel of the water and the Spirit that comes from it can make us complete beings. There is no truth besides this gospel that can strengthen one's soul, heart, thoughts, and body.

Paul did not plainly call the gospel "the gospel," but called it "my gospel." The gospel that Paul preached was the gospel of the water and the Spirit, revealed in both the Old and New Testaments. This gospel of the water and the Spirit is based on the gospel revealed through the prophets in the Old Testament and fulfilled by Jesus Christ in the New Testament. This is why Paul said that 'his gospel' was made manifest according to the revelation of the mystery kept secret in the prophetic Scriptures.

The gospel that Paul preached was implied in the sacrificial system in Pentateuch of the Old Testament, especially in Leviticus, and was completed by Jesus Christ in the New Testament as God's righteousness through His baptism, His death on the Cross and His resurrection. This is why Paul gave all glory *"to Him who is able to establish you according to my gospel."*

The gospel of the water and the Spirit establishes the saints and servants of God. Through this gospel, our faith, souls, thoughts, minds, and bodies are strengthened. How can our faith be strengthened? What makes us stand strong at all times when we are always weak?

Our faith becomes stronger and stronger because we have received the salvation of Christ, who took away all our sins through His baptism and the bloodshed on the Cross. We can say that we have no sin before God because our hearts have nothing to be ashamed of anymore, and with this unashamed spiritual faith, we can spread the gospel of the water and the Spirit to those who are still bound in sin.

The final admonitions

Paul ends chapter 16 with the closing prayer saying, *"To God, alone wise, be glory through Jesus Christ forever, Amen."* What glorifies God most of all? Preaching the righteousness of God in Jesus Christ glorifies God the most. We are also glorified when we serve the gospel with our whole hearts.

The essence of Paul's message in Romans 16 are these: greet one another, stay away from those who only fill their belly, spread the gospel to all nations. This was the last admonition that Paul gave to the church in Rome. The gospel of the water and the Spirit that Paul preached has the power to strengthen us in every way. This is what we believe in. The faith in gospel of the water and the Spirit is the same as the faith that the apostles in the Bible had and what our own church believes in right now.

Can you feel the sameness? I am amazed whenever I read the Bible and realize that we have the same faith as the biblical figures who lived two thousand years ago.

Have you thought about how many people we share the gospel with every day? We share the gospel with no less than two thousand people per day. This two thousand will soon multiply to ten thousand if the newly born-again saints in every nation preach the gospel to their neighbors, and the ten thousand people only have to share it once for them to become twenty thousand. As you can see, preaching the gospel to the entire world is not such an impossible task after all.

Of course, the key feature of our books on the gospel of the water and the Spirit is that they do not disappear but are stored, and their meanings do not change regardless of how many people read them. Where there is a book that contains the gospel of the water and the Spirit, many people will borrow and read it, and the gospel of God will spread. The day when the gospel will reach the entire world is not too far away.

The righteousness of God that you have by your faith is the gospel of the water and the Spirit that even those in the developed countries are not well aware of. The true gospel we want to share with the entire world is a mystery unknown to this world, and thus, we eagerly want to reveal the secret of salvation to all those who smother in their sins. This righteousness of God shown in the gospel of the water and the Spirit is so clear that whoever accepts this gospel will give thanks and glory to God.

Some people think it odd that we repeatedly talk about the gospel of the water and the Spirit. But no matter how many times we repeat it, it still stirs joy and thanks in our souls. Since there are so many Christians who are still bound to sin, we repeatedly preach the gospel of the water and the Spirit to the entire world. Because this gospel is the very gospel that was handed down by the apostles, including Paul, all souls should believe in this gospel. We need to listen and engrave the gospel of the water and the Spirit in our hearts because it is essential to every Christian.

We share the gospel with over two thousand people a day through our books, both printed and electronic, and web site. We are sure that if the seed of the truth falls on good soil, it will be able to produce a crop—thirty, sixty, or hundred times more than what was sown. One person can preach the gospel to dozens of people, and each of these people then can preach the gospel to dozens more, spreading the gospel to a vast number of people.

When we hear that our gospel is spread to over two thousand people a day, our hearts get filled with God's righteousness. I thank God for opening the way for us to deliver this gospel all over the world. I pray that God will strengthen even more the faith of His servants.

The gospel of the water and the Spirit that is now spreading all over the world is a new wave of truth for salvation. This gospel is the only way to receive the Holy Spirit and to enter the Kingdom of God. No matter how hard you search in secular religions, you will not find the gospel of the water and the Spirit.

People all over the world will thank God because they can now believe in His righteousness through the gospel of the water and the Spirit. Everyone who reads our book will exclaim, "Ah! This is how Jesus saved me from my sins!", for they had never heard this gospel before.

Those who want to be free from the bondage of sin and those who endlessly desire to receive the Holy Spirit will receive the complete forgiveness of their sins and the peace of their minds when they finally know and accept the gospel of the water and the Spirit. From this moment on, the gospel of the water and the Spirit will spread to every nation in the world.

My heart is filled with joy that the gospel of the water and the Spirit is spreading all over the world. Though I serve the gospel, I know that I am still full of weaknesses and shortcomings. But because I completely believe in the gospel of the water and the Spirit and know God's righteousness, I always receive new strength from the Lord so that I can continue to serve His gospel. The gospel has now entered more nations; more people have read our books and have been amazed by such perfect gospel.

Those who believe in God's righteousness all over the world are those who have been saved by believing in the gospel of the water and the Spirit. The reason why we can stand as whole and complete despite our weaknesses is because we believe in our Lord, the righteousness of God. We are God's workers. We do not seek to only satisfy our carnal bellies, but to spread the true faith all over the world. I bless and hope that many righteous believers will rise to our challenge to spread the gospel throughout the world.

Like Paul, we can spread the gospel of the water and the Spirit regardless of when the Lord comes. Let us work hard together for this Great Commission. When we spread the gospel to the ends of the earth, the Lord will come according to His promise and take us home. We must listen carefully to what Paul admonished us, greet and encourage one another. Although we lack in our deeds, we are greatly strengthened spiritually through our faith in God's righteousness. We come to know how fair and sure our faith in the gospel of the water and the Spirit really is. We really are believers in our Lord, who is the perfect righteousness of God.

When we look at this world with our faith in God's righteousness, we find that there is so much to do. We can all live our lives spreading the gospel throughout this world, praising God with our faith in Christ, who is the righteousness of God.

Hallelujah! I forever praise our Lord, the righteousness of God! ⊠

HAVE YOU TRULY BEEN BORN AGAIN OF WATER AND THE SPIRIT?

PAUL C. JONG

Among many Christian books written about being born again, this is the first book of out time to preach the gospel of the water and the Spirit in strict accordance with the Scriptures. Man can't enter the kingdom of heaven without being born again of water and the Spirit. To be born again means that a sinner is saved from all his lifelong sins by believing in the baptism of Jesus and His blood on the Cross. Let's believe in the gospel of the water and the Spirit and enter the kingdom of heaven as the righteous who have no sin.

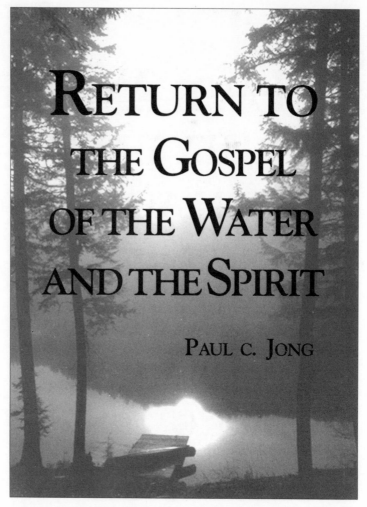

RETURN TO THE GOSPEL OF THE WATER AND THE SPIRIT

PAUL C. JONG

Let's return to the gospel of the water and the Spirit. Theology and doctrines themselves can't save us. Many Christians still follow them and are not born again. This book clearly tells us what mistakes theology and doctrines have made and how to believe in Jesus in the most proper way.

The Holy Spirit who Dwells in Me

A Fail-safe Way for You to Receive the Holy Spirit

Paul C. Jong

In Christianity, the most significantly discussed issue is salvation from sins and the indwelling of the Holy Spirit. However, few people have the exact knowledge of these two things, while they are most important issues in Christianity. Nevertheless, in reality people say that they believe in Jesus Christ while they are ignorant of redemption and the Holy Spirit.

Do you know the gospel that makes you receive the Holy Spirit? If you want to ask God for the indwelling of the Holy Spirit, then you must first know the gospel of the water and the Spirit and have faith in it. This book will certainly lead all Christians worldwide to be forgiven of all their sins and to receive the Holy Spirit.

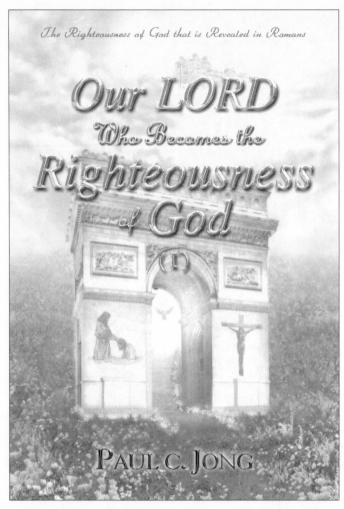

The Righteousness of God that is Revealed in Romans

Our LORD
Who Becomes the
Righteousness
of God
(I)

PAUL C. JONG

The words in this book will satisfy the thirst in your heart. Today's Christians continue to live while not knowing the true solution to the actual sins that they are committing daily. Do you know what God's righteousness is? The author hopes that you will ask yourself this question and believe in God's righteousness, which is revealed in this book.

The Doctrines of Predestination, Justification, and Incremental Sanctification are the major Christian doctrines, which brought confusion and emptiness into the souls of believers. But now, many Christians should newly come to know God, learn about His righteousness and continue in the assured faith.

This book will provide your soul with a great understanding and lead it to peace. The author wants you to possess the blessing of knowing God's righteousness.